Walter Hines Page

Published for the Organization
of American Historians

Ross Gregory

Walter Hines Page

Ambassador to the Court
of St. James's

The University Press of Kentucky

Standard Book Number 8131–1198–6
Library of Congress Catalog Card Number 78–94067

To Shirley

Contents

Illustrations   ix

Preface   xi

I. The Road to London   1

II. The Happy Time   27

III. Battle for Civilization Begins   49

IV. Harassing the British   63

V. Assault of the Barbarians   90

VI. Harassing the British Again   114

VII. The Worst Year   139

VIII. War at Last   173

IX. Victory and Death   197

X. The Ambassadorship of Walter Page   208

Bibliographical Note   219

Index   229

Illustrations

Walter Hines Page

President Woodrow Wilson and
Colonel Edward M. House

Sir Edward Grey

Arthur Balfour

between pages 108 and 109

Preface

WHILE WRITERS OF American history like to quote Walter Page, no one wishes to write about him. At least, no substantial work has appeared about this fascinating person since Burton J. Hendrick in the 1920s published *The Life and Letters of Walter Hines Page*. Doubtless the Hendrick volumes have been the discouraging factor, for they brought literary honor to the author. But this work, for all its success, should not remain the final word on Walter Page. Much a job of editing, these books were not exactly a biography and certainly not an objective history. Hendrick wished readers to remember Page as a significant person in American wartime diplomacy, if not the most important individual in the world at the time. It would have been impossible to write a thorough study of Page in the 1920s. Besides experiencing problems of time and perspective, scholars could examine only a smattering of sources pertaining to the ambassador and his period. Hendrick for the most part had to rely on information in Page's personal papers. Gradually over the years new material has become available, but for full access to manuscript and government collections of the period 1913–1918, during the ambassadorship of Walter Page, scholars have had to wait until the 1960s, nearly fifty years after the Great War had ended.

This study proposes to retell the story of Walter Page's ambassadorship in light of what seems full availability of sources, to reconsider Page's impact on American diplomacy as well as the impact of that diplomacy on Page. There is no attempt to rehash all aspects of British-American relations, but of course it is necessary to give attention to the major problems, at least those issues in which Page had an interest. While my primary objective is to concentrate on Page, I hope to introduce new material, especially from British Foreign Office collections, to broaden the view of this phase of history, and perhaps contribute to better understanding of foreign policy at the time of the First World War.

I would not have finished this work without assistance from several people, to whom I express deepest gratitude. At the top of the list is Professor Robert H. Ferrell, who gave unselfishly of time and advice to help in matters of style, substance, and other ways too numerous to mention. His assistance truly was indispensable. My friend and colleague Professor Otis K. Rice read portions of the manuscript and offered helpful suggestions. The editors of the Woodrow Wilson Papers, John W. Davidson and David W. Hirst, advised me freely about ways to get into the mass of Wilson Papers. The controller of Her Majesty's Stationery Office generously granted permission to use Crown-copyright papers in the Public Record Office, and the American Philosophical Society provided from its Penrose Fund a grant to help support research. Finally, I would like to thank my wife, who read the chapters, made excellent criticisms, and was a constant source of inspiration.

Chapter One

The Road to London

Like all southern lads raised in the second half of the nineteenth century, Walter Page grew up in the shadow of the Civil War. Born in the town his father had founded in north-central North Carolina, he was not quite six years old when Confederate batteries fired the first shots at Fort Sumter. His oldest memories were such tragic sights as soldiers' coffins, weeping relatives, the seemingly endless line of bluecoats that filed past his father's door in pursuit of fleeing rebels. He recalled soldiers camping in the yard, commandeering the property, and rummaging through the house, all of which appeared to the young observer as astonishing and culpable behavior. Invited one day to dine at the officers' mess, he retorted: "I'll starve before I'll eat with the Yankees."[1] Walter was ten in 1865, the year Sherman's troops came by, and only a dozen or so miles from his home, near Durham, the war virtually ended when General Joseph Johnston surrendered his battered Confederate army. Page grew to manhood during the years of Reconstruction, and since part of that time northern troops occupied the state and carpetbaggers ran the government of North Carolina, it was common to hear friends speak of the North as a foreign land and of a Yankee as someone despicable.

For too many years after 1865 northerners and southerners alike were slow to let the Civil War die. Republicans waved the bloody shirt as long as it served their political purposes, and southerners raised the banner of white supremacy, blamed their troubles on black Republicanism, and created myths about the grand historic past. Of the two sections, the South easily was the most depressed by the war. Classical liberalism was the dominant philosophy in the North, and at the center of the creed was the idea that man should have free movement and free thought, even if some men thought the wrong way. Hence the postwar North experienced, besides alarming political corruption and huge economic growth, great educational advance and intellectual creativity. The war did not soon change the mind of the South, at least the minds of many people in the South. To many southerners the northern victory had meant only that the North had more troops and rifles. Voluntary transformation to new thought and behavior would have been a confession that the South had been wrong. Every southern community, including Page's, had its supply of armless or legless veterans, or still more tragic, the widows and fatherless children. The loyal southerner could not admit that these brave heroes had fought for an unworthy cause. The best defense of the southern case seemed veneration of the noble soldiers and retention, as much as possible, of prewar southern society and thought. As Page later explained about his old home: "the school, like the war and the church was an institution; and I learned . . . at . . . early age, that nobody tells the truth about institutions."[2] While the postwar North awakened to numerous new ventures, the South, attempting to perpetuate false virtues,

---

[1] Burton J. Hendrick, *The Life and Letters of Walter Hines Page*, 3 vols. (Garden City, N.Y., 1924–1926), 1: 11; hereafter cited as Hendrick, *Page*. The factual biographical data of the first few pages come from chronology sheets in the Papers of Walter Hines Page, Houghton Library, Harvard University; Hendrick, *Page*, 1; and a later work of the same author, *The Training of an American: The Earlier Life and Letters of Walter Hines Page* (Cambridge, Mass., 1928). Page set down his memories of the Civil War in a semiautobiographical novel, written under the pseudonym Nicholas Worth, *The Southerner* (New York, 1909).

[2] *The Southerner*, 17.

slumbered in economic backwardness and intellectual conformity.

At least, such was what the southern environment came to seem
to Walter Page, and no less than most individuals he long felt the
influence of the old home. Convinced that in old habits it was
destined to a subordinate, colonial position, Page spent a major
portion of his life trying to change the South. Unsuccessful at
home, he went north and continued the campaign. The South
helped form Page's mind and also his career. It provided a theme
for his path to literary success; it drew him into friendship with
another southerner who thought similarly and who would appoint Page to high diplomatic office. A man with Page's talent
and initiative eventually would have found distinction in some
vocation; his career what it was, the southern background helped.

Southerners later disturbed at his seemingly treasonous behavior often wondered how Page went wrong. Clearly the first factor
was the family. Walter's father, like his grandfather, had been a
Whig moderate who regarded Henry Clay and not John Calhoun
his patron saint. Allison Page had acquiesced in the slave system
and even owned some Negroes, but he had been a hard-working
individual cautious not to let slavery destroy the inertia of the
master. He was one of the thousands of North Carolinians not
consulted when the time came for secession, and Walter once
heard his father remark that the Civil War was "the most fool-
hardy enterprise that man ever undertook."[3] If Allison Page contributed to the Confederate cause, it was not because he believed
it to be a crusade, and to his family he imparted the idea that the
southern position fell far short of infallibility.

The family influence also blessed Walter with an appreciation
for learning; and education, properly pursued, can lead one to
challenge the strongest idea. The principal benefactor was Mrs.
Page, a devout Methodist who deplored alcohol, tobacco, and
strong language. Walter did not maintain all his mother's convic-
tions, but he did profit from her gentle prodding for reading,

[3] Page to Edward M. House, Nov. 24, 1916, Hendrick, *Page*, 1: 6; also *The
Southerner*, 5.

often in English classics. From his mother's tutoring, improvised local schools, and a nearby private institution he also obtained a better-than-average education. And when the proper time came, the family expected Walter to go to college.

Page's first experience in higher education, at Trinity College in rural Randolph County (later renamed Duke University), was disappointing. He would have gone to the state university at Chapel Hill, except that the carpetbaggers insisted that if whites went to that school, blacks also would go, and the whites insisted that if Negroes went, they would not, and so in 1871 the university was closed. Walter's mother, hoping that her son would become a minister, doubtless encouraged his decision to enter Trinity, a nearby Methodist institution. Trinity in the 1870s showed no sign of becoming the great institution that it would grow to be. It was an inexpensive, backwoods school with an enrollment of about one hundred students who regularly attended chapel and drilled hard in the classical studies. Little remains about Page's stay except a respectable report card—he did best in sabbath school, worst in natural science—and a few letters in which the young man complained that the way to success at Trinity was cheating or apple-polishing; and Page would have nothing of either.[4]

Randolph-Macon in Ashland, Virginia, was somewhat better. Although the faculty and student body were overwhelmingly southern and Methodist, Randolph-Macon was an intellectual experience broader than Page had faced, and he began to develop new ideas about old subjects, especially religion. He participated in numerous social and cultural activities, and with friends—corncob pipes in their mouths—discovered that education often was more stimulating outside the classroom. Under the capable guidance of Thomas R. Price, he continued an emphasis on Greek studies, and with Price's encouragement, expanded in English literature. By 1876, when finished at Randolph-Macon, he

[4] The report card, dated Oct. 19, 1872, is in Page's Papers. For the gist of Page's letters see Hendrick, *Page*, 1: 19–20. A brief description of Trinity College is in Earl W. Porter, *Trinity and Duke 1892–1924: Foundation of Duke University* (Durham, N.C., 1964), 1–4.

had distinguished himself as one of the school's outstanding students.

Through a stroke of good fortune, Page made one further step in formal education. The year he left Randolph-Macon, Johns Hopkins University opened its doors in Baltimore. The president of that new school, Daniel Coit Gilman, insisted that Johns Hopkins begin by bringing together a select small group of professors and students in various academic disciplines. For the chair of Greek studies Gilman obtained Basil L. Gildersleeve, thought by many individuals to be the most capable American in the field. Gildersleeve, it so happened, was a friend of Price at Randolph-Macon. Through the influence of these two classicists, Page became one of the first twenty fellows at Johns Hopkins. The news came as a large surprise to the young man, who scarcely had heard of the Baltimore school and had no thought of making Greek his lifework. Whatever his future profession, Page could not pass up such an immensely flattering offer.

It was a wide-eyed Walter Page who stepped onto the Johns Hopkins campus. Baltimore was to him a large city, farthest from home and farthest north he ever had been. Younger than most of the students (he recently had turned twenty-one), pale, slender, a little awkward, he looked the unsophisticated rural lad that he was. What shocking things he encountered! Johns Hopkins required no prayer, no chapel, and the inaugural speaker was Thomas H. Huxley, the renowned, and by many individuals renounced, English Darwinian. Even so, Page had the ability to adapt to new situations, and whatever the environment, he had come prepared to concentrate on study. Shortly after arrival, he and a friend set out to find lodging. They obtained a room at a large old-fashioned house, the owner of which had five pretty daughters. The first evening there was a social affair and present, besides the daughters, were several other attractive young ladies. Back in their room later the young men grew (as the friend told the story) "excessively sentimental over those seductive sirens." The next day they decided that the atmosphere was too enticing for young men interested in scholarship, and so they started looking for another room, Page vowing he would accept no place where there was "a woman under three score and ten." They finally found a house in which lived "two ancient maidens," one of whom had a "most wrinkled and bilious visage and the other a nose and chin that nearly met." "This," said Page, "is just what we have been looking for."[5]

Page's intent to the contrary, there was abundant socializing at Johns Hopkins, all of which played an important part in the young man's intellectual maturation. Sessions with Gildersleeve were impressive, but Page found parts of classical study difficult, and being a practical person, he could not imagine himself a "professional Greek." The most inspiring hours were those spent in discussions in Page's room or some other meetingplace where the young man came into contact with individuals and ideas of wide variety. A growing curiosity led Page at the end of the first school year to spend a summer in Germany. The visit had no long-range effect on his thinking unless it was to strengthen the desire to abandon Greek and Johns Hopkins. He returned for a short while in autumn of 1877, then without taking a degree, he relinquished the fellowship and turned to face the world.

With Page, as with all individuals, formal schooling provided but a portion of his education. While the time in classrooms ended when he left Johns Hopkins, it would be some time before Page settled on a few central ideas that would propel his career. To be sure, his outlook was broader than it ever had been; he had abandoned many of his mother's fundamentalist principles and had heard so many new thoughts that he doubted if any idea was unchallengeable. But still he regarded himself a southerner, and he wished to live out his life in a southern state, preferably North Carolina. The problem was the choice of an occupation. Besides knowing Greek, he liked English literature, was a decent writer, and had developed a lively interest in current events. Use of these talents he apparently was willing to trust to fate.

Page spent the next few years in roving and experiment, attempting to find a profession and the place to practice it. Easily he preferred North Carolina and made several attempts to establish

[5] William White Jacques to Burton J. Hendrick, *The Training of an American*, 84–86.

there, but for various reasons—partly circumstances, partly Page's own behavior—the old state never made him welcome. His first employment was a summer job in the English department at the University of North Carolina, and he was willing to accept a permanent position, but the university did not offer one. Then came a position in English at Male High School in Louisville. In that city Page made a first venture into journalism when he began contributing articles to a short-lived periodical, the *Age*. That was the significance of the stay in Louisville, for he resigned the teaching job after a few months and wrote letters of application to almost every newspaper in North Carolina and several in Louisville and Baltimore, but received not a single offer. "I made up my mind to go into journalism," he commented. "But journalism didn't seem in any hurry . . . to admit me."[6] Jobless, almost penniless, he advertised for work and finally received an offer from an obscure newspaper in St. Joseph, Missouri, which he accepted. There he did a variety of tasks, reporting everything from politics to price of cattle; and while Page eventually became editor, he could tolerate the provincial St. Joseph environment little more than a year.

Then came a touch of success based on sheer nerve. In 1881 Page wrote the leading newspapers in New York, Boston, and Chicago that he was going to the South, and would send back reports he hoped the papers would publish. The scheme worked. The newspapers published all the essays, and Page felt he was "rolling in wealth."[7] The best luck he had had since leaving Johns Hopkins, this publication did not assure Page's future, but it introduced his name to the journalistic world of large eastern cities, and such self-promoted success gave a huge boost to the young man's confidence.

Even so, he had to jostle about a few more years. The letters from the South drew an assignment from the New York *World* to cover the Atlanta Exposition of 1882, where by chance, he met a struggling young lawyer named Woodrow Wilson. Thereafter he worked as correspondent and writer for the *World* and would

[6] Hendrick, *Page,* 1: 33.
[7] Ibid., 34.

have stayed longer except in 1883 Joseph Pulitzer obtained control. Knowing Pulitzer was going to change the *World* to an organ of sensationalism, Page and all staff members who regarded themselves respectable journalists resigned.

A final time Page attempted to settle in the old state. He became, in summer 1883, editor of a new Raleigh newspaper, the *State Chronicle*. At the time twenty-eight years old, he had spent most of the last ten years outside the state, and what he had seen in other parts of the United States made North Carolina seem a sorry sight. From its beginning, the *State Chronicle* was a vigorous organ of reform which struck sharply at some of the dearest local and sectional traditions. Page goaded provincialism and backwardness, directed sharp jabs at the Daughters of the Confederacy and high officers of the Civil War, called for scientific agriculture, industrialization, and education for all youngsters, black and white. It hardly was the tactful way of reforming North Carolina, but Page, as editor or ambassador, believed that the way to meet problems was head-on. Designed to assist the rebuilding of the old commonwealth, the *State Chronicle* editorials brought much abuse on their editor and caused a sharp decline in subscriptions. Page stuck it out a year and a half, then resigned and turned to the North. "There is no use in my trying to do anything down South any more," he wrote a few months later. "It proved disastrous every time."[8]

Distressed, angry at the way his state had rejected him, Page from his new home in New York sent back bitter letters to the *State Chronicle*. "The world must have some corner in it where men can sleep and sleep and dream and dream, and North Carolina is as good a spot for that as any," began one of the letters. "There is not a man whose residence is in the state who is recognized by the world as an authority on anything . . . . It is the laughing stock among the states." Whom did Page feel was at fault? "It is the mummies. And the mummies have the direction of things. Do you want examples? Count on your fingers the five men who fill the highest places or have the greatest influence on

[8] Hendrick, *The Training of an American,* 197. For the story of Page's days with the *State Chronicle,* see Hendrick, *Page,* 1: 42–48.

education in North Carolina. Not one of them is a scholar. Count the five most influential editors in the state. . . . Go around all the leading sources of power in the same way, and you will see what is the matter. Yet when a man tells the plain truth because he loves North Carolina the same fellows howl 'traitor'. . . . They are big men today in North Carolina. But they are mummies."[9]

In the North Page followed almost a steady path to success. After a few months of various newspaper work, he became in 1887 business manager of *The Forum,* a new journal trying to make its way into the New York literary world. For several months the magazine struggled along with only about 2,000 subscribers, hardly in the black. Then in 1891 Page became editor and it began to move. By 1894 it had almost 28,000 subscribers. The growth of Page's reputation paralleled that of his journal, and when in 1895 he relinquished his post with *The Forum*—he lost in a squabble for control—no longer did he need to search for a job. Ready for his services was the reputable Houghton, Mifflin and Company, publisher of *Atlantic Monthly.* Page joined the firm as literary adviser and in 1898 became editor of the *Atlantic.* While in the minds of many individuals this post was the peak of American periodical literature, Page did not stay long. Believing he was inadequately paid, that the reputation of the famous old journal eclipsed the editors who maintained it, Page resigned after a few months to accept a challenging invitation to help shore up the old publishing house of Harper.[10] The Harper experiment soon collapsed, but meanwhile Page had begun an association with Frank N. Doubleday, already prominent in the publishing business. The two men formed the publishing firm of Doubleday, Page and Company, from which emerged a new periodical, *World's Work,* with Walter Page as editor. There he remained until he received a call from Woodrow Wilson.

After a long, frequently difficult path which led from the sand-hills of North Carolina to many places in the United States and

[9] Letter dated Feb. 1, 1886, Hendrick, *The Training of an American,* 176, 180.
[10] Page explained reasons for leaving *Atlantic Monthly* in a letter to William Roscoe Thayer, Dec. 5, 1900, Hendrick, *Page,* 1: 68. Subscription figures of *The Forum* are from *The Training of an American,* 227.

finally New York City, Page had become a successful man. He had money in the bank, was part owner of a business, and above all editor of a journal he could run as he chose. He had a family. In 1880 Page had married Willia Alice Wilson, a girl who, born in Michigan, had spent most of her years near Page's home in North Carolina. Playmates as children, Walter and Alice had renewed the friendship on a different basis when Page lectured at the University of North Carolina in 1878. The Pages produced three sons and a daughter, whom they tried to give a good start in life. The sons went to Harvard, the daughter to Bryn Mawr. If a son flatters the father by following his profession, Page was so honored, for when he left *World's Work* for the London embassy, Arthur Page stepped into his father's shoes.

During those middle years in New York Page took on the physical appearance of a successful man. He was forty-five years old in 1900 and a far cry from the shy, gangling youth who had attended Randolph-Macon and Johns Hopkins. The corncob pipe of those lean, earlier days had been replaced with elegant and more prosperous-looking cigars. The eyelids still hung heavy over large brown eyes, but the face was fuller and the hair thinner and farther back on the forehead. There now was a mustache which helped somewhat, but even with that adornment, Page was not a handsome man. One feature which did not change—and Page doubtless wished that somehow it could—was his nose. Very large, it dominated his face. In years to come, when Page was ambassador, an incident occurred which demonstrated the prominence of his nose. Americans traveling in London preferred to have the English painter P. A. Laszlo do their portraits, but for some reason Laszlo did not want to do Page, and the ambassador could not understand. Colonel Edward M. House, a friend of Page and confidant of President Wilson, discovered the reason: "between us and the angels," House wrote a friend, "I found out it was because of Page's nose. . . . He did not want to put that nose on canvas."[11]

Page was such an interesting person, however, that people who

[11] House to Hugh Wallace, Feb. 16, 1916, the Papers of Woodrow Wilson, Library of Congress.

knew him rarely thought about his appearance. Honest, energetic, straightforward almost to the point of bluntness, confident almost to the point of dogmatism, he liked men with similar qualities. His success as editor was due in no small measure to the way he put personality into work. He scoffed at the stodgy men who thought it beneath their journal's dignity to solicit manuscripts and made the editorial desk almost a dispatch office whence went out requests for good articles. He liked to keep his journal, be it *The Forum, Atlantic Monthly,* or *World's Work,* abreast with the world. A student of the classics, he appreciated knowledge for the mere sake of learning, but his knowledge was more meaningful and had a broader appeal if it corresponded with a current issue. If *The Forum* and *World's Work* lacked the exclusive dignity of *Harper's Weekly* or *The Nation,* they attracted a more diverse public and were profitable.

Besides being an editor, Page was a capable writer. He had seen enough bad manuscripts to know good prose, and in his case the style was the man. His best compositions were letters sent from England during the World War, but before becoming a man of letters, he turned out a large number of articles for his journal or others. Whether editorial, article, or letter, Page's writing was brisk, frank, full of effective idiomatic English. A few years after Page's death, Rudyard Kipling asked a friend the source of such fine style. It came from study of the classics; "Page was a great Greek, Kipling," was the answer.[12] The training doubltess helped, but Page's style was largely a matter of transferring to paper a vigorous personality.

Even so, he did experience some literary disappointment. Having proved his talent as author of political and sociological articles he attempted to expand into new areas of literature. One time he even had visions of becoming a playwright. As editor of *Atlantic Monthly* he had had a part in publication of Mary Johnston's successful novel, *To Have and To Hold.* The work had just begun to appear as a serial in the *Atlantic* when Page

[12] Radio address, Herbert S. Houston (Page's former publishing associate), "Walter Hines Page: A Personal Tribute over the Air," CBS, Aug. 15, 1930, copy in the Papers of Edwin A. Alderman, University of Virginia Library.

suggested to Miss Johnston that he try his hand at preparing it for stage production. Working when he could squeeze in the time, he kept the manuscript over a year, and when he crossed over to *World's Work,* still had not completed the job. Meanwhile the story became a bestselling book and agents began to compete for stage rights. Miss Johnston, encouraged by the people of Houghton Mifflin, then wondered if it would not be better for Page to surrender the dramatization to someone with more time and experience. There followed some confused correspondence between Miss Johnston, Houghton Mifflin, and Page, at the end of which the author, a sensitive young lady, said Page could go on and finish the draft (he almost had finished) , and Page said he no longer cared to do so. He received nothing from the affair but experience and, as he wrote Miss Johnston, some hurt feelings: "For years I had given all my time to other people's work—in the awful, unspeakable drudgery of a magazine-editor (the galley slave is a free man in comparison) ; and now when I had become master of my own time, I was happier in trying my own constructive powers on this task than I had been since I was a boy. I believe that I should have succeeded too."[13] Never again did Page try to reach Broadway.

He did, however, try his hand at a novel. At least Page said *The Southerner* was fiction, but anyone who knew him could tell that large portions were autobiographical. He published part of the work in *Atlantic Monthly* in 1907, then expanded it into a book which he had his firm publish in 1909 under the pseudonym of Nicholas Worth. *The Southerner* was the story of a man with a background identical to Page who went to Harvard and returned to try to rebuild the old commonwealth. Using fraudulent election tactics and the cry of white supremacy, local stagnant interests kept Nicholas Worth from high office, but the hero persevered and lived to see the state adopt his ideas. Never a financial success, the book received little notice outside the South, where there was neither difficulty in identifying the author nor appreciation of the critical theme.

[13] Undated letter (about March 8, 1900) , the Mary Johnston Collection, University of Virginia Library. This episode comes out in letters between Page and Mary Johnston, Jan. 27–March 15, 1900, ibid.

The Southerner was but one bit of evidence that despite his status as an expatriate, despite new, stimulating friends, Page's principal interest still was the South. Few editions of *World's Work* came off the press without an editorial or article about the South, and Page contributed numerous other essays and speeches about southern problems. Whatever the audience, his approach was a direct attack: "The white man is not going to have what is called 'social equality' with the Negro," Nicholas Worth told a group of blacks. "The two races must live socially apart, yet side by side, and they must work together. And the white man must treat the Negro fairly. He has got to give him a chance to work, to buy land, to build a home, to raise his children decently. He's got to give him good schools."[14] Bitterness that Page felt in 1885, when chased from North Carolina, had vanished, but he had not abandoned the ideas. In *World's Work,* as in the *State Chronicle,* education and practical training for all individuals was the central theme, and Page usually proceeded with an assault on the religious, social, and economic forces which stood in way of this vital reform. Not unexpectedly, he received some verbal lashes from the mummies, but most important, Page helped bring national attention to the problem of southern education. The climax came when John D. Rockefeller agreed to found the General Education Board, on which Page served, and the great American billionaire endowed the organization with several million dollars, much of which went for southern education. In 1907 Page took a journey through the southern states similar to the trip in 1881, and when he saw signs of reawakening, like Nicholas Worth of *The Southerner,* he took it as personal vindication.[15] In view of the great change in race relations underway in the South at that time, this means that Page tolerated conditions a later age would regard as frightfully unjust if not unconstitutional. But then, so did the nation, and for a man with a southern heritage, Page's views on the Negro question were advanced.

Page reached full professional and intellectual bloom as the

---

[14] *The Southerner,* 243.

[15] Page to Willia Alice Page, Feb. 6, 1907, Hendrick, *The Training of an American,* 427. For Page's attack on southern problems see his collection of speeches, *The Rebuilding of Old Commonwealths* (New York, 1902).

United States began one of its most prosperous and exciting periods. The gay nineties had passed, but the early 1900s seemed almost as gay and much more inspiring. If nothing else, Theodore Roosevelt set a faster and much more colorful pace than such drab presidents as Harrison, Cleveland, and McKinley. Journalism rode the tide of the new era. Americans at last had become concerned about the problems created by industrialization, and journalists—the most opportunistic of which Roosevelt called muckrakers—were quick to discover that the problems made good copy. *World's Work* had much to say about reform, but Page put it on a middle course: less colorful and more scholarly than *McClure's* or *Ladies' Home Journal,* livelier than the old prestige journals. Readers who wished to be up-to-date but above the literary level of Lincoln Steffens or Ida Tarbell felt right at home with Page's journal and its essays from such scholars as Woodrow Wilson and Albert Bushnell Hart. The purpose of *World's Work,* said Page, was to make good literature "of the events of the day,"[16] and what a time it was. "If the truth were told," he wrote Wilson, "I suspect that the good old times had no match for it. It is refreshing, lifting—even bully."[17]

One of the movements that had aroused Page's interest was the nation's adventurousness in foreign affairs. In 1898 the United States had embarked upon a crusade against the decrepit Spanish Empire and from this conflict emerged with colonies, without knowing exactly why, where they were, or what to do with them. Many Americans had misgivings about turning the Spanish out of Cuba, but Page, then in his final months at *Atlantic Monthly,* was not one. The *Atlantic* of June 1898 had displayed an American flag on its cover and in an accompanying article the editor had defended the war against Spain. He viewed it as a result of large forces, of a people run out of western land for expansion, of a nation dissatisfied with influence only within its continent. "Shall we be content with peaceful industry," he asked, "or does there yet lurk in us the adventurous spirit of our Anglo-Saxon forefa-

[16] Interview with W. P. Kirkwood, The Minneapolis *Journal,* March 5, 1900, copy in Page Papers.
[17] Nov. 5, 1910, Wilson Papers.

thers? And have we come to a time when, no more enterprises awaiting us at home, we shall be tempted to seek them abroad?"[18] Page was not anxious for the United States to compete with major powers in the race for colonies or entangle itself in Old World alliances, but he wished his nation to be part of the world.

Page had not overlooked the way Britain had behaved during the little war with the Spanish. While continental monarchies had assailed the United States for bullying their weak sister, the British—for their own purposes principally, though Americans were slow to admit that fact—had encouraged the Americans, welcoming them into the community of colonial nations. For years Page had admired British literature and institutions. Of Anglo-Saxon blood, impressed with British government, he could view British colonialism as a civilizing movement. And now the United States, for the same humanizing purposes, had catapulted into the colonial picture. "The Spanish war made plain," Page wrote the British ambassador, "that English-speaking men are friends and friends for the larger purposes of civilization."[19] If by the start of the twentieth century Page did not possess yet the deep feeling about Britain that would dominate his actions in 1913–1918, he was on the way to becoming a complete anglophile.

In those secure times foreign affairs was a luxury Americans could take or leave as they chose, and for Page as for most of his countrymen, the primary interest was domestic issues. Since the Civil War American politics had been a dismal story of second-rate, often clownish candidates, many of whom danced on strings pulled by their industrialist bosses. Page was much concerned about the low state of political life, but he had spent so much time seeking a vocation and trying to reform the South that it was the late 1880s before he could set his mind on reforming the nation, and by that time there was indication the nation might be reforming itself. So it had seemed in 1885 when Grover Cleveland restored the presidency to the Democratic party after a twenty-five

---

[18] "The War with Spain and After," *Atlantic Monthly* 81 (June 1898): 721–27.
[19] To James Bryce, April 23, 1898, Hendrick, *The Training of an American,* 263–64.

year absence. Page had seen many admirable qualities in Cleveland, particularly honesty, frugality in government, and an insistence upon a sound money policy, but he came to see that Cleveland belonged to the nineteenth century, that he was plodding, unimaginative, unaware of the forces changing the nation.[20] Then the Democrats seemed to go haywire, choosing as their leader the artful, but emotional and undependable William Jennings Bryan. In the election of 1896 one was either for Bryan or against him, and while voting Republican meant supporting the "Old Guard," Page surely voted for McKinley, if he voted at all.

Disappointed with the past performance of both parties, Page from his new post at *World's Work* was delighted to watch the new century begin with rapid growth of the reform spirit. A member of that large, heterogeneous group called progressives, he was anything but a radical. Except for a lively interest in the South, Page's progressivism clearly was eastern. He wanted American society reformed and democratized, which meant that he supported the recent expansion of popular government and wished trusts policed to the point where the nation could proceed with fair and honest competition. He opposed broad government power; he opposed class legislation; he opposed irrational reformers such as Bryan and his followers from the Populist party. Roosevelt had been an acceptable president; even if he was more progressive in speech than in deed, it was great fun to have him in the White House. William Howard Taft was a respectable man, and with a decent party would have been a respectable president, but with the Rough Rider in Africa, Republican leadership slipped farther into the hands of the standpatters in Congress. To Page's chagrin, Bryan dominated the Democratic party for the first decade of the twentieth century. While he sometimes had voted Republican, Page wanted to be a Democrat, if the party would give him an inspiring leader. That is why he kept close watch on the career of Woodrow Wilson.[21]

[20] Anonymous article by Page, "Mr. Cleveland's—Failure?" *The Forum* 19 (April 1894) : 129–38.

[21] Page's views of politics and politicians are scattered throughout *World's Work*. Examples are the editorials of May 1911, Nov. 1911, Aug. 1912. See also "Mr. Cleveland's—Failure?" and "Political Career and Character of

If Page and Wilson had not met in 1882 it would have been another time, for circumstances destined that their paths frequently would cross. Both were southerners; both went to Johns Hopkins, attained success in the North, and looked back on the old area with hopeful objectivity. Free traders at the time of their first meeting, they shared ideas about politics, government, and literature. Page as editor sought the type of article Wilson wrote, and was one of the first individuals to recognize the rising young scholar's style and perception. He kept an eye on the brilliant Virginian, delighted to see that at least one southerner was leaving his mark as a scholar, and perhaps would do so as a statesman.

Wilson and Page saw little of each other the few years after introduction at Atlanta. Page was moving about attempting to find someone who recognized his journalistic talents, and Wilson, unsuccessful at law, had entered Johns Hopkins to study for a doctorate in political science. Publication in 1885 of Wilson's penetrating dissertation, *Congressional Government,* caught Page's eye. At the time with the Raleigh *State Chronicle,* Page wrote such a flattering review that Wilson sent a word of thanks and comment that he was "sincerely glad to hear that you have a special appetite for serious political and economic study." Wilson complained that "here [Bryn Mawr] I have no associates who are more than mildly interested in the topics I care most for."[22]

While by 1885 the two men were acquaintances, it was Page's ascension to a New York editorial post which laid the basis for a stronger association. His searches for good manuscripts frequently led him to Wilson, and more often than not the professor fulfilled the request. On one occasion Page tried to lure to Houghton

---

David B. Hill," *The Forum* 26 (Nov. 1894) : 257–69. Page said many things about Bryan. To an associate he wrote what he thought could happen if Bryan were elected in 1896: "The paralysis of industry would be something frightful, but the free coinage (of silver) plan is so absurd that it could not be tried. During the four months between Mr. Bryan's election and his inauguration the panic would produce much disastrous effects that the whole country would suffer a violent revulsion of opinion, and demands too strong to resist would be made upon the incoming President and Congress to take action to restore confidence." To J. Lawrence Laughlin, Aug. 11, 1896, Hendrick, *The Training of an American,* 254–55.

[22] Oct. 30, 1885, Page Papers.

Mifflin Wilson's *History of the American People*. Letters of those years concerned articles, books, professional matters mostly. Page was the most verbose. Wilson wrote friendly letters which answered questions and expressed gratitude for flattering remarks; almost never did he introduce new topics or broaden the discussion. If there was mutual respect between the two men, it was not, nor did it ever become, an intimate friendship. Much the warmer personality, Page probably would have enjoyed a close relationship, but Wilson did not have many close friends—Page once remarked that he lived too much alone and in company of women —and evidently did not wish any.[23]

Undisturbed by his friend's reserve, Page always was ready to urge Wilson to academic and political success. He marched in the parade that in 1902 inaugurated Wilson president of Princeton University, and watched the university come alive under new leadership. As Princeton's president, Wilson's popularity so broadened that when the election of 1908 approached, word circulated that the Democrats might draft him as their presidential candidate. Page thought the rumor irresponsible, ill-founded, and not a bad idea. In 1907 he wrote: "If the Democratic Party should come to its senses again next year and assert its old doctrines and take on its old dignity, and seek real leadership (and pray Heaven; it may) leaving its Bryans and Hearsts alone . . . , suggestion of President Wilson is logical, sound, dignified and decent. He is a man of practical mind and he knows men as well as books. He uses our language with both strength and charm; he has a sense of humor and he is a Democrat of the best tradition. What if a political miracle should happen and the long lost old party should find itself by nominating such a man?"[24]

The Democrats did not leave Bryan alone in 1908, and Bryan did not leave the Democrats alone, but two years later the party in New Jersey (with assistance from some Republicans) selected

[23] Page offered for the first volume: 10 percent, first $5,000; 12½ percent, second $5,000; 15 percent, third $5,000; 17½ percent, fourth $5,000; 20 percent, over $50,000. Undated note, Page Papers. For examples of other letters see Page to Wilson, June 22, 1896, March 10, 1897, Wilson to Page, May 20, 1895, Oct. 24, 1895, June 17, 1902, ibid.

[24] *World's Work* 13 (Jan. 1907): 8377.

Wilson as governor. A factor in his decision to enter politics was a squabble at Princeton over control of the graduate school. While Wilson lost the battle, he said that his was the democratic position, and during the progressive era one had to be democratic to be successful in politics. Page kept in touch with the "grad" controversy. He wrote his friend at Princeton that although he did not know much about the problem, from what he could tell Wilson was "eternally right."[25] And when the issue assisted Wilson's introduction into politics, Page was all the more satisfied.

In view of his high regard for Wilson's political and intellectual talent, it comes as no surprise that Page was a first mover in the Wilson presidential boom in 1912. For many years—one associate has said as early as 1886—Page had regarded Wilson as presidential timber,[26] but he knew that candidates traditionally came from the ranks of military heroes or party professionals, that no one had moved from the campus to the White House. A governor, especially the governor of a state in the populous East, was a different matter, and Wilson had little more than settled in New Jersey's executive house when Page and a small group of friends began to meet in New York to plan a campaign for the presidential nomination. The first task was to spread Wilson's name, little known except in the East, to all sections of the United States. For publicity agent, Page chose the newspaperman Frank P. Stockbridge, to whom he explained: "Academically and as a matter of practical politics, he [Wilson] has the keenest appreciation of its value; personally he does not understand the principles of publicity at all. The people will like him once they know him. The question is: How can we get them to know him? It is a problem of publicity, and that is why I have sent for you."[27] The strategy was to have Wilson go west and make speeches about political principles. A question soon arose about an invitation to speak at Lin-

[25] Feb. 11, 1910, Wilson Papers.

[26] Page in 1886 reportedly told a fellow journalist, Josephus Daniels: "Keep your eye on Wilson. His is the best mind in America studying political questions. One day he may be President of the United States." Daniels, *The Wilson Era: Years of Peace 1910–1917* (Chapel Hill, N.C., 1944), 4.

[27] Related by Stockbridge to David Lawrence in Lawrence's *The True Story of Woodrow Wilson* (New York, 1924), 45–47.

coln, Nebraska. That was Bryan's state, a place, some advisers thought, which might prove embarrassing to Wilson. The group decided to ask Page and abide by his advice. Page scoffed at their fears.[28] Within a short time Wilson was traveling west and over large portions of the nation. The presidential machine was in motion.

Besides helping plan strategy, Page made *World's Work* an organ for promotion of Wilson's candidacy. He sent the journalist William Bayard Hale to observe Wilson in his executive duties, and the May issue of *World's Work* was a special Woodrow Wilson edition, which pictured the candidate on the cover and featured Hale's article. With work in publicity and organization, advice to Wilson and the small group of promoters, Page in the initial stages of the movement was a central figure, if not the person most responsible for getting the campaign moving.

Once the campaign had gained momentum, however, Page's participation declined. In his journal he continued to trumpet Wilson's virtues, and when Champ Clark rushed past his candidate seemingly on way to the nomination, Page warned his readers that selection of Clark would mean a disaster for the Democratic party.[29] But Americans did not then—nor do they yet—select their presidential candidates directly, and outside the few states which had presidential primaries, the task of choosing a nominee was a matter of persuading delegates. Not a professional, having little influence within the party, Page could do little, even in the states he knew best. Since he was far from popular with the professionals in the old home, the planners decided that Wilson's cause in North Carolina would go better if Page's brothers, not Page himself, handled matters.[30] A resident of New York, Page could make no dent in the party organization of that state, and

[28] Frank Parker Stockbridge, "How Woodrow Wilson Won His Nomination," *Current History* 70 (July 1924) : 563.

[29] *World's Work* 24 (June 1912) : 130. Letters between Wilson and Page about the campaign are too numerous to mention. Examples are Wilson to Page, June 7, 1911, Page to Wilson, Jan. 22, 1912, Page Papers.

[30] See Edward M. House to Woodrow Wilson, Dec. 15, 1911, Wilson to House, Dec. 22, 1911, the Papers of Edward M. House, Yale University Library.

the Wilson backers had to watch the convention begin without the support of the huge, Tammany-controlled New York delegation.

The course of the Democratic Convention in Baltimore is familiar to scholars of the period. Wilson supporters felt great distress on the tenth ballot, since Clark with over a majority of votes seemed assured of victory; then four ballots later, Bryan—at that critical stage even Bryan's support was pure delight—cast his lot with Wilson; thereafter the Wilson men held firm and slowly began to turn the tide. At the time of the forty-sixth ballot Page stood with Stockbridge in Times Square watching the bulletin board flash news of Wilson's victory. The two men then crossed to the Knickerbocker Hotel to eat. "Well, Stockbridge," said Page with great satisfaction, "it looks to me as if we started something."[31]

What Page had started was the election of a president. Wilson mounted a vigorous campaign for the rational economic and political reform which Page thought was true progressivism; Page supported Wilson in *World's Work;* but while the campaign was impressive and Page's support beneficial, the Republicans were Wilson's chief benefactors in the election of 1912. Denied the nomination, Roosevelt bolted the party to head his own ticket. Going in two directions, the Republicans paved the way for a Democratic victory.

The election of Wilson was one of the most important events of Page's life. It was, first of all, a great source of encouragement to see the people abandon mediocre politicians and flashy generals and choose as their leader a man of Wilson's caliber. Page had much confidence in the president-elect. As he explained to a friend: "I have a new amusement, a new excitement . . . and as we all who really believe in a democracy—a new study, a new hope, and sometimes a new fear; and its name is Wilson." Intellectually brilliant, politically pure, Wilson seemed the high priest of the reformist spirit changing the United States. But amidst this large optimism, Page had to confess some doubt as to whether

[31] Stockbridge, "How Woodrow Wilson Won His Nomination," 572.

brilliance and honesty were enough to rule a world of self-seeking and often illogical men. Was politics, as some people said, exclusively a business for practical professionals? "Will he do it?" Page asked. "Can he do it? Can anybody do it?" Anxious to help, Page prepared memorandums about some of the problems Wilson would face. "I sent him some such memoranda. He came forth with a note of almost abject thanks. I sent more. Again such a note—written in his own hand. Yet not a word of what he thinks. The Sphinx was garrulous in comparison. . . . Wise? Yes. But does he know the men about him? Does he really know men? Nobody knows. Thus twixt fear and hope I see—suspense. I'll swear I can't doubt, I can't believe. Whether it is going to work out or not—whether he or anybody *can* work it out of the haze of theory—nobody knows; and nobody's speculation is better than mine and mine is worthless."[32]

"What ought to be done with Bryan?" Page asked. "What can be done with Bryan?"[33] Disposal of party benefactors and other people who assisted in the election, which included Page, was the first matter to which Wilson had to address himself. Bryan was the most troublesome problem, for while neither Wilson nor his associates respected the Great Commoner, they knew it unwise, by denying him patronage, to antagonize the large bloc of Bryan Democrats in Congress. After much indecision, Wilson decided that Bryan could do the least harm and receive the most glory as secretary of state. In that position the president could keep close watch on Bryan; besides, nobody expected the administration to face any major foreign problems.

If it took longer, the placement of Page was not so delicate a matter. Although a group of friends urged Wilson to give Page a high post, there would have been no political danger in ignoring the editor entirely. It would not have been fair, however, to leave out Page. He was a friend who could boast long support, devoted service in the campaign, and was a capable person. Of what he was most capable, Wilson could not decide. By time of the election Colonel Edward M. House had worked his way into Wilson's

[32] To Edwin A. Alderman, Dec. 31, 1912, Alderman Collection.
[33] Ibid.

confidence and became the principal adviser on appointment.
House's conversation with the president-elect, the gist of which
the colonel recorded in a diary, shows that the thinking seemed
this: Page was a likely candidate for the cabinet or other high
position. After handing out political spoils and placing a few men
in positions for which they were qualified, if something was left it
should go to Page. In a sense, Page competed with himself, for he
was both a possible appointee and an adviser on appointment.
While he never expressed a preference, there is some indication
he expected, and perhaps desired, to become secretary of agriculture. He frequently had written about farm problems, particularly the problems of southern farmers, and much of the information he sent Wilson concerned agriculture. For a time Wilson
considered giving Page that post, but he gave it instead to a man
Page had recommended, David F. Houston. When Houston objected on financial grounds, Page—"in his characteristic way,"
said House—solicited enough money from private sources to
guarantee Houston $30,000 a year for four years. And if that
amount was not enough, he promised to get as much as was
needed.[34]

Page nearly entered the cabinet as secretary of the interior.
That post had been jostled for weeks from one possible appointee
to another, finally offered to Newton D. Baker, who turned it
down. With the agriculture post filled, Wilson in late February
1913 decided to make Page secretary of the interior and commis-
sioned House to make the appointment. Discovering that he was
in North Carolina, House telegraphed that Page should return.
Meanwhile, some individuals began to complain about a southerner's heading the department which administered pensions for
veterans of the Union army. Wilson dropped the idea, with some
reluctance, but that left the problem of what to tell Page who,
without knowing why, was on his way back from North Carolina.
Wilson suggested that House take a list of prospective appointees

[34] House diary notation, March 14, 1913, the Diary of Edward M. House,
Yale University Library. Too numerous to mention, references in House's
diary to the appointment of Page began shortly after Wilson's election in
November 1912 and continued until Page received a post in the latter part of
March 1913.

and ask Page's advice, to make it appear that such was the reason for the telegram. When Page saw the list he thought it was mediocre, objecting to Louis Brandeis, the brilliant attorney then slated as secretary of commerce and labor, and to Josephus Daniels, future secretary of the navy. "You do not seem to think that Daniels is Cabinet timber," remarked House. "He is hardly a splinter," Page answered. The plan went off nicely. Not until House confessed a few days later did Page learn how near he had come to being a member of the cabinet.[35]

If Page was disappointed at failure to receive a cabinet position, he did not show it, for he went about his work as though he would spend the rest of his life at an editorial desk. He just had settled down to work one morning near the end of March when the telephone rang. "Good morning, your Excellency," said the voice. It was House who had called to say that Wilson wished to appoint him ambassador to Great Britain. Page knew that Wilson recently had been considering such a move. He knew also that the president had offered the post to Richard Olney, the aged former secretary of state and a man with diplomatic experience, and to Charles W. Eliot, former president of Harvard. Even if it was thirdhand merchandise, the offer was exciting news.[36]

Page might have questioned the wisdom of this appointment, had he not been involved personally. A believer in selecting qualified personnel, he could not deny that this was a case of fitting the post to the man, not the man to the post. Page had not the slightest diplomatic experience, and his interest in foreign affairs had been skimpy. At that late stage of the appointment process, his principal recommendation was that he did not have a position and the London post was open. If these grounds might seem flimsy, they were quite in line with the United States's traditionally haphazard manner of awarding diplomatic positions. Page in fact was better suited than many American repre-

---

[35] House Diary, Feb. 1913. The issue is similarly discussed in Charles Seymour, ed., *The Intimate Papers of Colonel House*, 4 vols. (Boston, 1926–1928), 1: 109–13; hereafter cited as Seymour, *Colonel House*. The story best unfolds in House's diary notations of the last days of February 1913.

[36] Essay, "The Ambassadorship," Page Papers. House recorded the incident in almost identical words, Diary, March 26, 1913.

sentatives who had gone to the Court of St. James's, which was as much a social as diplomatic position. By 1913 he had obtained some social finesse, was reasonably educated, and if he knew little about diplomacy, he could talk at length about Shakespeare and Keats. Anticipating nothing in way of controversy with Britain, Wilson wanted a man who would keep relations friendly between the two countries. Page met this modest requirement. Had the president possessed a hint of the diplomatic problems in store for the United States, he surely would have reconsidered the placement of Bryan, probably also of Page.

While there was no serious doubt that Page would accept, he did allow himself a few days to think of reasons why he could not go to Britain. He would have to leave *World's Work,* a secure, prosperous, by-no-means unsatisfactory position. He had heard stories about the expenses of high officials abroad and wondered if he could afford it. Ignorance of his role caused some concern. Another reservation mentioned to House was that his daughter, Katherine, was near graduation at Bryn Mawr, and he did not wish her to have so much contact with foreigners that she would marry one. The colonel suggested that Katherine spend most of her time in the United States. "I did not tell him so," House noted, "but I thought the fact that he was a man of very small means would probably protect her more than anything else."[37] In truth, Page found a clear answer to none of these questions, but it made no difference. He was so flattered and determined to serve his president and nation that he would have accepted almost any position Wilson offered. "I have decided to turn my face towards the East," he told House.[38]

Before leaving for Britain Page took a few weeks to prepare. He received a call from the British ambassador, attended a farewell banquet given by Doubleday and associates, arranged financial and family matters, and called on the president for instructions. The last task turned out to be the simplest: there were no instructions. The president, Page noted, "knew no more about the task

[37] House Diary, March 26, 1913; see also "The Ambassadorship," Page Papers.
[38] House Diary, March 28, 1913. Page officially accepted in a letter to Wilson, April 1, 1913, Wilson Papers.

that awaited me than I knew. Of course the Secretary of State knew nothing; his ignorance was taken for granted. But the President seemed to have in his mind only this idea—that he wanted somebody in London whom he knew and upon whose judgment he could rely. That was complimentary, but it lacked definiteness. The upshot of it all was that I had no idea what I was to do, where I was to live, nor what it would cost me."[39]

He set sail the middle of May 1913, a pleasant time to travel the Atlantic. The challenge of a new role in a foreign country caused only the slightest uneasiness. Challenges never frightened him. The North at one time had appeared almost a foreign land and he had succeeded in New York without great difficulty. Ignorant of the terrible days ahead, Page was very excited. "Even things never dreamed of come true—in this glad year," he had written.[40]

[39] "The Ambassadorship," Page Papers. Wilson stated his reasons for the appointment to Page: "It would give me the deepest satisfaction to have in London a man . . . with character and ability to comprehend a situation and the men who formed a part of it." March 28, 1913, ibid.

[40] Written on the margin of Wilson's letter offering the appointment, March 28, 1913, ibid.; Hendrick, *Page,* 3: 18–19.

Chapter Two

The Happy Time

Lᴏɴᴅᴏɴ ɪɴ 1913 was more than a large and cosmopolitan European city; it was the focal point of a sprawling empire that since has vanished, capital of a people proud of that empire and a long history of cultural and political progress. For an American like Page, accustomed to looking to the future rather than the past, the transition to a world where tradition was important, where noble blood somehow was redder, or bluer, might have seemed difficult. It did not turn out that way. Indeed Page merged into London society with ease. During those first months on the job he learned that the life of an ambassador can be enjoyable, especially when he represented a great nation like the United States in time of peace; one even might say that the first months in London, to August 1914, were a vacation. He did meet some diplomatic problems, such as Mexico and the Panama tolls, but these were minor and did not force him to unpleasantness with the people at the Foreign Office. He could deal adequately with Anglo-American relations while enjoying the diplomat's role of fostering friendship in the nation of his embassy.

Before having to undergo the harassing years of war, Page thus had some happy times moving about London and the countryside pursuing the light side of an ambassador's job. Social life of major diplomats involves entertaining, often in reciprocity with a nation's social and political elite. Before going to London, Page had associated with important people in the United States and of course was a friend of the new president, but appointment as ambassador to the Court of St. James's cast him into a society unlike anything he had encountered before. He now rubbed shoulders with dukes, earls, even the monarch himself, George V. He took these new experiences in stride. Though a confirmed democrat, he found the protocol and ritual amusing sights. Especially exciting was the glitter about the monarchy, for with his knowledge of British government Page was able to view the king as chiefly a ceremonial official and no obstacle to democracy.

Even so Page did experience some trying moments while learning the steps of social and diplomatic ritual. On one occasion he became absorbed in discussion, ignorant that other guests could not leave until the ambassador had moved on. Seeking to behave better, at another gathering he overlooked the presence of royalty, moved too quickly, and left a royal person standing without an ambassadorial conversation.[1] A reception of the king called for special dress. Most officials fortunate enough to receive an invitation wore flamboyant uniforms, which Page could not do. He had to wear a black suit with knee breeches and "a funny little tin sword." The ambassador at first felt strange in such costume but came to enjoy the knee breeches, "nice and comfortable," though "a devil of a lot of trouble to put 'em on." Nor was he oblivious that as an ambassador he was a diplomatic agent of first rank, a more august personage than a minister: "The Ambassadors come in first and bow and the King shakes hands with them. Then come the forty or more Ministers—no shake for them."[2] It was all new and pleasant and Page was able to write, "I am having more fun than anyone in the world."[3]

The society that Page adorned was not all politeness and pageantry, as the ambassador soon discovered, for Page had arrived

[1] Described in House diary notation, June 19, 1913, Seymour, *Colonel House,* 1: 188. See also Page to Wilson, Oct. 25, 1913, Hendrick, *Page,* 1: 147.
[2] Page to Robert Newton Page (a brother), Dec. 22, 1913, Hendrick, *Page,* 1: 156–57.
[3] To David F. Houston, undated, ibid., 151–52.

in England at a time of marked change in politics, when the nation seemed almost on the verge of civil war. Emotion had lingered over the Parliament Act of 1911, which virtually had eliminated the House of Lords as a lawmaking body, an act that one Conservative politician referred to with some exaggeration as "an instrument of Parliamentary government . . . for which . . . you will find no parallel in the whole record of human folly since the world began."[4] That crisis had come about because of the steeply graduated tax policy of Chancellor of the Exchequer David Lloyd George. One Tory lady told Page she no longer could invite Liberal friends to her house: "I have lost them—they are robbing us, you know."[5] To pass the Parliament Act the Liberal government had used the Irish vote; in return Liberals pushed through a Home Rule bill for Ireland, which would place Protestants of Northern Ireland under Catholics of the South. Long an explosive issue in British politics, the Irish question again raised tempers to a pitch. If these problems were not enough, the movement for woman suffrage was at its peak in the British Isles. The suffragettes led by the dynamic Pankhurst sisters were fasting to the point of starvation, smashing windows, mobbing members of Parliament, using all the ingenious female methods of disturbance at their command.

For a man of his temperament and political inclination, Page's letters on these issues show remarkable restraint. The ambassador talked with members of both political parties, listened to the case for each element of British society, and, playing the true diplomat, avoided sides. On one occasion he slipped and voiced a word of praise of Sir Edward Grey to a duke. "Yes, yes," the duke snapped, "no doubt an able man, but you must understand, sir, that I don't train with that gang."[6] Another "old Tory" talked him deaf abusing the Liberal government:

"You do this way in the United States—hate one another don't you?"

"No," said I, "we live like angels in perfect harmony except for a few weeks before election."

[4] Speech by Bonar Law in the *Times* (London) , May 28, 1913.
[5] Page to Woodrow Wilson, Oct. 25, 1913, Hendrick, *Page,* 1: 145.
[6] Ibid.

"The devil you do. You don't hate one another? What do you do for enemies? I couldn't get along without enemies to swear at."[7]

Page dealt mostly with Liberals, since they were in office, and compared the Liberal party with the Democratic party, but rarely expressed himself on issues. He could witness these goings-on and retain faith in the British system and nation. As with the monarchy, he was more amused than troubled.

The first problems in London were not diplomatic, but domestic household concerns which caused inconvenience and considerable embarrassment. The United States provided its ambassador no permanent residence at that time, and there arose immediately the problem of a house and also a suitable place of business. The chancery at 123 Victoria Street was in a dingy, dilapidated section of the city where Page's predecessors had spent as little time as possible. When he saw the building his heart sank: "I knew that Uncle Sam had no fit dwelling there." He lived three months at the Coburg Hotel ("a crowded and uncomfortable nightmare"[8]), and in time obtained a house at 6 Grosvenor Square, with twenty bedrooms, seven drawing rooms, a large ballroom and large reception hall—"no frills," said Page, "but . . . simply the kind of house in which . . . an American Ambassador should be housed."[9] That took care of a residence, but the place of business still was the old chancery, and for several months Page was embarrassed to meet anyone there. "It's a damned mean outfit, your American Government," one Briton remarked.[10]

Of greater importance was the huge personal expense Page had to incur while handling the normal functions of his post. His allowance of $17,500—a diminutive sum compared with the $85,000 the British government provided its ambassador in Washington—fell far short of the costs of a respectable London embassy. This fact need not have been much of a surprise, for previous American representatives, particularly men of modest

---

[7] Page to Robert N. Page, Dec. 22, 1913, ibid., 159.

[8] Essay, "The Ambassadorship," Page Papers.

[9] New York *Times*, Aug. 26, 1913.

[10] Page to House, Feb. 13, 1914, Hendrick, *Page*, 1: 233; also Page to Wilson, June 8, 1913, Wilson Papers.

means, had encountered the same problem; it was common belief that only a wealthy person could handle the posts at London, Paris, and one or two other capitals. Page's first year cost about $30,000 of personal savings and forced such a drain on his resources that he wrote President Wilson in June 1914 he could not continue unless he received funds.[11] The president at that time was so delighted with Page's performance that he would not permit so paltry a problem as money to cause the loss of his ambassador in London. Aware of Congress's reluctance to face up to the expenses in the foreign service, Wilson searched for an unofficial source of aid, and his old and wealthy friend Cleveland H. Dodge came to the rescue with an offer for Page, annually, of $25,000. The money went to Colonel House who sent it to Page's son Arthur. Content that his benefactor should remain anonymous, the ambassador never learned the source of assistance.[12]

Meanwhile Page went on with the numerous, albeit uninspiring tasks of diplomatic routine expected of all foreign representatives. He had to keep his government informed about Great Britain and give advice on policy. It was his duty to represent Americans and their government—signing passports, bailing compatriots from jail ("when they are jugged"), obtaining tickets to races, making speeches. He had the task of explaining American politics and government to all classes of Britons. (He had to explain that all Americans were not rich; one lady complained that she had only $1,250,000—"nothing like all you Americans."[13]) Page went about these chores with remarkably few signs of boredom. He liked speeches and private discussion, for they gave him opportunity to trumpet the virtues of the new American president and pound some elementary democracy into Britons.

Fortunately he came to London when there was a surfeit of friendship for the United States, which helped the ambassadorial duties of fostering friendship. It had not always been this way, and perhaps an explanation for the state of Anglo-American affairs in 1913–1914 was that times had changed and by the turn

[11] June 5, 1914, Hendrick, *Page,* 3: 79–87.
[12] Explained in House Diary, Sept. 5, 1914; also Page to Wilson, Nov. 5, 1914, Page Papers.
[13] Page to Robert N. Page, Dec. 22, 1913, Hendrick, *Page,* 1: 155, 160.

of the century the British were learning to value the people and government of the United States. British insecurity, so obvious after the World War began, scarcely was camouflaged beforehand. Preceding decades had seen the Union Jack carried to new lands in Asia, Africa, the Near East, an expansion that had enhanced imperial prestige and British commerce but not without attracting a multitude of incidents with nations trying to do the same thing. The traditional "splendid isolation" made no sense in the new twentieth-century era of crisis and power alliances, and so His Majesty's government had cast about for allies.

Participation in the diplomatic chess game inevitably affected relations with the United States. The record after the 1890s showed increasing restraint toward the American government, far different from earlier days when such men as Lord Palmerston occupied the Foreign Office. The Venezuela boundary dispute of 1894–1895 had ended with arbitration; in the Spanish-American War, Britain encouraged the United States; in 1901 the second Hay-Pauncefote Treaty gave in to the United States on building a Panama Canal; two years later Britain agreed to arbitrate the Alaska-Canada boundary dispute in the manner President Roosevelt had described with an outcome in total accord with American wishes. If there was a sign of bellicosity in any of these incidents, it was all on the side of the Americans. With a similar language, culture, and tradition, with huge economic wealth, and an impressive navy, the United States was a nation well worth cultivating.

Many individual Americans took pleasure in this new rapprochement. Some persons like Henry Adams, who in historical studies had "flung himself into the arms of the Anglo-Saxons in history," based friendship on a sense of racial superiority. Theodore Roosevelt loved the British when he was not preparing to fight them, and felt warmth for such people as James Bryce, ambassador to the United States during the term of President Taft, and especially Bryce's successor Sir Cecil Spring-Rice. President Wilson was an admirer of British literature and government. Another anglophile was Walter Page.

It is doubtful that any Briton could have served Anglo-American friendship better, had greater influence with Page, than the man directing the Foreign Office in 1913, Sir Edward Grey, for during the long period in which Grey was foreign secretary, from 1905 to 1916, one of his principles was to maintain good relations with the United States. A Liberal and, like Page, concerned for both the common and the cultivated man, equally at ease discussing English classics or foreign affairs, this cultured diplomat had a profound influence on all Americans who met with him—a quiet, pensive individual who, while observing the ritual of Old World diplomacy, privately admitted to Page that much of it was superficial or silly. The two men soon established a friendship that confounded old methods of diplomacy; they discussed world problems in frequent confidential conversations during which neither man withheld anything, so Page felt. Before the war the two men were able to help smooth out all possible misunderstandings between their nations.[14]

When Page arrived in London he found the problem of Mexico on the docket, and so while attending parties, meeting important people, and beginning to feel important himself, he was getting his feet on the ground in the serious part of diplomacy. While it seemed important at the time, the Mexican situation was never a critical issue between Britain and the United States; it did not threaten British security or the balance of European power, and Grey could be friendly and cooperative. Solution of the Mexican problem in American-British relations, and the manner of solution led Page to believe that this was what diplomacy was or should be, perhaps a poor analogue for later years.

President Wilson had inherited the Mexican problem from Taft, and it gave opportunity to test the moral diplomacy of the new administration in what seemed a simple series of Mexican events. President Porfirio Díaz had ruled Mexico for many years, from 1877 until 1911, at which time Francisco Madero forced out the aging dictator and took over the government, but Madero was unable to maintain himself and brought in a drunken if efficient soldier, General Victoriano Huerta, to put down revolutionaries, whereupon Huerta turned on his sponsor, signed an agreement

[14] For Grey's attitude toward the United States and Page see his *Twenty-five Years, 1892–1916*, 2 vols. (New York, 1925), 2: 86–89, 96–102; also George M. Trevelyan, *Grey of Fallodon* (Cambridge, Mass., 1937), 102.

with the revolutionaries, and permitted the murder of his former chief in February 1913. Huerta in Wilson's eyes was merely one of many Mexican revolutionary leaders, and the president believed the unrest had gone on long enough. The Mexican tyrant became the focus of a new American foreign policy: that governments should come to power peacefully and rest on support of their citizens. Inasmuch as Huerta did not meet these qualifications, Wilson defied traditional diplomatic procedure, refused to recognize Huerta, and put on pressure to oust the general.

Some diplomatic difficulty then arose with Britain. British interests in Mexico stemmed largely from investment, particularly the oil wells of Lord Cowdray which produced fuel for the Royal Navy. British policy required protection of these concessions and the lives of subjects in Mexico. Less concerned than Wilson about what the Mexican government was, or how it came to power, Grey could see no moral difference between Huerta and the factions wishing to depose him. The foreign secretary believed the reports of his agents in Mexico which said that order—hence protection of British interests—best could come through a Huerta government or a government with his support.[15] By the time Wilson became president Britain had recognized and was doing business with Huerta's regime.

It became the duty of Page to explain Wilson's policy to the British and persuade them to withdraw recognition, which Wilson and Page hoped would cause the dictator's fall, presumably the first step toward Mexican democracy. The ambassador's conversation with Grey was thoughtful and friendly, but at first not heavy with result. At times he wrote Wilson of irritation: "I can't get away from the feeling that the English simply do not and will not believe in any unselfish action—further than the keeping of order. They have a mania for order, sheer order, order for the sake of order."[16] Like Wilson, the ambassador was disturbed at

[15] The minister in Mexico (Stronge) to the foreign secretary, Aug. 27, Sept. 2, 1913, Foreign Office Papers, Series 371, Vol. 1676, Public Record Office, London. Hereafter citations from the Foreign Office Papers will read, for example, F. O. 371/1676. See also Grey, *Twenty-five Years*, 2: 99–100.

[16] Nov. 16, 1913, Hendrick, *Page*, 1: 188. For other criticism of British policy see Page Diary, Nov. 1913.

Britain's inability to understand the president's high moral purpose in Mexico.

The Mexican situation gave the first hint of Page's ideas on foreign policy; it showed he was, if anything, a more enthusiastic exponent of idealistic missionary nationalism than Wilson. He agreed that undemocratic countries should adopt American principles but was willing to go farther than the president to boost undeveloped nations into progressivism and popular government. That these people might not want American interference seemed of little importance. He wrote exuberant letters to Wilson and House about a new world order under American leadership and occasionally disclosed some of these ideas to Grey. Meeting the foreign secretary in October 1913, he gave some unofficial thoughts of how he would like to see the Mexican problem treated. Page spoke of the growing suspicion that British interests had financed Huerta (which Grey denied), and explained that the United States probably would have to intervene. "In that event," he said, "the United States would go into Mexico, and they would hold the elections with bayonets round every polling station to ensure that the people voted secretly and with freedom, so that the result of the election might be the choice of the people." Cautioned that such action would be a large operation, Page replied that "however many millions it cost, if the American people decided to act they would vote anything that was required." The ambassador expressed belief that the United States, in Mexico as in Cuba, should intervene as often as necessary to ensure a democratic society.[17] Grey—much more the realistic diplomatist—listened to these ideas with interest and considerable amusement. "Remember," Spring-Rice once warned his British colleagues, "that Christ if he had been an American would have run for the governorship of Judaea with the sermon on the mount for his platform."[18]

Like many nationalists and expansionists, Page believed that

[17] Grey to Spring-Rice, Oct. 28, 1913, the Papers of Sir Cecil Spring-Rice, Public Record Office, London.

[18] Spring-Rice to Sir William Tyrrell, Feb. 3, 1914, the Papers of Viscount Grey of Fallodon, Public Record Office, London.

American greatness partly was attributable to kinship with the British nation—a matter of racial, not solely national superiority —and as he devised schemes for remaking the world he did not hesitate to invite the British to join in. One time he proposed to Wilson that the United States and Britain jointly announce intervention in Mexico, apparently believing this proclamation would frighten the Mexicans into stable government. Another time he wrote House: "If I could outdo these folk at their game of courtesy and could keep our treaty faith with 'em, then I could lick 'em into the next century on the moral aspects of the Mexican Government . . . and you know what it would lead to—even in our lifetime—to the leadership of the world; and we should presently be considering how we may best use the British fleet, the British empire, and the British race for the betterment of mankind."[19]

When the time came for solving the dispute over Mexico, Page was less ambitious, and his negotiation with Grey was partly responsible for settlement of Anglo-American differences. Solution did not come until many Americans, including the president, became aroused over continued British recognition of Huerta. Wilson had become convinced that British oil interests, which he felt were dictating British policy, stood in the way of Huerta's fall. The British government had aggravated the issue in July 1913 when it appointed Sir Lionel Carden as minister to Mexico. Carden had been unpopular with the American government for some time, and the Taft administration previously had asked his removal from Cuba because of reputed anti-Americanism. Bitterly opposed to Wilson's Mexican policy, he now made some indiscreet public statements which the American press exaggerated, and Wilson came to believe that Carden was giving assistance to Huerta.[20]

Several factors then combined to relieve tension and induce Grey to place the Mexican situation in Wilson's hands. Among

[19] Nov. 2, 1913, Hendrick, *Page*, 1: 189–90. Page set down his proposal in a memorandum he sent to House to give Wilson, Aug. 25, 1913, ibid., 194–95. For a similar proposition see Page to Grey, March 11, 1914, Grey Papers.

[20] House to Page, Nov. 4, 1913, Page Papers.

these factors was Page's amicable and persistent explanation of Wilsonian diplomacy. During the illness of Spring-Rice, Grey sent his private secretary, Sir William Tyrrell, to talk with the president and secretary of state. Tyrrell had little success with Bryan, but he managed to remove some of the president's suspicion that oil interests dictated British policy. As for Wilson's policy, he could get only the now famous presidential statement: "I am going to teach the South American Republics to elect good men."[21] But the conversation eventually permitted a settlement. Grey offered to urge Huerta to retire, if he could get a promise that the United States would recognize and protect British rights if chaos followed.[22] In December the foreign secretary explained to Page that these rights included, besides protection of British citizens, concessions granted before the Huerta regime. He would not insist upon privileges granted by Huerta, nor large or "political" concessions. Page "entirely agreed" to these conditions, and explained that Wilson did not wish to deny legitimate commercial enterprise, but opposed far-reaching activity, such "perhaps" as the oil wells of Lord Cowdray.[23]

In months to come, Grey maintained restraint despite dreadfully little evidence of improvement in the Mexican situation. Carden, who smothered the Foreign Office with reports of disorder and savagery, wished to make public statements to expose the absurdity of Wilson's meddling. One Foreign Office official concluded from reading the dispatches that "it is evidently the intention of the U.S. for some ulterior object to introduce a state of complete anarchy & misery in Mexico."[24] Even so, Grey held firm, kept quiet, and instructed Carden to keep his thoughts to him-

[21] Cited in Hendrick, *Page,* 1: 204.

[22] Page to the secretary of state, Nov. 13, 1913, *Papers Relating to the Foreign Relations of the United States, 1913* (Washington, D.C., 1920), 860–61.

[23] The foreign secretary to Ambassador Spring-Rice, Dec. 8, 1913, F. O. 371/1679; see also Wilson to Tyrrell, Nov. 22, 1913, cited in Arthur S. Link, *Woodrow Wilson and the Progressive Era* (New York, 1954), 119.

[24] Notes by Mr. Spicer accompanying Carden's message to the foreign secretary, Dec. 7, 1913, F. O. 371/1679. Other reports by Carden include the messages sent Dec. 6, 8, 15, 1913, ibid.

self.[25] He believed no more than Carden that Wilson's ambitious venture would be successful, but did not wish to see Mexico the cause for Anglo-American difficulty. And in time Carden left the scene. Reports from Spring-Rice about the attitude in Washington and Page's gentle prodding led Grey to call the diplomat home for consultation in spring 1914.[26] In a few weeks Carden returned to Mexico but only to make preparation for permanent departure. While Grey maintained that the transfer was merely fulfillment of Carden's original appointment, few individuals doubted that he acted to please the American government.[27] If Mexico was to be a worrisome problem with Wilson for several months thereafter, by spring of 1914 it was no longer an important issue in British relations.

Page was delighted. "An abler man could have done it better," he noted, "but as it was, I did it."[28] Of course, Page did not solve the problem alone nor did he mean to imply he had. Tyrrell's visit had helped. Most important was Grey's desire for American friendship, willingness to regard Mexico as a United States sphere of influence. Page's performance was important enough, however, that he rightfully could give himself a passing score on his first diplomatic test, and he then could devote full attention to the other problem of Anglo-American relations, the Panama tolls issue.

The Panama controversy dated at least to the year 1850 when Britain and the United States in the Clayton-Bulwer Treaty agreed to joint construction and operation of a canal in Central America. Neither nation did anything for a half century, at which time the United States felt pressing need for a link between the Atlantic and Pacific oceans. The Hay-Pauncefote Treaty of 1901

[25] Grey told Carden that the only alternative to long drawn-out disorder was American intervention, "as they will certainly not abandon their settled purpose to eliminate . . . [Huerta]. But I cannot urge the United States to intervene." Dec. 9, 1913, ibid.

[26] Spring-Rice to Grey, Feb. 6, 1914, Grey Papers; Page to House, Nov. 23, 1913, Hendrick, *Page,* 1: 212; House Diary, Dec. 6, 1913.

[27] The foreign secretary to Ambassador Spring-Rice, April 2, 1914, Grey Papers.

[28] To Frank Doubleday and others, Dec. 28, 1913, Hendrick, *Page,* 1: 166–67.

put exclusive right of construction in the hands of the American government, stipulating that the canal be free and open to ships of all nations and that tolls be equal. In seeming violation of the final provision, Congress in 1912 passed and President Taft signed a bill that exempted American coastal shipping. The dubious reason for this measure was that the term "all nations" did not apply to the United States. Distressed at what it considered an act of bad faith, the Foreign Office had protested to the State Department in December 1912; and throughout 1913 Page had to read British editorials that assailed the tolls act.

Page built a dream edifice on the tolls problem, viewing its equitable solution as the veritable foundation of future American policy. Even before leaving the United States he had decided the legislation was wrong; what he heard in London strengthened this belief. When he posed the question to the foreign secretary in June, Grey expressed strong feeling that the issue involved more than a technicality, that American shipping stood to gain and British shipping to lose if the law remained in effect. The foreign secretary said he would accept arbitration if there could be no better solution, but hoped the new Congress would repeal the measure. Page said he understood Grey's position, ventured a guess that Congress would abolish the law, and tried to explain how domestic American politics complicated the issue.[29] He kept the White House informed of the British (and his own) view that the United States had acted dishonorably: "We made a bargain —a solemn compact—and we have broken it . . . this . . . matter stands in the way of everything. It is in their minds all the

---

[29] The foreign secretary to Ambassador Spring-Rice, June 12, 1913, F. O. 371/1702. In this interview with Page, Grey explained that British shipping might suffer the following ways:
  1. Exemption of United States ships would place a heavier toll burden on ships of foreign nations.
  2. Goods that normally traveled from Liverpool to San Francisco or other Pacific ports (on British ships) might now be sent to New York and from there be sent on American ships.
  3. American coastal shipping might have aboard goods of foreign as well as local trade.
  4. American ships on return voyage might pick up goods in Central or South America which ordinarily might travel in British vessels.

time—the minds of all parties and all sections of opinion."[30] Page believed the tolls act prevented revolutionary progress in American foreign relations. "If the United States will have a home here and repeal the Canal-toll discrimination, we can command the British fleet, British manufacturers—anything we please," he wrote House. "Till we do these things, they'll regard us as mean and stingy and dishonorable on occasion and, therefore, peculiar and given to queer freaks."[31]

Repeal might have been simple had it been a controversy between American political parties, had, let us say, the Wilson administration come to power in 1913 with the opportunity to discredit the Republican administration of President Taft by reversing the tolls act. But the question had cut across party lines, and in the campaign of 1912 the Democratic platform and presidential candidate had favored the exemption law. Wilson did this in ignorance. The campaign stressed domestic issues, with Wilson and Roosevelt arguing what to do with trusts, not foreign affairs. Once he gave the matter serious study, the president decided to have the act repealed.

Even so, Wilson had to move cautiously. Anglophobes in the United States, aroused by the British press, stood ever ready to resist generous gestures to the British government, and among these individuals were some Democratic politicians whose votes Wilson needed to place into law important New Freedom measures. The issue inevitably became embroiled with the difficulty in Mexico, and once Grey had yielded to Wilson on that problem, the president had to avoid the impression that he was trading concessions. The British ambassador (James Bryce; Spring-Rice had not arrived) frequently mentioned the tolls issue to Wilson and Secretary Bryan, but the best he could report was that while the United States wished to be just and honorable, Britain would have to wait until the president chose to act.[32]

Page's job was to see that the British government did nothing to

[30] Page to Wilson, Sept. 10, 1913, Page Papers.
[31] Aug. 28, 1913, ibid.
[32] Ambassador Bryce to the foreign secretary, March 18, 24, April 1, 14, 18, 1913, F. O. 371/1702.

make Wilson's task more difficult. It was an easy undertaking, for Bryce long had cautioned patience, and simple logic said that further protest could do nothing more than endanger the end Grey desired. Colonel House was in Europe in summer 1913, and Page, after explaining the colonel's relation with the president, arranged a meeting with Grey. House repeated that Wilson had decided upon repeal, and joined Page in suggesting it might be wise for the British to be silent. Though much disappointed at the delay, Grey agreed, and through the controversy which lasted until June 1914, the only official British protest remained the note of December 1912.[33]

Unfortunately Page—perhaps the person most anxious to see the president's views prevail—was the individual who caused Wilson some of the greatest difficulty. The ambassador in March 1914 went before a London audience to make some off-the-cuff, half-serious comment about a number of things including the Panama Canal and Monroe Doctrine. He observed that while the United States had not built the canal for Great Britain, knowledge that the British would profit most (because they had the largest merchant marine) "added to the pleasure" of its building. He said the United States would prefer that European countries acquire no new territory in the western hemisphere. When fragmentary reports filtered into the United States some individuals interpreted Page's words to mean that while the United States "preferred" European countries to acquire no territory in the western hemisphere it would not object if they did, that the administration wished repeal of the discriminatory tolls law so Britain could profit more from the Panama Canal.[34]

For one of the few times in his ambassadorial career Page received front page coverage in the eastern press. William Randolph Hearst devoted almost the entire editorial page of the New York *American* to a jubilant attack on Page, Wilson, and the repeal bill. The Senate, led by Chamberlain of Oregon, passed a resolution demanding the text of Page's remarks, and Chamber-

[33] House diary notation, July 3, 1913, Seymour, *Colonel House,* 1: 193; Hendrick, *Page,* 1: 245–46.
[34] New York *Times,* March 13, 1914.

lain, O'Gorman of New York, and a few other senators demanded Page's recall.[35] Perhaps proof that Page had become an international figure came from the fact that he merited an assault from Mr. Dooley, the mythical political philosopher created by Finley Peter Dunne, who devoted his entire page in the New York *Times* to the problem of diplomatic indiscretion: "I am wondhrin'," said Dooley to his friend Hennessy, "if we can't find some way f'r our ambassdures to England to entertain th' English people without speakin' in public. It's a tur-rble sthrain on them, it's a tur-rble sthrain on us, an' it's a good deal iv a sthrain on th' English people. Not that I care much what happens to our hereditary inimies or cousins, but it makes me onaise to wake up in th' morning an larn that th' American Ambassdure in ordher to amuse th' annyoial meetin' iv th' Hon'rable Guild iv Deck Hands had offered to turn over Michigan to th' Canajen governmint because iv th' gratichood he feels toward Willum Shakespeare." Dooley while on the subject explained the selection and duties of an ambassador to Britain. In the "good old days" the successful candidate had to have "knowledge in burglary an' a good poker face." Nowadays the president went down a list of acquaintances of the campaign and selected a man who had saved a little and could afford a vacation. So appointed, the ambassador went for instruction. "There ain't anny. 'Don't bother ye're head about matthers that don't consarn ye,' says the Prisidint. 'Run along an injye ye'ersilf. See Shakespeare's tomb, dhrop in at Westministher Abbey, have a good time. Be light hearted an gay. Amuse th' British popylace. If ye can sing or whistle so much th' better.' " So instructed, the ambassador crossed the Atlantic bent on entertaining the English. He visited a few places, tried several stunts, but could not get a rise. "So," continued Mr. Dooley, "he's dhriven to greater an' greater lengths to get a hand, an before he's through he's offerin' to cancel the Declaration iv Indypendence an' pull down th' Bunker Hill monymint. Mind ye, there's no harder task in th' wurruld thin to make a hearty Briton laugh without ye break a leg or set down on ye'er hat." Finally, "in a fit iv desp'ration, he took up th' Monroe Docthrine an jumped on it. 'It

35 Ibid., March 14, 1914.

don't mean annything,' he said. 'It's a joke. I niver heerd iv it till I come over here. If ye want South America take it. It ain't mine to give, but ye can have it annyhow. Take annything we've got. On'y smile. For hiven's sake, smile.' " Dooley did not blame Page for what he said about the Monroe Doctrine; the stolid English audience drove him to it.[36]

Aside from angering people who disliked the British anyway, and leaving in the public mind a vague identification of Page with anglophilism, the matter had no far-reaching effect. The furor quieted when the ambassador sent a copy of the address as best he could remember it, with explanation that part was jocular. Common judgment was that newspapers had interpreted Page incorrectly, and while the canal and Monroe Doctrine were not matters to joke about, the speech was harmless.[37] The president did have to answer allegation that Britain was pressing him. But in no way did the incident undermine Wilson's high regard for his ambassador. Wilson wrote that though the speech was probably ill-timed Page should not worry, and that he was pleased with the job Page was doing.[38] A few days afterward House reiterated the president's attitude: "I would have given a great deal if you could have heard what he said of you to Cleveland Dodge. He also spoke of your letters to him to me as classics and said they were the best letters as far as he knew, that anyone had ever written."[39] Above all, Page's speech did not change the outcome of the tolls controversy. Faithful to his promise, the president hurled determination and talent for leadership into the struggle. He asked for a repeal bill, then demanded it, quarreled with Republicans, quarreled with Democrats, used patronage and other powers to their fullest, and in June 1914 emerged victorious without a party split.[40]

Page came out of the episode pleased, somewhat surprised at the trouble he had caused, but little wiser. If he recognized his

---

[36] Ibid., March 22, 1914.
[37] Ibid., March 14, 19, 1914.
[38] March 25, April 2, 1914, Page Papers; Hendrick, *Page*, 1: 262–63, 265–66.
[39] April 19, 1914, Page Papers.
[40] A good summary of the controversy appears in Arthur S. Link, *Wilson: The New Freedom* (Princeton, N.J., 1956), 307–12.

flair for outspokenness, he did not consider it a liability in London. "Of course what some of the American newspapers have said is true—that I am too free and untrained to be a great Ambassador," he wrote the president, "but the conventional type of Ambassador would not be worth his salt to represent the United States here now, when they are eager to work with us for the peace of the world, if they are convinced of our honour and right-mindedness and the genuineness of our friendship."[41] The forbearance of Grey in the Mexican and Panama tolls issues convinced him that the foreign secretary was anxious to work frankly with the United States. Page based his diplomacy on friendship, not suspicion, and in doing so was an effective representative for the United States so long as diplomatic problems were not serious.

Serious problems, however, were closer than most people suspected. Concerning the European situation in 1914, it has become customary to cite obvious signs of danger—commercial competition, the naval race, the alliance systems—and wonder how people and governments could have been so foolish. Only from the present day, with Americans accustomed to huge defense budgets, when almost any diplomatic crisis might lead to world war can one understand the European attitude of that bygone day. Still, this newly acquired enlightenment does not subtract from the danger in 1914. If Europeans had learned to live with crisis and huge armament expenditure, the detached observer easily could catch the senselessness of the Old World atmosphere.

Page, for a time, saw Europe not merely with the eyes of an outsider, but as citizen of a nation richer than any European power and in some ways richer than all Europe, a nation aloof from armament races and balances of power. All these factors made a deep impression on the ambassador, a nationalist and idealist anxious to improve the world. It was clear that Europe could not work out its own problems. Leadership would have to come from the United States. "There's no future in Europe's

41 "Right or wrong," continued Page, "the American ambassador here is put in a class by himself and given liberties that European ambassadors have never taken and are denied by their armed and jealous governments." March 18, 1914, Page Papers.

vision," he wrote House, "no long look ahead. They give all their thought to the immediate danger."[42] Idealism was a feature of the Wilson administration: the president had spoken of putting the nation at the service of humanity; but the task of the presidency left him no time to devise anything specific in the way of international organization. For the first year and a half of the administration Wilson thought nationally, not internationally. Page's position permitted time and perspective for broad speculation and he frequently sought a system whereby Europe could turn its energies toward world peace and material betterment of humanity, with the United States leading the way.

Page's favorite scheme for peace and world reorganization involved Anglo-American cooperation. Standing together the two Anglo-Saxon nations could show such great power that no nation would dare go to war without their permission. Wilson, he felt, could make a step in the proper direction if he visited England, and the ambassador wrote the president about it. "The old Earth would sit up and rub its eyes and take notice to whom it belongs," he noted. "This visit might prevent an English-German war and an American-Japanese war."[43] Page had in mind at least a treaty of friendship, and while he used the word *alliance* cautiously, aware of the distaste Americans traditionally held for it, there is much to suggest he would have favored a military tie with Britain. He wrote House that he could see no hope of the United States making a mark on the world "so long as we choose to be ruled by an obsolete remark made by George Washington."[44]

If nothing came of Page's dreams before the World War—Wilson politely rejected the idea of a visit to England—House did make a meager attempt at a world plan when he journeyed to

[42] Aug. 28, 1913, ibid.; Hendrick, *Page*, 1: 271.
[43] Undated memorandum "about the President's coming to England," Page Papers. Page mentioned the idea to Wilson, July 9, 1913, Hendrick, *Page*, 3: 96.
[44] Jan. 2, 1914, Hendrick, *Page*, 1: 283. Pondering the question further Page asked himself "why the U.S. and G't Britain (and specifically all the English colonies) sh^d not make a hard-and-fast alliance; then invite all other nations in on an invitation gradually to disarm; and thus gradually reduce the world to a peace basis—why not?" Page Diary, Jan. 4, 1914.

Europe in the summer of 1914.[45] Perhaps Page's letters helped influence the colonel to undertake this "mission." House decided in the latter part of 1913 that he should go abroad and search for a solution to world tension, and received Wilson's blessing, so he thought. The colonel hoped he might create sympathetic understanding, perhaps a disarmament pact between Germany, France, Britain, and the United States. He proposed to go first to Germany and speak with the kaiser and if the results were encouraging he could continue to France and Britain.[46]

House's plan, fortunately or otherwise, was not the sort Page had in mind. "House proposes to go see the German emperor to try to reach any agreement about limiting armaments," he noted. "I doubt it; but let him try."[47] The ambassador, who preferred discussing problems intimately with Grey, did not feel this method would work with continental diplomats. He could not see how the quiet colonel could divert the suspicious powers, particularly the Germans, from their dangerous course. While House planned his trip Page kept up a stream of letters about Anglo-American cooperation. Unfriendly with European balance of power, he felt that an alliance between Britain and the United States—a concentration of power—would best prevent war.

It is needless to go into the details of House's well-meaning but futile journey. In Germany and Britain, diplomats were cordial, expressed vague interest, but contributed nothing. The French were so occupied with other matters that House did not stay in Paris.[48] No one tried to help him, not even Wilson. Nor did Page give much assistance: the ambassador was happy to see his friend in London and encouraged him, without hope of success. The colonel noted in his diary on June 12: "He [Page] was kind enough to say that he considered my work in Germany the most

[45] "I must say that I agree with your arguments for [a visit abroad] . . . ," wrote Wilson on Sept. 11, 1913, "and yet the case against the President's leaving the country . . . is very strong and I am afraid overwhelming." Page Papers.

[46] House to Page, Dec. 13, 1913, Hendrick, *Page*, 1: 277–78; House diary notation, Dec. 2, 1913, Seymour, *Colonel House*, 1: 242–43.

[47] Diary, Dec. 24, 1913.

[48] For details of this journey see Seymour, *Colonel House*, 1: 248–74.

important done in this generation." Page evidently showed House more enthusiasm than he felt and a few weeks later gave another view of the mission: "When House's plan first came to me, I wrote him a letter to show the utter futility of his idea. The next day I wisely burnt it because it was foolish, perhaps wicked, to discourage any such effort made by anybody; and I sent him another letter instead."[49] The task of staving off war was gigantic for anyone, let alone a man with as little prestige as House in 1914. His proposals hardly touched the underlying causes of the war which involved problems the colonel scarcely understood. In its beginning stages the plan merely called for discussion, and here was perhaps the proper beginning, yet no one was willing to take this first step to prevent a war everyone feared.

Summer 1914, with the first signs of war visible, marked the end of the idyllic period of Page's embassy. On the whole the first year in London had been a fruitful experience. There had been diplomatic and personal problems, but the ambassador had dealt with almost all of them. Perhaps the most enduring irritant was the State Department; like individuals before and after his time Page found the department uncooperative, an almost impenetrable thicket which repeatedly leaked confidential messages and kept its foreign diplomats in a haze about policy.[50] Fortunately the ambassador enjoyed a special relationship with Wilson, which allowed him at times to bypass the State Department, send messages direct to the president, and also point out the department's deficiencies. Wilson seemed entirely understanding and helpful. He wrote his ambassador as often as he found time and in every letter expressed delight at the tasks Page was undertaking.[51] The president had confided to a friend that Page was "for the present at any rate, an indispensable man in the right management of our foreign relations. I would not know what to do if I were obliged to part with him. . . . He has furnished me with more light on

[49] Page to Wilson, Sept. 6, 1914, Hendrick, *Page*, 3: 138.
[50] Page frequently complained about this problem; see, for example, Page to the secretary of state, Oct. 22, 1913, copy in Wilson Papers; House Diary, June 19, 1913, April 9, 1914.
[51] For example, see letters of Nov. 21, 1913, Feb. 24, 1914, March 7, 1914, Page Papers.

difficult foreign matters than all my other informants and advisers put together."[52]

In many respects, one might conclude, Page was like many men cast into a new position of prestige and importance. He had boundless enthusiasm, wished to do a great deal in a short time, simplified the solutions to complicated problems. He enjoyed his work and saw his position as an opportunity to serve his nation and the world. He liked working with the foreign secretary on a basis of confidence and hoped to establish such ideals in Anglo-American diplomacy. In characteristic manner Page went about this task boldly, perhaps too much so, for his friend Colonel House privately had predicted that unless Page proceeded with discretion he would cause trouble.[53]

[52] To Cleveland Dodge, July 12, 1914, Ray Stannard Baker, *Woodrow Wilson: Life and Letters*, 8 vols. (Garden City, N.Y., 1927–1939) , 4: 33.
[53] Diary, June 30, 1914.

Chapter Three

Battle for Civilization Begins

A s July marked the end of the social season and beginning of a slow time in official circles, Page closed the London house and took a place about an hour's travel from the city where he planned to spend several weeks playing golf, resting, and catching up on correspondence. Among the letters was a folksy missive July 22 to his brother, Robert, congressman from North Carolina. Looking back on the first year as a diplomat, he allowed some boastfulness. "I think I kept this Gov't from making possibly embarrassing protests about the Canal tolls," he wrote. "I've kept them right about Mexico too & induced them to refrain from embarrassing us in certain ways that they might quite innocently have done." He knew that nearly a month earlier an assassin had killed the heir-apparent to the Austro-Hungarian throne, but that needless and tragic act seemed to carry no special meaning; people had ceased to talk about it, and Page said nothing about the murder to his brother. Who could think about world events in such secluded, pleasant surroundings? "Trees & grass and flowers grow as they grow nowhere else," he continued. "All round this place are roses & geraniums (as big as roses) and sweet peas & hundreds of other flowers, and the gardener goes with the place."

He had brought along all the servants; aside from two or three trips a week to the embassy, there were no duties; and he looked forward to "a very happy, quiet time for three months."[1]

The quiet time lasted little more than a few days, for the armies of the Hapsburg monarchy then fired the shots which started Europe on the path to the First World War, and the ambassador had to rush back to a city far different from the London he had left. Inasmuch as it took a week thereafter for all the major powers to become involved—Britain did not go to war until August 5—the observer in London had a broader field of vision than if war had come at a single stroke, and Page had several days to make the rounds of diplomats and watch their reaction to an exciting series of events.

Little now escaped his eye, and fortunately much of what he observed found expression in letters to friends in the United States, which surely must have been some of the most moving prose at the time. Witness his description of the beleaguered diplomats: "I went to see the German Ambassador at three o'clock in the afternoon. He came down in his pajamas, a crazy man. I feared he might literally go mad. He is of the anti-war party and utterly failed. This interview was one of the most pathetic experiences of my life. . . . I shall never forget Sir Edward Grey's telling me of the ultimatum [which led to Britain's declaration of war upon Germany] while he wept; . . . nor the King as he declaimed at me for half-an-hour and threw up his hands and said, 'My God, Mr. Page, what else could we do?' Nor the Austrian Ambassador's wringing his hands and weeping and crying out 'My dear Colleague, my dear Colleague.' "[2] Several days later the ambassador still showed his excitement: "The world's gone mad & is burning up—blowing up. Nero in Hades must blush for shame that his achievements were so tame. The Goths and Huns and Huerta & Villa were mere novices and played for mere penny stakes—childish performances. Old Huerta landed here the other day & the papers gave him 2 lines.

[1] To Robert Newton Page, The Papers of Robert Newton Page, Duke University Library.

[2] To Woodrow Wilson, Aug. 9, 1914, Hendrick, *Page*, 1: 306, 309.

His show is no more than a tatoed [*sic*] Fiji Islander in a side-tent, 10 cts. admission."[3]

The bewilderment and anxiety Page met in the Foreign Office, embassies, or streets of London had its counterpart in the American embassy. War caught many Americans—as many as 60,000—in Britain or on the Continent on holiday, business, or some errand, and almost all wished to return home. Most Americans in Britain and many from the Continent (when they could get to England) dumped themselves on the embassy and pleaded or demanded action. It became the duty of Page and his staff to help find funds, lodging, and transport to the United States. "God save us! What a week it has been!" the ambassador described the scene. "Those first two days, there was, of course, great confusion. Crazy men and weeping women were imploring and cursing and demanding—God knows it was bedlam turned loose. I have been called a man of greatest genius for an emergency by some, by others a damned fool, by others every epithet between these extremes. Men shook English banknotes in my face and demanded United States money and swore our Government and its agents ought all to be shot. Women expected me to hand them steamship tickets home."[4] It was a chore that required, as one newspaper noted, "the wisdom of Solomon and the Patience of Job," for all types of Americans came to the embassy—those with no money, others with wealth and status who expected preferential treatment, others who wished to profit by the abnormal situation. One individual who had lived in England twenty years applied for passage to the United States, casually explaining he thought he would like to see the old folks at home.[5]

While he did not satisfy everyone Page did an admirable job organizing the American exodus. He acquired additional office space and enlarged his staff, several of whom were American volunteers, had the applicants cataloged so he could deal with them efficiently and democratically. The government sent the warship *Tennessee* with gold bullion to finance American nation-

[3] To Arthur W. Page, Aug. 23, 1914, Page Papers.
[4] To Wilson, Aug. 9, 1914, Hendrick, *Page,* 1: 303–305.
[5] New York *Times,* Sept. 1, 1914.

als, and then the ship set up ferry service between England and the Continent. Within a few days order returned to Victoria Street, but for well over a month a stream of Americans straggled into the embassy, many desperate, frustrated, some wearing the only possessions they had salvaged.

In addition to marooned compatriots there was the task of representing belligerent countries. It was to be one of the ironies of war that Page, who became intensely anti-German, acquired responsibility for German affairs in the British capital, was in a sense the German ambassador, for Germany and later Austria-Hungary asked the United States to take over their London embassies. Occasionally the State Department had a complaint of the ambassador's indifference toward this chore, but evidently the complaints were unmerited, for if Page was not enthusiastic he was scrupulous.[6] Most work was routine—such problems as German citizens in England, or prisoners of war—and Page could handle it while devoting most of his energy to representing the United States.

The detachment of the American people and government was so overwhelming that for a while it seemed to Page that his simplest task would be that of representing the United States. Virtually no American wanted anything to do with the war, unless it was to stop it or keep the conflict from spreading. Almost automatically Wilson had Bryan inquire if the good offices of the United States would be of value. Page's answer was not encouraging; he already had asked Grey if the United States could help, and repeated the offer, but the foreign secretary was evasive, asking if the American government had made a similar offer to Berlin, Vienna, or St. Petersburg. Page felt that the United States could do nothing at the time, and that to continue peace over-

---

[6] One message from William Bayard Hale to Secretary Bryan complained that Page "felt very slight concern as to this duty." Sept. 5, 1914, Bryan-Wilson Correspondence, National Archives. Wilson told Bryan that he thought Hale's report was completely untrue. Ibid. The ambassador in Berlin, James W. Gerard, later wrote House that Page was doing great work and that the Germans were convinced their prisoners were well treated in England. July 20, 1915, copy in Wilson Papers.

tures would lessen the chance to act later.[7] Wilson on August 4 made America's position public with a declaration of neutrality, and supplemented this statement on the seventeenth with an appeal for the American people to suppress their emotions and be neutral in thought as well as in deed.[8] The president and secretary of state moved to assure that an ocean separated their country from war. Bryan discouraged loans to belligerents, and Wilson refused to protest Germany's bombing of Belgian cities for fear he would be acting unneutrally.[9] Here was the simplest interpretation of neutrality—impartiality, treating each nation alike. Since neither Wilson nor Bryan was schooled in international law, such response was the only one they thought of. Then too, the president and secretary experienced emotions similar to most Americans: gratitude that this was not an American war.

Despite an environment much different from the secure Washington atmosphere, Page was in full agreement with his government's position. He could not fail to be impressed with London's confusion and urgency, the newspapers which called for volunteers to save country and king, the patriotic young men who lined up at recruitment stations. The tragedy of the scene overwhelmed him, and for that reason his earliest response was similar to the way most Americans responded—shock, horror, relief that this war did not involve the United States. In letters he thanked Heaven for the Atlantic Ocean and in a public statement virtually divorced his nation from anything to do with the war.[10] "How wise our no-alliance policy is," he wrote Wilson. In those days he explained the war in broad terms such as racism, "the Slav against

[7] Page to the secretary of state, Aug. 3, 1914, *Papers Relating to the Foreign Relations of the United States, 1914, Supplement* (Washington, D.C., 1928), 37; hereafter cited as *For. Rels.;* Page to the secretary of state, July 31, 1914, ibid., 24–25; the secretary of state to Page, July 28, 1914, ibid., 19.

[8] Both messages, ibid., 547–52.

[9] The secretary of state to J. P. Morgan and Company, Aug. 15, 1914, ibid., 580; President Wilson to the secretary of state, Sept. 4, 1914, *Papers Relating to the Foreign Relations of the United States, The Lansing Papers 1914–1920*, 2 vols. (Washington, D.C., 1939–1940), 1: 33; hereafter cited as *The Lansing Papers*.

[10] New York *Times,* Aug. 6, 1914.

the Teuton," nationalism, "Russians, Germans and even French-
men are . . . yet in that stage of evolution where the 'glory' of war
makes a strong appeal to them," and commercial rivalry. The first
letters seemed to say that one side was almost as bad as the other:
Page disliked Germany, suspected Russia, and was indifferent
toward France and Austria-Hungary.[11] It was clear that Britain
would enter the war to fight Germany, and while the clash between these two nations soon would dominate Page's attitude
toward the war and American neutrality, in the first days of
August he spoke as an American who could stand at a distance
and watch Old World powers battle it out.

For a man visibly touched with the dreadful affair, the ambassador viewed the war with remarkable opportunism. Irrational as
the conflict seemed, he saw it as perhaps the event which would
catapult the United States to a position of international leadership. At times during the first year in London he had expressed
desire for the United States to open an era of disarmament and
general world improvement, by itself or in collaboration with
Great Britain. British participation in the war meant that the
United States was the only great nation with perspective for a
settlement beyond vindictiveness or power politics. He seemed to
be watching Europe, waiting for the Old Continent to tear itself
apart so the United States could step in and assume leadership.
Fearing his country might return to old ideas of foreign affairs
and play a passive role, he counseled the president to "be ready;
for you will be called on to compose this huge quarrel. Now when
all this half of the world will suffer the unspeakable brutalization
of war, we shall preserve our moral strength, our political powers,
and our ideals."[12]

Aside from producing a much-needed prod for moral guidance,
Page felt the war would help the United States in a practical way
if the nation would refrain from policy of the days of Washington
and Jefferson. Earlier than most Americans he anticipated the
boost the war would give American commerce. Without misgiv-

[11] Page to Wilson, Aug. 2, 1914, Hendrick, *Page*, 3: 129–30; also Page to
Wilson, July 29, 1914, ibid., 127–28.
[12] Aug. 9, 1914, ibid., 1: 310–11; Page to Wilson, Aug. 2, 1914, ibid., 3: 130.

ings about war profits, indeed without any idea of the problems a neutral nation could encounter in wartime, he hoped the United States would expand its merchant marine to handle the huge business that inevitably would come. Whatever the course of the conflict, whoever the victor, peace would expose an exhausted and bankrupt Europe that would beg for American economic intervention.[13]

These ideas, practical and moral, represented Page's first hasty efforts to fit the international situation to his idea of a great and influential America. The World War was an extraordinary occurrence, and if it would be a disaster for Europe, the United States should exploit the situation and make the world what it should be. Europe, having proved itself incapable of managing even its own affairs, would have to yield moral, political, and economic leadership to the United States.

It is difficult to determine when Page made the transition from a detached observer to a partisan of the British cause, if indeed there was such transition. It might be helpful to note that the nations entered the war one-by-one over a period of approximately a week, and that Page was most aloof in the hectic days before Britain, the last great power to become involved, entered the war; but for several months the ambassador's thoughts ran along two not fully reconcilable paths. He saw the war as both an insane slaughter from which the United States should remain apart, and a British crusade for liberty and righteousness, which seemed to mean that someone had to destroy the murderous Germans, but the Americans should not do it.

Thus after a brief period of emotional detachment, and while expressing delight at American neutrality, Page went on to explain the great issue in the conflict. In not one letter or diplomatic dispatch did he delve into the negotiation of the days of July and August, and allocate blame. He looked for—and to his satisfaction found—the war's "larger meaning." This view held that the conflict was a clash between the British democracy and German autocracy. Page saw Germany attempting to attain the glory which late unification had prevented, trying to emulate

[13] Ibid.

nations which had had their time of continental supremacy—Caesar's Rome, Napoleon's France, the Spain of Philip II. This, thought Page, was an intolerable prospect. If the kaiser's armies won the European war it only would whet the Teutonic appetite. Thereafter no nation would be free of German influence, perhaps German attack, not even the United States which would have to maintain large military forces to defend the western hemisphere. As he later wrote House: "If German bureaucratic force would conquer Europe, presently it would try to conquer the United States; and we should all go back to the era of war as man's chief industry and back to the domination of kings by divine right. It seems to me therefore, that the Hohenzollern idea must perish—be utterly strangled in the making of peace."[14]

However much Germany represented what was undesirable in Europe, Great Britain represented everything good. Seldom to nonparticipants did war seem so clearly a matter of black and white as to Page in 1914. Early letters described Britons as vehicles of democracy and humanitarianism, not imperialists in a derogatory sense, the best fighters in Europe but no militarists. "It isn't an accident that these people own a fifth of the world,"[15] he would write; or "this English nation . . . [has] a quality that is invincible. I thank Heaven I'm of their race and blood."[16] One scarcely could determine that Alliance battled Entente. When he spoke of the Allies he rarely mentioned France and showed outright suspicion of the third partner, Russia. Britain was the nation he loved, and in his mind the fate of the world turned on its success.

It would be an overstatement to say that the ambassador's thoughts were solely a result of his relations with Grey, but the foreign secretary did have great influence on Page; and no one knew this fact better than Sir Edward. The foreign secretary also appreciated the importance of the nation Page represented, if not as an ally, at least as Britain's major source of supply. The United

[14] Sept. 22, 1914, ibid., 1: 327–28; Page to Wilson, Sept. 6, 22, 1914, ibid., 137–46.
[15] To Wilson (undated), ibid., 339.
[16] To House, Sept. 22, 1914, ibid., 334.

States, he later recalled, was "in a category by itself . . . so potentially important that its behavior might be decisive in deciding the war in favour of either set of belligerents."[17] Grey's prewar relations with Page provided an ideal foundation for efforts to obtain the correct position of the United States; and the foreign secretary was cautious to assure that the war caused no change. Page kept close touch with Grey during the critical days of July and August, and his admiration for the foreign secretary swelled to proportion of hero-worship. One dramatic meeting took place July 28, the day Austria-Hungary went to war with Serbia, when a general war seemed fully possible. "I think I shall never forget yesterday," Page wrote Wilson of the interview. "There sat this always solitary man—he and I, of course, in the room alone, each, I am sure, giving the other his full confidence. He looked ten years older than he looked a month ago." Page went on to explain the attributes of his friend: "He is, I imagine, the foremost Foreign Secretary in Europe . . . a forward-looking, liberal-minded man—a sort of sad and wise idealist, restrained and precise in speech and sparing in his use of words, a genuine clear-thinking man whose high hopes for mankind suffer sad rebuffs but are never quenched—a grave philosopher who feels the prodigious responsibility he carries."[18] England's day of decision was August 4 when Grey sent an ultimatum demanding that Germany stay out of Belgium or face war with Britain. He called in Page that afternoon to explain his act and indicate what likely would happen. The ambassador listened sympathetically, noting each move and expression so profoundly that he could have described them at any time the remainder of his life: Grey stood first against the mantlepiece in the Foreign Office, calm and dignified; now he sat in a chair, arms on the arms of the chair, hands folded under the chin, sad; now he rose quickly, eyes flashing determination characteristic of English gentlemen to declare that Britain would not permit Germany to violate Belgian neutrality; reverting to depression, he tearfully explained that the war party had control in

[17] *Twenty-five Years, 1892–1916*, 2 vols. (New York, 1925), 2: 168; also George M. Trevelyan, *Grey of Fallodon* (Cambridge, Mass., 1937), 356.
[18] July 29, 1914, Hendrick, *Page*, 3: 126.

Germany, that war was inevitable. "Thus the efforts of a lifetime go for nothing," he said.[19]

It is hardly accurate to think that Grey was out of character in those touching interviews. Never boisterous, the foreign secretary felt many of the emotions Page attributed to him. But it would be naïve to assume that these meetings, if reflecting a true state of mind, were not conscious diplomacy, providing an atmosphere for Page. It was highest flattery to hear news at firsthand which would occupy the next day's headlines, or some information so confidential that newspapers would not learn of it. Grey's manner of fatalistic determination touched Page, more let us say than a diplomat of the old school—a Bismarck, or a sometimes impetuous, belligerent individual such as Page's counterpart Spring-Rice in Washington with whom Secretary Bryan had to deal. The ambassador came away dazedly from the meeting of August 4, an indelible picture in his mind. Thereafter he saw Grey frequently, gave the foreign secretary complete confidence, believed Grey equally frank.

It is doubtful that the foreign secretary was as uninhibited as Page believed. Grey was an experienced diplomat who knew when to color some ideas and slide over others, as he did in explaining Britain's reasons for going to war. In his memoir he had kind and grateful words for Page, but his assessment of the American ambassador does not compare with Page's worshipful description of Grey.[20] Colonel House later wrote of Page that he was so honest he thought everyone equally honest. For that reason House often failed to tell Page all he knew.[21] Grey sometimes found it best to confer that way with Page, and he could do it while appearing to treat the ambassador as a confidant.

When one considers Page's background, the atmosphere in London, and in addition to Grey, the other people he faced, it

---

[19] Memorandum, Aug. 4, 1914, Page Papers; Hendrick, *Page*, 1: 313–15.

[20] *Twenty-five Years*, 2: 101–102. In the interview of August 4 Grey explained on high legal and moral ground that Germany violated a treaty and wronged an innocent neighbor when it attacked Belgium. Not exactly a misstatement, this explanation said little about practical and strategic reasons for war. Hendrick, *Page*, 1: 313–14.

[21] House to Wilson, March 9, 1915, Wilson Papers.

would be difficult to imagine his taking a view other than pro-British. There was no reliable source from which he could receive an opposing view of the war. Britons he met felt, like Grey, they were fighting civilization's battle. Those persons closest to Page at the embassy—his secretary, the temporary counselor Chandler P. Anderson, in fact, the entire staff—were of similar view. Aware that the British were kinsmen and parents of much that was worthwhile in American culture and institutions, the ambassador did not wish to see these creative people die as a nation and as shapers of the world's destiny.

Convinced of the sanctity of Britain's cause, Page set about trying to keep American policy "correct" within the scope of a formal neutrality. As representative of a neutral nation in a belligerent state he was under obligation to display outward neutrality. Apparently he did well at this; he said he did; certainly newspapers printed nothing to make one believe otherwise. Confidentially he made no attempt to be impartial, but sought to portray Britain as the peace-loving defender of democracy and decency, Germany as a nation determined to use any means, however inhumane, to conquer the world.

A case in point was the numerous stories of atrocity which spread almost from the beginning of hostilities. If a huge majority of these reports condemned the Germans for barbarous conduct in Belgium and France, Wilson and his advisers in Washington received other news which denied the truth of the charges, or accused the Allies of warfare anything but chivalric. One such message from the consul general at Aix-la-Chapelle (in a general area of the supposed atrocities) denied that the Germans had become drunk, relating instead how Belgian civilians had ambushed German troops. Conceding that reprisals were extreme, this American official believed investigation would expose causes which "may have extenuated, if not as the Germans claim, justified their conduct."[22] There were so many conflicting and unverified stories that Wilson wisely refused to take a position on any of

[22] The consul at Aix-la-Chapelle to the secretary of state, Sept. 17, 1914, *For. Rels., 1914, Supp.,* 799–801. For other charges and countercharges see ibid., 791–809.

them.[23] Page's sources were neither confused nor contradictory. He read frightening accounts in London newspapers and every day Londoners told him what the Germans were doing in Belgium and France. Overwhelmed with the unanimity and savagery of the reports, he cabled the State Department in September about "some of the most barbarous acts in human annals." The message told of German soldiers violating young Belgian girls, severing tendons in arms and legs of Belgian boys, cutting noses off English soldiers lying wounded in the field: "The violators of the Belgian treaty, the sowers of mines in the open sea, the droppers of bombs on Antwerp and Paris to kill anybody they may hit, have taken to heart Bernhardi's doctrine of the glorious enjoyment of war. It is impossible longer to doubt the wholly barbarous conduct of the Prussians."[24]

Besides dispatches to the State Department and letters to Wilson, Page tried to reach the president through Colonel House. "Put the President on his guard," the ambassador cautioned when it appeared that Wilson might attempt to mediate the war. A consistent opponent of mediation, Page felt—as did Grey—that war had to continue until Germany lost, or someone would have to do the job later.[25] The ambassador thought he had a receptive pupil, for Wilson long had admired the English, and the president had shown great pleasure in Page's letters of previous months which had spoken in strong terms about Anglo-American cooperation. Page knew Wilson had said something about neutrality in thought, but he surely believed that those words were for public consumption and did not apply to him.

The president was more serious about neutrality than Page had imagined. Deeply troubled at the outbreak of war and, almost at the same time, the death of his beloved wife, the last thing Wilson wished was for Americans to do anything which might involve their country in the holocaust in Europe; his neutrality statements represented an initial, honest judgment of what the posi-

[23] President Wilson to the secretary of state, Sept. 4, 1914, *The Lansing Papers*, 1: 33.

[24] Page to the secretary of state, Sept. 11, 1914, ibid., 395.

[25] Sept. 10, 1914, Hendrick, *Page*, 1: 411; Page to the secretary of state, Sept. 7, 1914, *For. Rels., 1914, Supp.*, 99.

tion of the nation should be.[26] As war continued the president, like most Americans, learned that he could not avoid a personal preference, and occasionally confided to close friends that he favored Britain.[27] But he considered these thoughts aside from his role as president, having no bearing on the position of the United States. Struggling to keep such ideas to himself and not permit them to affect a policy that he hoped would keep the nation out of the war, the president did not like to hear ideas contrary to this policy, especially from officials of the United States, and so Page's communications were not as welcome as they once had been. Wilson said nothing at the time—he did not write Page at all during the first weeks of war—but he knew that his eloquent ambassador would bear watching. Having proclaimed neutrality, the president had turned again to American problems, content to let the European powers fight it out, if they must.

At that stage of the conflict—late August, early September 1914—few individuals in Europe were concerned about the American attitude. All thoughts were about the ferocious fighting on the Continent, where the German military machine was grinding its way toward Paris. On September 7 the Germans were so close that the government moved the capital to Bordeaux. Page, Grey, and the Londoners watched nervously, amid gloomy reports of friends who had lost their lives with the hastily organized British expeditionary force. The tide turned near Paris, where the Allies held and began to push back the German armies. In the first crucial test they had halted the German advance.

Among the people who breathed easier after the Battle of the Marne was Page, whose tendency for hasty conclusion was never more evident than his evaluation of the war at that juncture. In a letter to Wilson during the turn of events on the battlefield he heaped guilt on Germany, discouraged a negotiated peace, pre-

[26] It is difficult to overstate the effect on the president of his wife's death. House's diary for as late as November 14 had this notation: "When we reached home he began to tell me how lonely and sad his life was since Mrs. Wilson's death and he could not help wishing when we were out tonight that someone would kill him."

[27] For an example of Wilson's pro-Ally thought, see House Diary, Aug. 30, 1914: "He gives even further than I in his condemnation of Germany's part in this war."

dicted with astonishing optimism how the war would end: "France will give the Germans the best tug they can this autumn and wear them down somewhat, and Russia will finish Austria. Meanwhile England will drill a million, perhaps a million and a half men, and have them as a fresh army in the spring. I shouldn't wonder if Kitchener himself [British minister for war] will take command; and these are the fellows who will take Berlin; and Kitchener, if he goes, will dictate the terms of peace; it'll be an English (not a French or Russian) victory. These English are the only people in Europe who have the habit of success and who know the art of managing great things."[28]

Thus after several weeks of confusion and suspense, conditions had calmed in London, and to Page the future looked bright. The conflict was an immediate catastrophe, but since it would bring an end to the despicable German system, civilization should profit in the long run. The United States should profit also, if the nation, as Page suggested, took advantage of new opportunities. Even the ambassador's working quarters had improved, for the landlord of the Victoria Street embassy, trying to raise the rent, had forced the Americans out and into much nicer accommodations at the Grosvenor Gardens.[29] Lost souls who turned up at the embassy there met an efficient staff, schooled in ways to facilitate transport to the United States. Page anticipated no difficulty between his country and the British. President Wilson had no desire to handicap his ancestral country in its struggle for survival; he recently had told Spring-Rice that "everything . . . I love most in the world is at stake . . . ," and "if they succeed, we shall be forced to take such measures of defence as would be fatal to our form of Government and American ideals. A dispute between Britain and the United States," the president had said, "would be 'the' crowning calamity."[30] And the Foreign Office, fully aware of the importance of the United States, would not be so foolish as to give cause for offense. Page had only to do routine duties, keep Wilson informed, cause Grey as little inconvenience as possible, and wait for victory.

[28] Sept. 22, 1914, Hendrick, *Page*, 3: 144.
[29] New York *Times*, Sept. 18, 1914.
[30] Spring-Rice to Grey, Sept. 3, 1914, Grey Papers.

Chapter Four

Harassing the British

THE BRITISH AMBASSADOR to the United States spoke with as much truth as sarcasm when he remarked in 1915 that most of the American people "want to make money and not to make war."[1] There seemed little reason why the United States should not trade with nations at war, for the powers of Alliance and Entente, each wishing to draw on American resources, welcomed commerce with the industrial giant. After some hasty statements, the government announced that it was legal, that merchants and shippers could sell almost anything they had. The State Department did say the government could not send war materials to the belligerents, but private individuals and firms could do so; and the administration would not stand in the way of private financial arrangement, such as credits, needed to keep the traffic flowing.[2] If this official policy represented a departure from the president's initial detachment, it was based on sound legal precedent and, providing one did not object to profit which came from the slaughter of humanity, was a happy situation. It was, however, to lead to serious controversy with both sets of belligerent powers.

The problem was that America's customers all were greedy. Each wanted to trade with the United States while keeping its enemies from doing so. Though vastly complicated with new weapons and new principles of sea warfare, the situation the United States found on the seas in 1914 and 1915 bore some resemblance to problems with which Adams, Jefferson, and Madison had struggled during the era of the French Revolution and Napoleon. Americans hoped that a hundred years' experience would allow them to avoid involvement in another European war, to persuade belligerents to accept a code that set down what neutrals and belligerents could do. At the outset of war, the Declaration of London of 1909 appealed to the State Department, since it seemed to meet these requirements. This Declaration—an attempted clarification of decades of controversy and uncertainty in international relations—was in a sense the latest word on neutral rights. The United States saw much benefit in its distinction between contraband and noncontraband goods, for there was a liberal "free" list of items not subject to seizure. A provision on neutral-to-neutral commerce further weighted the Declaration of London in favor of neutral nations. Although it was the most recent pronouncement on maritime warfare, it was outmoded in 1914, for such "free" articles as copper and rubber had become essential in manufacture of munitions, thus meriting classification as contraband. None of the belligerents had ratified the Declaration of London by 1914, and the British Parliament had turned it down.

The guns had been firing in Europe scarcely more than a week when the State Department in a routine way asked if the nations at war would hold themselves to the rules of the Declaration.[3] The first response was encouraging. Germany and Austria-Hungary, largely land powers, offered to comply if their opponents did.[4] The opponents were not so cooperative, as Bryan and his advisers might have expected, for the Allies, aware of their naval superiority, looked forward to keeping large quantities of supplies

[1] Sir Cecil Spring-Rice to Dominick Spring-Rice, Sept. 17, 1915, Spring-Rice Papers.
[2] Public circular issued by the secretary of state, Oct. 15, 1914, *For. Rels., 1914, Supp.*, 573–74.
[3] The secretary of state to Page, Aug. 6, 1914, ibid., 216. Identical messages were sent to other belligerent countries.
[4] Ambassador Gerard to the secretary of state, Aug. 10, 1914, ibid.

from the enemy. They were not anxious to commit themselves to a list of rules which would nullify that advantage. The British, who usually established maritime policy for the Allied nations, made approval of the Declaration of London "subject to certain modifications and additions . . . indispensable to efficient conduct of . . . naval operations."[5] Rebuffed, the State Department dropped the matter for the time and waited to see what the problems were going to be.

By mid-September the course of the war and some of its effect on the United States was becoming visible. On the eastern front the Germans had repulsed a Russian advance into East Prussia and were beginning to drive back the huge armies of the tsar. In the West, the gay September foliage of the French countryside became obscure amid ugly shellholes and systems of trenches, as the armies prepared for artillery barrages and suicidal infantry charges. Sudden blows to overwhelm the enemy and end the war had failed on both fronts and it was becoming evident that it was going to be a long struggle in which such factors as supply and resources would be more important than battlefield strategy. The Royal Navy, with ability to protect friendly shipping and intercept vessels headed for the Central Powers, began to prove its worth. The British followed their own interpretation of sea warfare, often to the detriment of commerce of the United States. At first the Foreign Office lengthened the list of absolute contraband. At the beginning of war the list included twelve items. By October there were twenty-one.[6] The British insisted that traditional material of war and also such new items as rubber, metallic ores, and chemicals not reach Germany. Besides stopping ships headed for Germany, the Royal Navy halted vessels destined for Holland or the Scandinavian countries, alleging that since these neutral countries had not embargoed these products, the enemy might receive them by transshipment via routes outside British control.[7]

[5] Page to the secretary of state, Aug. 26, 1914, ibid., 218–20.
[6] For the lists see Page to the secretary of state, Aug. 6, Sept. 30, Oct. 9, 1914, ibid., 215–16, 236, 244–46. Besides contraband goods, the lists contained a growing number of items classified as conditional contraband.
[7] Britain first set down this argument in the message of Aug. 26, 1914, ibid., 218–20. It was repeated many times thereafter.

For American shippers it was a bewildering and frequently expensive situation; there was no definition of what rights they had and did not have, except for Britain's published contraband list which the United States had not accepted as legal.

Page watched these goings-on, unaware that the first diplomatic controversy of the war was about to unfold. He transmitted the State Department's request that Britain adhere to the Declaration of London, cabled Washington regarding the way the Foreign Office proposed to modify that document, and sent along the expanded contraband lists. Grey had explained it all to him: why Britain could not accept the Declaration, how the navy might be stretching international law, but that it was necessary if Britain was going to prosecute the war. If there were some minor legal disputes, the countries could settle them peacefully, like gentlemen. The foreign secretary was supremely polite and made it clear that he wished to cause the United States as little inconvenience as possible. That made sense to Page. After all, the British were fighting for their lives against a group of heathens, certainly no time to become aroused about an unimportant technicality and lose sight of the meaning of the war. There was no danger of that happening, Page thought. "Everything is going well here, I think," he wrote House on September 15. "The British Government is most considerate of us in all large ways. These smaller questions of ships and prizes, etc., are really in the hands of the Admiralty—really, tho' not nominally—and they are conducted on a war basis."[8]

In Washington there was a different attitude as officials began to understand what the British planned on the seas. Unable to ignore the protests pouring in, the State Department believed it had to define the limits of British policy and let the Foreign Office know that Americans were disturbed. So felt Robert Lansing, counselor of the department and, in absence of Bryan, acting secretary of state. Also of that opinion, Wilson asked the State Department for a message with "teeth in it." Evidently the first draft had too many teeth, because it underwent several revisions

[8] Seymour, *Colonel House*, 1: 305; also Page to Wilson, Sept. 22, 1914, Wilson Papers.

before the president would permit its going off to London. When the draft came from the department, it alarmed House. He took the message to the British ambassador, who suggested that one or two sentences seemed discourteous. Then Lansing wrote a new note which House and Wilson again altered before they sent it to Page for use in informal discussion.[9]

Appropriate as it seemed to the American government, the message of September 28 was the basis of the first Anglo-American dispute of the war, a controversy which stunned the American ambassador into realizing that the view from London might not be the attitude in Washington, that although he favored one view he represented the other and found himself between the two. The note had two purposes: to caution the British government against allowing the navy so much freedom that American resentment would force the government to a policy it preferred not to take. The ambassador thought that part reasonable and wise. The message also suggested a solution—Britain should accept the Declaration of London.[10] There was the rub for Page and the Foreign Office. Britain had rejected that proposal. The ambassador was aware of the sound legal argument against the Declaration, and the practical fact that if followed, His Majesty's ships would have to stand off and watch huge quantities of war material enter Germany, directly or indirectly, to become part of the kaiser's military machine. If Page could not understand his government's request, he dutifully explained the American position to Grey. He knew what the answer would be, and this he cabled to the United States. That should be the end of it, he thought. But Lansing persisted. Back came another cable to point out that Britain could accept the Declaration and lengthen the contraband list, and explain that if Britain altered the document the

[9] This complicated story comes out in House diary notations, Sept. 27, 28, 1914, Seymour, *Colonel House*, 1, and House to Page, Oct. 3, 1914, Hendrick, *Page*, 1: 378–79. Although House said he and Spring-Rice revised the message, the British ambassador left no such impression. Spring-Rice wrote Grey that he read the note "hurridly" and pointed out one or two bad sentences. Sept. 28 and Oct. 1, 1914, Grey Papers.

[10] The secretary of state to Page, Sept. 26, 28, 1914, *For. Rels., 1914, Supp.*, 225–33.

Central Powers would not accept it. He could not do it, Grey explained for the third time. True, Articles 23 and 25 did allow a longer contraband list, but they did not permit items on the free list (which included several new products of war) to do anything but remain free, out of the navy's reach.[11]

It was not an acrid controversy. Each message was friendly. House and Wilson had gone out of their way to remove offensive phrases. Certainly Grey was polite and anxious that the countries agree, as well he might be, for Britain stood to lose a great deal if the United States did not abandon its dubious proposal.

Page was very disturbed. Unable to know how far either side would go, he could imagine the worst things happening—a diplomatic breach, perhaps even war between his native land and the country he had come to love. He thought it needless, useless, that the United States could quarrel over a few cargoes of copper and lose the future of the world; that his government could insist that Britain accept rules which were illegal and might wreck the entire British war effort. Convinced the work was the doing of Lansing, a lawyer obsessed with legal finery, Page determined to educate Wilson and put an end to the nonsense.

The ambassador's warning was twofold: a letter to Wilson on October 15 which would follow the slow-moving steamship route, and the same day an urgent telegram through the State Department marked "for the President." The latter message was a frank statement that the United States pressed a useless issue, because the British had conceded everything except admitting war material into Germany. "That it will not yield," he pleaded. "We would not yield it if we were in their place. Neither would the Germans. The English will risk a serious quarrel or even war with us rather than yield. This you may regard as final." Page described the controversy as "academic," for in what he called a clash between English civilization and Prussian military autoc-

---

[11] This controversy is described in several messages between Washington and London, the most important being: Page to the secretary of state, Sept. 29, Oct. 3, 9, 1914, the foreign secretary to Ambassador Spring-Rice, Sept. 28, 1914, the secretary of state to Page, Oct. 1, 4, 1914, ibid., 233–46. See also Grey's dispatch to Spring-Rice telling of a conversation with Page on Oct. 29, 1914, F. O. 372/601.

racy precedents had "gone to the scrap heap." He believed the United States should not raise controversy that it could avoid or postpone, and recommended "most earnestly the substantial acceptance of the new order in council or our acquiescence with a reservation of whatever rights we may have."[12] The letter to Wilson carried much the same message in language even more blunt. "The upshot of it is . . . we've got to submit to this—or fight," he told the president. Page cautioned Wilson about permitting Lansing to concoct American foreign policy out of law books. He realized the counselor was overworked, that the war was on everyone's nerves, but Lansing's messages were pitifully inhuman and had a bad effect. They sound, he wrote, "like a sort of Hague-book in time of peace."[13]

Page did not have to wait long to learn how Washington had received his urgent recommendation. His telegram arrived at the State Department on the morning of October 16. That afternoon Lansing cabled the government's latest proposal, a message that expressed hope for friendly settlement, allowed a major concession on trade with European neutrals, and called again for acceptance of the Declaration of London. Do this in a personal way, Lansing instructed; do not say it is an official proposal.[14] The ambassador must have exploded when he read the dispatch. No mention of his cable of the previous day, not even verification the State Department had received it, and Lansing persisted in the same absurd course. Moreover, the counselor seemingly attempted to give Grey the impression that the idea was Page's. Furthermore, a few hours later he received a message from the president. Do not consider the American position "merely academic," Wilson cabled. He felt that "contact with opinion this side the water would materially alter your view," and urged Page to use his most persuasive efforts for an understanding with Britain in the manner the United States had suggested, meaning, of course, the Declaration of London.[15]

Some of the most depressing days of Page's ambassadorship—

[12] *For. Rels., 1914, Supp.,* 248–49.
[13] Hendrick, *Page,* 3: 179–80.
[14] *For. Rels., 1914, Supp.,* 249–50.
[15] Ibid., 252–53.

and there were many sad times to come—were those days of mid-October 1914, which were fraught with difficulty over the Declaration of London. The president had rebuked him; Lansing had ignored his recommendation; the countries seemed headed for a crisis. It had burst on him like a thunderstorm in the midst of a sunny day, completely unexpected, an event for which his months in London had provided neither precedent nor guidance. By his own confession, he had difficulty adjusting. His eyelids, already heavy, drooped lower, and circles beneath them became darker and deeper. Appetite dwindled and digestive organs ceased their proper functioning—a deficiency aggravated in ensuing months, which eventually would lead to his death. Ceaselessly he turned over the matter in his mind. Could he be wrong, he asked Laughlin, his secretary, and Chandler Anderson, his legal adviser? They said he was right. There was nothing to do but see Grey again, give him the message, try once more to alert the president, and, if nothing helped, resign and get out.[16]

Page set forth painfully on what he thought might be some of his final acts as ambassador. If it was an uncomfortable task, the visit with Grey did not take long. Repeating Lansing's proposal, he not only refused to accept responsibility but also told Grey he strongly had urged Wilson to accept the British position. The somewhat puzzled foreign secretary repeated that he would accept the Declaration of London only by retaining the right to modify it.[17] Page knew that; he would not have it any other way. Then he turned to the problem of Wilson and carefully penned another missive to explain that American treatment of the subject, not the subject, seemed academic. He did not mean to be critical of Lansing, he said, but surely the counselor did not know where his proposal would lead. The ambassador again urged acceptance of the British position.[18]

[16] Memorandum by Page shortly after the controversy, Hendrick, *Page,* 1: 385–87.

[17] Grey to Spring-Rice, Oct. 17, 1914, Grey Papers; Page to the secretary of state, Oct. 19, 1914, *For. Rels., 1914, Supp.,* 253–54. By saying the proposal was his idea, Page would not have jeopardized his standing with Grey, for the foreign secretary had learned from Spring-Rice of Lansing's instructions to proceed in that manner. Spring-Rice to Grey, Oct. 17, 1914, Grey Papers.

[18] Oct. 21, 1914, Hendrick, *Page,* 3: 181–85.

How Page felt he revealed to House, desperately attempting to move the president through his close friend and adviser. First an urgent telegram: "God deliver us, or can you deliver us from library lawyers. They often lose chestnuts while they argue about burns. See our friend and come here immediately if case be not already settled. Of utmost importance."[19] Next came a letter which contained an elaborate review of the controversy:

"We set out on a comprehensive plan to regulate the naval warfare of the world and we up and ask 'em all, 'Now boys, all be good, damn you, and agree to the Declaration of London.' "

" 'Yah,' says Germany, 'if England will.' "

"Now," Page continued, "Germany isn't engaged in naval warfare to count, and she never even paid the slightest attention to the Declaration all these years. But she saw that it would hinder Britain and help her now, by forbidding England to stop certain very important materials from reaching Germany. 'Yah,' said Germany. But England said that her Parliament had rejected the Declaration in times of peace and that she could now hardly be expected to accept it in the face of this Parliamentary rejection. But to please us, she agreed to adopt it with only two changes."

"Lansing's method is the trouble," Page continued. "He treats Great Britain to begin with, as if she were a criminal and an opponent." The ambassador feared that if someone did not stop the counselor, a break with Britain might result and the United States would lose the only friendship in the world worth having. And to show his desperation, he declared: "If Lansing again brings up the Declaration of London—after four flat and reasonable rejections—I shall resign. . . . I pray you, good friend, get us out of these incompetent lawyer-hands. Why doesn't the President see Spring Rice? Why don't you take him to see him?"[20]

In view of the calm with which the men in Washington considered this first controversy with Britain, in view of the ease with which they smoothed it over, one must wonder if there should not have been a way to inform Page and spare the beleaguered ambassador some of his exhausting anxiety. When the telegram about "library lawyers" came to House, the colonel did not even

[19] Oct. 21, 1914, Seymour, *Colonel House*, 1: 305.
[20] Oct. 22, 1914, Hendrick, *Page*, 1: 380–84.

know what Page was talking about. Relaying the message to Wilson, he commented: "I hardly know to what he refers, but perhaps you do. It may be the Declaration of London. Page evidently is disturbed."[21] The administration had no idea of pressing the issue, as Page feared. The attitude in Washington seemed to be that the Declaration was worth a vigorous try, but if not acceptable, it should be given up.

Suddenly the controversy stopped, with neither party fully aware of the terms, outside abandonment of an unmodified Declaration of London. Stating the final British position on October 19, Grey had proposed a proclamation that would accept the Declaration of London with two reservations—pertaining to extension of the contraband list and commerce with neutral European countries, to be followed by a new list. The United States did not have to accept the proclamation, merely withhold protest while reserving rights under international law and take up cases as they occurred. Retaining everything Grey wished, the proposal rephrased British policy to sound as much as possible like the American plan. Page had advised that course several times and again urged its acceptance as "an emergency working plan," with request that if the United States could not do so, the president should send House to London.[22] Lansing, almost casually, it seems, advised Wilson on October 20 that due to the "rigid attitude" of the British government it would be useless to insist on the Declaration of London.[23] With the president's permission the counselor cabled Page that the United States was reverting to international and treaty law as basis for its rights as a neutral.[24] Overjoyed, Page carried the news to Grey and virtually apologized for his government's behavior. "He assured me," Grey wrote, "that it had not been, and was not their intention to give us trouble."[25] Seemingly then, while Britain had accepted the Declaration of London with two reservations, the United States had abandoned it entirely. If that

[21] Oct. 22, 1914, Wilson Papers.
[22] Page to the secretary of state, Oct. 19, 20, 1914, *For. Rels., 1914, Supp.,* 253–56.
[23] *The Lansing Papers,* 1: 255–56.
[24] Oct. 22, 1914, *For. Rels., 1914, Supp.,* 257–58.
[25] The foreign secretary to Ambassador Spring-Rice, Oct. 23, 1914, F. O. 372/602.

seemed confusing, it merely was a preview of uncertainty the two nations would have in the months ahead.

The administration could have followed no other course, since at that juncture in the struggle for neutrality, Britain had much the better case. It was one of the few times in the months to come the British had legality on their side. The document was not international law and the United States had no reasonable way to make it so. The free list was totally unrealistic. The Declaration prohibited practices the United States had insisted upon when at war (as the British government had pointed out) and might want to insist upon again. If Washington held Britain to this code Germany would benefit—an important fact when one considers that almost all important members of the Wilson administration were pro-British.

If the preceding points are true, one must wonder why Wilson permitted the State Department to suggest that dubious proposal. Some reasons are obvious: the United States stood to profit from the large free list and other provisions favorable to neutral nations; the document was the product of an international conference that Americans could view as having superseded all others, and a logical starting point. The Declaration of London emerged from the hectic first week of August when Americans were attempting to regain the equilibrium lost at news of the war. The president, struggling to bear his wife's illness and soon her death, felt more detached than at any other period. Neutrality largely meant treating belligerents equally. Experience soon taught that he could not treat all powers alike; he did not encounter the same problems with each. He would have to define neutrality in relation to problems with each nation at war, and this afforded some flexibility. Wilson's withdrawal from the Declaration of London provided a fortunate meeting ground of his desire for neutrality and his preference for the British. This stand was favorable to Britain, yet was legally neutral, and in fact it would have been illegal to hold Britain to the Declaration. Even so, one wonders what Wilson's position would have been had the geography of Europe been different, had the president faced a situation highly prejudicial to Germany.

It is somewhat more difficult to explain why the administration persisted so long and why Page's recommendations received such unfavorable response. The ambassador was correct in his suspicion that the president did not give foreign affairs the attention they needed. Occupation with domestic and personal problems, and ignorance of international law shielded Wilson from learning that he could concede a major point to Britain and still be legally neutral. And if Wilson was pro-British, his anglophilism in autumn 1914 differed from that of Page. The ambassador had accepted the British view almost entirely and was willing to aid Britain in all measures short of fighting. He wanted Britain to win. Convinced that the future of the United States depended on British victory, he could understand no other view. Not so the president, who hated the war and would have been happy to see it end with no victor. Wilson was concerned not so much that Britain win as seeing it not lose. Whatever his personal feeling, he was obligated to press the case for the United States, and for several weeks the American case was the Declaration of London. If yielding marked a first reconciliation of Wilson's feeling for Britain and the United States, it did not indicate complete conversion to the crusade for British victory.

Perhaps the most durable result of the episode was its effect on relations between Washington and the London embassy. Page's opinion of the State Department, barely cordial when war began, turned to disgust; he was convinced that men such as Bryan and Lansing were by temperament or training incapable of conducting American foreign policy. The ambassador did not feel that way about Wilson, but he did find disturbing the president's unwillingness to view the war as he saw it, and the boisterous faith in Wilson which Page had carried about London began to lose its force. The ambassador became convinced that officials in Washington lacked perspective, were not quite trustworthy, that to keep American policy correct he might have to modify it. Correspondingly Page's influence in Washington began to dwindle. His messages probably helped induce the administration to withdraw from the Declaration of London, but for the future the ambassador did himself more harm than good.[26] Prolonged praise

[26] Burton Hendrick gave Page credit for the American withdrawal, saying that the threat to resign caused Wilson to drop the Declaration of London

of Britain produced suspicion that the ambassador's view came less from examination of the merits of the Declaration of London than fear that adherence would weaken the British. Lansing recorded that the State Department ignored Page's attitude, and the counselor's cables support that comment.[27] Wilson noted the incompatibility between the ambassador's dogmatic messages and the presidential request for spiritual neutrality. As he wrote House on October 23, "I am a little disturbed by the messages Walter Page is sending recently. We are very much helped by his advice but I hope that he will not get into an unsympathetic attitude . . . it would be very unfortunate if he were to . . . forget the temper of the folks at home, who are exceedingly sensitive about every kind of right."[28] A little later the president wrote Page almost the same thing. He thanked the ambassador for the letters, said they helped, but stressed the need to emphasize the American view.[29] House also wrote Page and he was sympathetic, feeling that nothing could go wrong with "all of us feeling as we do," but the colonel explained that Wilson had to consider public opinion.[30]

American withdrawal from the Declaration of London cleared the air in London. Page's friends started speaking again and stopped those glances which had made him feel like a misfit.[31] If the ambassador nursed wounds, they were the product of American stupidity, not hostility at the Foreign Office. Fuming at the State Department, he loosed a blast in a letter which he advised House to destroy: "I don't know that you can do anything about

---

(*Page*, 3: 237). It is extremely unlikely that Page's resignation would have made that much difference. This is a superfluous point anyway, because it is possible in another way to disprove Hendrick's contention. Page threatened to resign in a letter to House October 22. Two days earlier Lansing and perhaps Wilson had given up on the Declaration. While Lansing's message of surrender was on its way to London, Page's letter still was in the British capital.

[27] Robert Lansing, *War Memoirs of Robert Lansing* (Indianapolis, Ind., 1935), 119.

[28] House Papers; also Wilson to House, Oct. 29, 1914, ibid.

[29] Oct. 28, 1914, Wilson Papers.

[30] Oct. 29, 1914, Page Papers.

[31] The atmosphere, wrote Page, was as different "as Arizona sunshine is from a London fog." Memorandum, Hendrick, *Page*, 1: 390.

it; but I have an irresistible impulse to tell you that the St. Dept. lacks guts."[32] These were private feelings. He wrote the secretary of state and president of delight at the American action, boasting to Wilson that within forty-eight hours the British released every ship and cargo but one, and he felt that one would be free in another forty-eight. "Sir Edward and I had a little tilt at compliments today," he continued. "I have to see him every day now."[33]

Page also felt inspired, momentarily, to fight for the American view, which by November 1914 meant that he should protest seizures and other violations of international law, try to speed release of detained ships, and obtain settlement. There were no threats of what might happen if Britain ignored these representations, procrastinated, or tightened controls. The ambassador was without a weapon when he argued with Grey, but in truth he did not wish any.

It was fortunate that diplomatic problems eased, for the struggle on the Continent was sad enough that it could have occupied Page's full attention. The fields of France, marked with ruts of wheeled vehicles and tracks of men who sludged their way to the battleline, bore witness that the war had entered its first winter. A growing group of realists predicted it would not be the last. The western front fairly well had stabilized along a vast irregular line from the North Sea to the Alps, with Germans on one side, British and French on the other. If one side or the other gained momentary advantage, nothing changed much territorially, for the struggle in the West had become a war of trenches, machineguns, and artillery—a bloody, gloomy stalemate with no sign of early end. Page kept close touch with the battle reports, and since many of the casualties were close friends or acquaintances, suffered almost as much as the British. Now he heard about the death of young Britons who used to attend his daughter's parties, now news about American volunteers slain on the fields of France. Page's young former secretary, Harold Fowler, was on the front at that time. Fowler had asked advice about joining the British army. The

[32] Oct. 25, 1914, Page Papers.
[33] Oct. 28, 1914, Hendrick, *Page*, 3: 189–90; Page to the secretary of state, Oct. 23, 1914, *For. Rels., 1914, Supp.*, 258.

ambassador would not tell him what to do, so Fowler enlisted. "I couldn't advise you to do this Harold," Page responded, "but now that you've settled it yourself I'll say this—if I were a young man like you and in your circumstances, I should enlist myself."[34] Page thought that Fowler had done a noble thing, but knew as well that the next casualty list might contain the name of his young friend. "It isn't the work that tires," he wrote Wilson. "It's the war. . . . The war gets between my eyes and the printed page. It gets between your golf club and the ball."[35] In the same depressed mood he wrote his son: "We don't know the day of the week or of the month, nor where we are, nor where we will be tomorrow—it's a sort of dark, blind, un-sign-board world we travel, going nobody knows whither. I shall never wish to see Europe again. It is the saddest chapter in human history and the most discouraging."[36]

But it was a grand inspiration to Page that despite long casualty lists, gigantic expense, and personal deprivation, a heroic people did their best for the cause of humanity. Never before had Britain so showed itself a masterful nation; never before did the United States so much need to understand the British cause. "Depression hangs over everybody like a London fog," Page wrote the president. "But all these are incidental—are as nothing, if we keep fair and considerate dealing—these two governments with one another; for upon this hangs the destiny of the world."[37] Within the Europe from which he placed the United States apart, Page did not include Britain. Europe was decadent, Britain progressive. Europe was tearing civilization apart, Britain fighting to preserve it. He felt his private expressions of sympathy for the British did not violate American neutrality, nor affect his willingness to argue with Grey.

Unfortunately the responsible men in the United States could not agree with Page's definition of a neutral ambassador; indeed misunderstanding and suspicion continued to limit understand-

[34] Hendrick, *Page*, 1: 358.
[35] Nov. 30, 1914, ibid., 3: 194.
[36] To Ralph Page, Nov. 29, 1914, Page Papers.
[37] Nov. 30, 1914, Hendrick, *Page*, 3: 196.

ing between London and Washington long after the Declaration of London had vanished. For one thing, the administration tired of Page's attitude. House made this fact clear when he forwarded a request from Wilson that Page not express unneutral feelings "either by word of mouth, or by letter, and not even to the State Department." The colonel said that Bryan, Lansing, and Wilson feared the ambassador's attitude would lessen his influence.[38] Theirs is diplomacy of the old style, Page thought. It is useless at this time and place. He snapped back to House: "Is an ambassador a man sent to keep another Government friendly and in good humor with your government so that you can get and give all sorts of friendly services and make the world better? Or, is it his business to snap and snarl and play smart and keep 'em irritated —damn 'em—and get and give nothing?"[39] And there was Wilson's almost perpetual interest in mediation, which Page could not understand and about which he had sent discouraging messages. When in December the president again appeared ready to end the war, Page considered crossing the Atlantic to lay his ideas before Wilson, but fortunately for the ambassador the matter blew over.[40]

Page's most harassing problem was American commercial rights, British treatment of those rights, the ambassador's wish to please both countries, and his evident inability to please either. Countenanced by the Foreign Office, the Royal Navy cheerfully exploited the large area of operation which remained after the United States abandoned the Declaration of London. American officials in London might have encouraged these moves, for in late October word had circulated about the Foreign Office that the embassy was surprised at Britain's readiness to surrender to demands about contraband. One American reportedly had said that the British conceded more than the United States asked, much less expected—"an interesting revelation," remarked Arthur Nicol-

[38] Dec. 4, 1914, Seymour, *Colonel House,* 1: 312; Hendrick, *Page,* 1: 362.

[39] Dec. 12, 1914, Seymour, *Colonel House,* 1: 312.

[40] House Diary, Dec. 15, 1914: "Arthur Page telephoned that his fater [sic] sailed on the *Lusitania* today. . . . I take it he wants to say if we offer our services for mediation, we will offend Great Britain and will not serve any purpose whatsoever." The report, however, turned out to be false.

son, Grey's colleague at the Foreign Office.[41] In any event, Britain virtually cast aside the fear of American retaliation. As one official cabled Spring-Rice: "The threat of an embargo against exports to the U. K. is not likely to come to anything. The U. S. trader won't want to cut off his nose to spite his face: besides we have luckily the means of retaliation by preventing goods of which the Allies have complete control from going to the United States."[42] The contraband list stretched again, and in practice Britain made almost no distinction between absolute and conditional contraband. In shipments of foodstuffs—traditionally conditional contraband—there was no distinction at all: the fleet received orders to seize all foodstuffs destined directly or ultimately for Germany.[43] The navy stopped cargoes addressed to neutral companies and individuals and hauled them into port in violation of the law of visit and search. Even if not carrying contraband, American shippers suffered losses due to deterioration of goods not to mention the general expenses of their ships' lying idle. Grey's explanation was that the navy had to bring ships to port because it was impossible to search large modern vessels on the sea and, because of German submarines, unsafe to do so; moreover, goods deposited in certain neutral countries easily could find their way to Germany. He said that some American shippers brought trouble on themselves by mislabeling cargoes or hiding war material beneath a thin surface of innocent produce (the Admiralty could recite many stories about hollow masts, cotton in flour barrels, and the "onions" which, dropped on the deck, bounced ten feet in the air).[44]

Page's position was difficult, for he had to handle the cases ship by ship, cargo by cargo, attempt to wring enough concession from

[41] Foreign Office Minutes by C. J. B. Hurst, note by Arthur Nicolson, Oct. 19–20, 1914, F. O. 372/602. The American official was not named, but impression was that all embassy personnel were so inclined.

[42] Draft telegram by Mr. Sargent, Nov. 24, 1914, F. O. 368/1162.

[43] The Foreign Office to Agents of the Committee on Restriction of Enemy Supplies, Sept. 29, 1914, F. O. 372/601.

[44] Page to the secretary of state, Nov. 13, Dec. 6, 1914, *For. Rels., 1914, Supp.*, 345–46, 356–57. See also statement by Rear Admiral Sir Dudley de Clair (former commander of blockade in the North Sea), *Times* (London), May 1, 1916.

Grey to satisfy the State Department, but not so much that it would enable the United States to supply the German warlords and endanger the British effort. "I fight Sir Edward about stopping cargoes," he wrote. "Literally fight. He yields and promises this or that. This or that doesn't happen or only half happens."[45] And again: "I am trying my best, God knows, to keep the way smooth as possible; but neither government helps me. Our Government merely sends the shippers' ex-parte statement. This Government uses the Navy's excuse."[46] One of the many conferences with Grey occurred December 5, at which time Page confessed deep concern about feeling in the United States. He was "most anxious to smooth it over." After much "friendly conversation" Page suggested the British ease difficulty by inducing neutral nations to prohibit export of certain items.[47] These arrangements, which eliminated the need to detain American ships, were satisfactory to the United States; at one time Bryan also had encouraged such arrangements.[48] Even so, the issue touched off another little outburst between Page and his superiors. The ambassador cabled the State Department about talks with representatives of the neutral states, without explaining the nature of the discussion. Bryan cabled that he should stop, that the United States could not assist Britain in working out agreement with nations bordering Germany.[49] Angered again, Page wrote to House: "Now what damfool in the State Department supposed I was making agreements with any Gov't or that I was doing anything but trying day and night to get an American cargo released and to prevent more from being stopped—I don't know, nor care to know. . . . But you can't help doubting the *intelligence* of a man (whoever he is) that breaks loose with a sermon about my making 'agreements with other governments'; and you don't know just how much

---

[45] To House (undated), Hendrick, *Page*, 1: 365.

[46] To House, Dec. 12, 1914, ibid., 422.

[47] The foreign secretary to Ambassador Spring-Rice, Dec. 5, 1914, F. O. 368/1162.

[48] So Spring-Rice wrote Grey, Oct. 6, 1914, F. O. 372/601.

[49] Page to the secretary of state, Nov. 6, 1914, the secretary of state to Page, Nov. 12, 1914, *For. Rels., 1914, Supp.*, 395.

dependence to put in the next telegram about something else, that comes from the same source."[50]

While there was much to be said in sympathy of Page's uncomfortable position, the State Department had no easy task representing the interests of the American people. In some cases the department obtained satisfaction for a client, but often it was slow and expensive, and in far too many cases the fate of American shippers rested with the generosity of a prize court. Protests came in steady flow, and many of them, especially from German sympathizers, were abusive, accusing the American government of selling out. As Bryan in mid-December explained to the ambassador in France, public opinion demanded broader action: "The situation produced by the wholesale seizure and detention of American ships by the Allies, particularly by [the] British, on grounds denied in international law, has reached a stage calling for vigorous action on part of this Government in opposition to their course."[51]

"Vigorous action" took the form of a note to Britain on December 26, which, like the message of three months earlier, underwent much departmental revision. It had come first to the president on the seventeenth, from the pen of Cone Johnson, and Wilson thought it unclear and harsh. Incorporating some of the president's suggestions, Bryan and Lansing revised it, received Wilson's approval, then sent it off to Page. The press received it on the thirty-first—the United States's first public protest of the war.[52]

While rumors of a protest to Britain had created much public anxiety—fear with anglophiles, hope with Germans and pro-Germans—a quick reading of the message showed no justification for

[50] Dec. 12, 1914, Seymour, *Colonel House,* 1: 311.
[51] The secretary of state to Ambassador Sharp, Dec. 15, 1914, *For. Rels., 1914, Supp.,* 363–64. For some of the protests see ibid., 278–304.
[52] House noted the president's response to the original note: "I can see we will have to revise this." Wilson began correction and then gave up: "It is not right to impose such a task upon me. They have not written good and understandable English, much less writing it in a way to avoid offense." House Diary, Dec. 18, 1914. See also the secretary of state to President Wilson, Dec. 17, 1914, *The Lansing Papers,* 1: 257–58.

these feelings. A polite and friendly dispatch, it said nothing new. It questioned British treatment of commerce with neutral nations, the practice of taking ships into port, pointed out that British policy was unclear and inconsistent, cautioned that continuation might arouse popular hostility. The note made no threat of what might happen if Britain persisted.[53] Small wonder that the London *Daily News* called it "eminently friendly," and the pro-allied New York *Times* had similar comment.[54] Perhaps ultimate proof of the note's friendliness was the attitude of the American ambassador in Britain, who on this rare occasion wrote Bryan a genuinely decent and respectful letter: "It is an admirable paper, & it is a pleasure to present it."[55]

It is difficult to imagine what satisfaction the administration expected from such message, outside knowledge that it had refused to sanction British policy and could demonstrate to the American people how it had made gestures on their behalf. Certainly the British government found nothing threatening about it. The note, said Spring-Rice, was "for consumption of Congress, German vote and commercial interests."[56] And so Grey regarded it. The foreign secretary replied to his ambassador that while he never had lost sight of American public opinion, he promptly would send a preliminary reply to "show that we are prepared to deal with questions in such a way as to minimize inconvenience."[57] If the reply, delivered January 7, 1915, had the friendly tone Grey had promised, it carefully avoided hint of change in basic problems. Lansing thought the message conciliatory but illogical, "without . . . any assurance that trade conditions with neutral countries will be relieved." Wilson felt the two governments were in basic agreement and that "it is not worth while debating details."[58] There the matter stood. While international

[53] The secretary of state to Page, Dec. 26, 1914, *For. Rels., 1914, Supp.*, 372–75.
[54] Both opinions in New York *Times*, Jan. 1, 1915.
[55] Dec. 28, 1914, *The Lansing Papers*, 1: 259.
[56] To Grey, Dec. 29, 1914, F. O. 368/1162.
[57] Dec. 31, 1914, ibid., Jan. 2, 1915, F. O. 382/2.
[58] The counselor for the State Department to President Wilson, Jan. 11, 1915, *The Lansing Papers*, 1: 261; President Wilson to the secretary of state,

law drew at least general limits for belligerents dealing with neutral nations, it did not dictate what a neutral nation should do if a belligerent violated its rights. It was for the neutral to choose, and in this case Wilson chose not to quarrel.

If the American note pleased Page—certainly he did not wish to quarrel with the British—he could not be sure that American policy always would be sensible. When the president took a hand in foreign affairs, American policy showed clarity and perspective. The recent note was acceptable, Page wrote his wife, "because the President went over it and made it the letter of a gentleman to a gentleman."[59] But to his mind Wilson continued too great a detachment from the war, and in absence of his guiding hand policy emerged from the mind and prose of the shortsighted if not incompetent people in the State Department. To compensate for their deficiencies, to shield Grey from the crudity of the department, Page had undertaken responsibility for rephrasing unclear wording, changing passages unduly harsh. Beyond that, the ambassador occasionally collaborated with his friend in the Foreign Office in ways which Grey conceded "were of the greatest value in warning us when to be careful or encouraging us when we could safely be firm."[60]

The clearest evidence of Page's cooperation with the foreign secretary was the case of the *Dacia* of January and February 1915, an episode which dated to the first stages of war when the United States discovered there were not enough merchant vessels to handle the increasing American commerce. Construction of new ships would take time. No Allied vessels were for sale. There were, however, a large number of German merchantmen which, for fear of British capture, had laid up in American harbors. Seeking to assist acquisition of a merchant fleet, the administration had an act passed in August 1914 which permitted transfer of titles from

---

Jan. 14, 1915, ibid., 266. For the note see Page to the secretary of state, Jan. 7, 1915, *Papers Relating to the Foreign Relations of the United States, 1915, Supplement* (Washington, D.C., 1928), 299–302.

[59] Jan. 7, 1915, Page Papers.

[60] *Twenty-five Years, 1892–1916*, 2 vols. (New York, 1925), 2: 110; see also Hendrick, *Page*, 1: 391.

foreign to American registry, and Congress began work on a bill to allow the government to purchase some of the interned vessels. The secretary of state defended these measures on moral and practical grounds. Bryan told a British official "that special cases had to be met by special measures, that United States trade was being completely strangled, that neutral countries were clamouring for bread, not only to feed their own people, but the thousands of American citizens who were there, that [the] United States, though neutral, were [*sic*] being ruined and their [*sic*] citizens would have to be heavily taxed to meet deficiencies in customs receipts, all because it pleased others to settle their differences by force of arms." The British embassy cautioned the Foreign Office that if Britain ran counter to the project, "we must be prepared for a violent and general outburst against us."[61]

Indeed Britain did intend to oppose the American scheme, for Grey saw it as potentially harmful to the Allied cause. The foreign secretary cabled his embassy that he did not wish to place obstacles to the United States's obtaining a merchant marine, but could not tolerate activity which gave "material assistance to Germany during the war and [was] thereby . . . in effect a departure from neutrality and international rules." Page met Grey on August 21 to learn more of the foreign secretary's position. The ambassador, who at first had approved the ship registry act, assured Grey that the United States had intended Britain no ill will, offering the exaggerated, if not untruthful, explanation that Wilson was interested in the ships partly to keep Britain supplied with food. Asked if he objected to Germany's receiving money for the vessels, Grey replied he would not press that point and confessed—he asked Page to tell only the president—that before the United States became involved, Britain "had gone some way" with a scheme to obtain the ships for Britain. What caused the foreign secretary "grave anxiety" was the use new owners might make of the vessels. If they carried supplies to German cities or such neutral ports as Rotterdam, Grey would regard change of

[61] The counselor of the British embassy (Colville Barclay) to the foreign secretary, Aug. 19, 20, 1914, F. O. 372/578.

registry a transaction to benefit Germany and would feel compelled to object.[62]

The issue then laid dormant for several weeks, until the *Dacia* came on the scene to test how firm the two governments would hold to what seemed irreconcilable positions. A ship of the Hamburg-Amerika line, the *Dacia* was purchased by an American, Edward N. Breitung of Michigan; on January 4, 1915, he transferred it to American registry. Breitung made clear his intent to use the vessel to ship cotton to Bremen (later changed to Rotterdam, although the cargo would continue to Germany). As the vessel followed a slow, much-interrupted course from its berth at Port Arthur to Galveston to load the cotton, to Norfolk and with the government's blessing across the Atlantic, a debate grew up in British and American newspapers and in correspondence between the two governments. To the British, Breitung, son of a German, was a tricky businessman, pro-German, and probably a tool of the kaiser's government. He had paid for the *Dacia* no more than one-third the ship's value.[63] Grey made clear the *Dacia* was a test case, that if Britain permitted her through it would lead to purchase of all interned German ships. He offered to buy the cargo, or have it unloaded and shipped to Holland; it was not the cargo that concerned him but the ship, and he left no doubt that if the *Dacia* sailed, the Royal Navy would seize her.[64] The incident, said the New York *Times,* was "likely to become of international importance."[65]

Much to his discomfort, Page again found himself suspended in a dispute between the United States and Britain. Conversation in the Foreign Office had destroyed an earlier attraction to the ship-purchase act and he soon came to see it promised nothing

[62] The foreign secretary to Ambassador Spring-Rice, Aug. 20, 1914, Memorandum "Printed for the use of the Cabinet," ibid.

[63] These points were set down in a summary of the *Dacia* case by Mr. Hugenson, Feb. 17, 1915, F. O. 382/183.

[64] The foreign secretary to Ambassador Spring-Rice, Jan. 13, 20, 1915, F. O. 372/728. For other correspondence on this issue see *For. Rels., 1915, Supp.,* 678–89.

[65] Jan. 4, 1915.

but trouble for British-American relations. Even so he probed about, attempting to find something to offer the American government while doing nothing to weaken Britain's position. Would the British government object if Americans used the ship for innocent commerce, such as coastal traffic or trade with South America and Great Britain? The answers were not consistent: Lord Haldane said these arrangements were satisfactory; Grey said he would have to consult the cabinet. On one point all British officials were emphatic: the *Dacia* could not sail to a port which had access to Germany.[66] Henceforth Page followed the twofold approach adopted during the controversy over the Declaration of London: try to calm feelings of the ruffled British diplomats and create an air of urgency in cables to the United States. "Everything was going to pass quite pleasantly,"[67] he told Lord Haldane, and at the same time wrote the State Department in a much different tone. Newspapers and people he met had the same attitude: unfriendliness, if not belligerency, like the "atmosphere just before an earthquake." "They regard the *Dacia* as a German ship put out of commission by their navy," he cabled and went on to warn that if the United States permitted the ship to sail, "a very large part of English opinion will regard us as enemies."[68]

There is little reason to believe—or to feel Page believed—that the *Dacia* was leading to an impasse in Anglo-American relations. What disturbed the ambassador was fear that the nearsighted attitude of the United States, the "spinelessness of the [State] Dep't," again was interfering with his efforts to promote Anglo-American friendship.[69] As he saw it, the administration stood to gain nothing from pressing the case, except perhaps some dubious support from German-Americans; it stood to lose the precious good will of the British nation. Threat of deadlock, if it ever existed, had vanished by the latter part of January 1915. Page

[66] Memorandums of conferences with Page by Lord Haldane, Jan. 15, 1915, and Sir Edward Grey, Jan. 21, 1915, F. O. 372/728.

[67] Haldane's memorandum, Jan. 15, 1915, ibid.

[68] Page to the secretary of state, Jan. 18, 1915, *For. Rels., 1915, Supp.*, 682–83.

[69] Page Diary, Jan. 16, 1915.

could see from diplomatic dispatches that while the United States insisted the *Dacia* should sail, it showed no inclination to create serious disturbance if Britain seized the ship.[70] And whatever the attitude of his government, the ambassador thought he had devised a way to avoid confrontation: let the French take the *Dacia* and get Britain off the hook. As Page's biographer told the now well-known story, the ambassador conceived the thought late one night as he sat before the fireplace. The next day he took the idea to Grey who, delighted to learn such a simple solution (but perhaps perturbed that he had not thought of it), immediately set the plan in motion. Page's suggestion, wrote Burton J. Hendrick, was "little less than genius. . . . one of the great inspirations of the war."[71]

Indeed a French cruiser did stop the *Dacia* on February 27, and with this act the controversy ended peacefully; but events did not unfold as Hendrick (and Grey in his memoirs) left the world to believe.[72] In the first place, Page was not the only, and perhaps not the first, individual to suggest that the French should take the ship. Records of the Foreign Office contain letters from at least ten private British citizens, written during the final two weeks of January 1915, which had the same advice.[73] It also is fully possible that other individuals communicated this idea orally to Grey or that the foreign secretary thought of it himself. All these factors suggest that Grey's appearance of grateful enlightenment in the heralded interview with Page (if Hendrick's description is accurate) was merely another performance. But the most curious feature of the *Dacia* affair is that Grey failed to accept the advice offered from so many quarters. He never conspired to have the French take the ship. Nor were his colleagues convinced it was a worthy scheme. As one adviser commented: "It is not at all a bad idea, but the French would hardly see the force of pulling chest-

[70] For the attitude of the American government see the secretary of state to Page, Jan. 14, 23, 1915, *For. Rels., 1915, Supp.*, 678–79, 684–87.

[71] *Page*, 1: 392–95.

[72] Grey in his description of the episode did not say exactly that he had acted on Page's advice, but he was vague enough to allow readers to believe he had. *Twenty-five Years*, 2: 111.

[73] These letters, dated Jan. 16 through Jan. 26, 1915, are in F. O. 372/728.

nuts out of the fire for us." Arthur Nicolson agreed: "Personally I would prefer that we would capture her—if she be captured—I don't like the idea of shoveling off the responsibility."[74] To be sure, Grey and his colleagues pondered the matter a few days and considered such questions as: If the French took the ship, whose responsibility should it become? Should they take it to a French or British port? Grey settled the matter by saying that events should take a natural course. "We should say nothing to the French & certainly should not prompt them to seize the ship," he added. "If they do so on their own . . . she must go to a French court."[75] There was no agreement between the two governments, not even a strong British suggestion, that France take up this diplomatic burden. Fully prepared to stop the vessel, the Foreign Office gave the Admiralty clear instructions including, on the day of the *Dacia*'s capture, a reminder to bring the ship to Liverpool.[76] That the Royal Navy did not do so is due to the simple fact that the *Dacia* sailed into the French zone of patrol.

The episode thus is significant not because it showed Britain's delicate treatment of American commerce and public opinion, but because it demonstrated Page's collaboration with Grey and reflected the foreign secretary's interpretation of relations with the United States at that stage of the war. Grey did not conspire with the French because he thought the American attitude not stringent enough to deem it necessary. Spring-Rice had cabled that Bryan cared more for the cargo than the ship, that the secretary of state had agreed the ship would have to go to a prize court. Owners of the cargo already had begun to quibble about price, hoping the British would pay what consignees in Germany had offered.[77] Grey knew it would have been inconsistent for the

[74] These notes, dated Jan. 18, 1915, accompanied one of the letters sent by a British citizen to the Foreign Office; ibid.

[75] Foreign Office note, Jan. 23, 1915, ibid.

[76] See Grey's note of Jan. 24, 1915, about a conversation with Winston Churchill (First Lord of the Admiralty), and the Foreign Office to the Admiralty, Feb. 27, 1915, F. O. 372/728, 729.

[77] Summary of the *Dacia* case by Mr. Hugenson, Feb. 17, 1915, F. O. 382/183. The summary reiterated that "it has been decided to say nothing to the French with regard to the possible capture by them."

United States to take a hostile stand on the *Dacia* when that government had been so flexible on the Declaration of London and in the recent exchange of notes. The foreign secretary understood relations with the United States to mean not that he must curtail any practice of trade restriction, but that he should provide reasonable legal argument and perhaps financial adjustment. While the *Dacia* at one time might have seemed an exceptional case, Grey came to see he could treat it as he had handled other problems.

The peaceful passing of the *Dacia* affair brought to an end the first phase of Anglo-American relations of the war, and they had been very meaningful months for Wilson and Page. The president had been able to conduct British relations as a solitary aspect of American diplomacy, not yet complicated by Germany's repulsive submarine warfare. Faced with highly dubious measures of sea warfare, he chose not to quarrel with the British, preferring to rest his case on a flexible legal foundation which permitted large restriction. For the moment matters appeared safe enough to Page, but glancing back to the troublesome previous three or four months he could see that his job was not going to be the uncomplicated task it had appeared in the first weeks of war. If experience warned of difficult days ahead, the trouble stemmed largely from Page's interpretation of his role as, in different ways, representative of both nations.

Chapter Five

Assault of the Barbarians

WALTER PAGE WAS out of bed earlier than usual May 9, 1915, for that morning he had to perform one of the most unpleasant tasks of his ambassadorship. Before 6:00 A.M. he was at Euston Station to greet and offer his services to American survivors of the *Lusitania,* the large British passenger liner torpedoed two days earlier. As passengers stepped off the train and proceeded into the small crowd awaiting, their expressions told of the terrible experience two days before. Occasionally a weary face brightened at sight of a relative, but for the most part the people walked hypnotically, eyes to the ground or straight ahead. A reporter asked one individual for comment: "Don't ask me about it," he said. "I wouldn't talk for a guinea a word."[1] That seemed the consensus among survivors, and Page felt the same way. As he watched the dazed figures, perhaps the ambassador imagined the Cunard giant lying on the bottom only a dozen or so miles off Old Head Kinsdale, over 1,200 of its passengers still aboard or scattered about in the water—the deed of a barbaric people.

Sinking of the *Lusitania* introduced with dramatic clarity a new era in Page's diplomacy, and the ambassador discovered that rather than lessening his chores the submarine onslaught greatly increased the burden and strain of his office. Already deeply involved in his role of crusader for the Allied cause, at-

tempting to dissuade the American government from pressure on
the beleaguered British, when the Germans for their own purposes began to assail American rights on the seas, Page took it
upon himself to demonstrate what inhuman people the Germans
were, and to assure that his government responded with indignation appropriate to the challenge. The ambassador believed that
the submarine tested as never before the ability of the United
States to have its rights respected, to prove itself a powerful and
moral nation. The sinking of the *Lusitania,* he once wrote, was a
turning point in American history.[2]

The outrage of May 7, 1915, was part of a huge controversy in
which the Wilson administration had found itself embroiled at
the beginning of February. The German government, acting, so it
said, in retaliation for Britain's mining of the North Sea, announced that the area around the British Isles was a war zone in
which submarines would operate freely. Alarmed at the huge
quantities of supplies which entered Britain from abroad, unable
to challenge the Royal Navy on the surface, Germany resorted to
the new but increasingly effective sea weapon. The Germans did
not plan a deliberate assault on American shipping, but they did
warn that "it cannot always be avoided that neutral vessels suffer
from attacks intended to strike enemy ships."[3]

President Wilson had replied that he would countenance no
violation, however accidental, of American rights on the seas.
Wilson insisted that the submarine, an unorthodox weapon, adhere to orthodox rules of visit and search, promising that the
United States would hold Germany to "strict accountability" for
violation of neutral rights and "take any steps . . . necessary . . .
to safeguard American lives and property and to secure to American citizens the full enjoyment of their acknowledged rights on
the high seas."[4] Those had seemed almost fighting words; certainly they were stronger than anything sent to Britain, and they
delighted anglophiles such as Page. But coupled with the Allies'

---

[1] *Times* (London), May 10, 1915.
[2] Page to the secretary of state, Feb. 17, 1916, *The Lansing Papers,* 1: 706.
[3] Ambassador Gerard to the secretary of state, Feb. 4, 1915, *For. Rels., 1915,
Supp.,* 94.
[4] The secretary of state to Ambassador Gerard, Feb. 10, 1915, ibid., 98–100.

maritime restrictions, which became increasingly severe in the spring of 1915, Germany's use of the submarine pointed to a difficult future for American foreign relations, almost, it seemed, a repetition of a century earlier, the problem of orders-in-council and Napoleon's decrees.

Just as the prospect had looked so dim for the United States, it appeared for a while that there might be a way out; the belligerents, attempting to blame their measures on the enemy, let out a false hope that there could be compromise. Page had cabled on February 17 that Britain might refrain from making foodstuffs absolute contraband if Germany agreed to stop sowing mines and not attack merchant ships.[5] About the same time the German government hinted that if Britain halted its "murderous method of conducting maritime war," observed the Declaration of London, and permitted foodstuffs and raw materials to enter Germany, it would reconsider submarine policy.[6] These messages were vague and promised nothing, but together they seemed to ask about the same thing; they represented the most encouraging ideas the United States had seen, and well worth exploring. Bryan seized the opportunity when with Wilson's approval he proposed an agreement for Germany to employ submarines only under rules of visit and search while Britain permitted foodstuffs through to Germany. The United States offered to designate an agency which would assure that goods reached only the German civilian population.[7]

It soon became evident that the belligerents wanted no such agreement. Gerard cabled from Berlin that the German government unofficially seemed favorable to the idea with modification: primarily that raw material as well as foodstuffs enter Germany. A few days later the official response interpreted raw material to mean items permitted in the Declaration of London: copper, rubber, and other material of war which Britain would not let into the German Reich.[8]

[5] Ibid., 111.
[6] Ambassador Gerard to the secretary of state, Feb. 17, 1915, ibid., 112–15.
[7] The secretary of state to Page, Feb. 20, 1915, ibid., 119–20.
[8] Ambassador Gerard to the secretary of state, Feb. 24, March 1, 1915, ibid., 123, 129–30.

The German position did not matter anyway, for the American proposal had run aground in London. Page had new discussion with Grey and the foreign secretary now appeared unwilling to let even foodstuffs go through. Grey's hesitation destroyed Page's interest in the plan and the ambassador wanted to drop it. He cabled it was hopeless, blaming failure on the Germans who with proclamation of submarine warfare had forced Britain to retaliate by keeping all goods out of Germany.[9] Only through the urging of Colonel House, then in London, who told Page that Wilson wanted the proposal presented "with all the emphasis in his power," did the ambassador agree to do anything. This was a considerable overstatement of the action Page took, since he "had no stomach" for the plan and felt it neither wise nor acceptable to Britain.[10]

It was no use. The Foreign Office, seeing no benefit for Britain, gave the proposal but scant attention. Believing the Germans would reject the plan, officials decided to delay an answer and by these means place blame for failure on the enemy.[11] Grey responded to Page in friendly but noncommittal manner and said he would have to consult the cabinet. The formal reply came later, but Britain's position became public on March 1 when in conjunction with France the British announced they would "prevent commodities of any kind from reaching or leaving Germany," and "hold themselves free to detain and take into port ships carrying goods of presumed enemy destination, ownership, or origin."[12]

For the moment the American proposal for a *modus vivendi* disappeared. It had been a fair and honest attempt to introduce order to the maritime problem, and if adopted would have assured safe sailing for part of American commerce. Britain had

[9] Page to the secretary of state, Feb. 20, 1915, ibid., 118–19; see also Page to Wilson, March 10, 1915, Wilson Papers.

[10] House Diary, Feb. 22, 1915.

[11] Copy of the proposal Page submitted to Grey, Feb. 22, 1915, with Foreign Office notes by C. J. B. Hurst, E. Crowe, A. Nicolson, and Edward Grey, F. O. 382/185.

[12] The British ambassador to the secretary of state, March 1, 1915, *For. Rels., 1915, Supp.*, 127–28. For Grey's response see Page to the secretary of state, Feb. 23, 1915, ibid., 122.

good reason for refusal. Hypersensitive to any measure which tampered with use of the Royal Navy, the British would not surrender the advantage they had in the war—ability to deprive the enemy of important supplies. The submarine had not yet demonstrated how costly it would be to Allied shipping, and this manner of warfare provided opportunity to embroil Germany with the United States. As one Foreign Office official explained, he could see no reason why Britain should enter into an agreement which would relieve Germany "of the consequences of her own illegalities."[13] German assaults on American shipping indeed would take pressure off British restriction. What is least understandable is the position of Ambassador Page, unless, and this seems to be the case, he was more interested in satisfying the British than the Americans. Knowing Britain would refuse the plan, Page seemed afraid the Germans might accept and present Britain to the world in a bad light. As events showed, Allied policy made unrestricted submarine warfare only more justifiable to the Germans. Soon there began a series of controversies with the United States that would end only in war.

However scrupulous the German regard for rights of American citizens (and at first it was not scrupulous), it was inevitable that the submarine would produce incidents to strain German-American relations. The chance of accident was high, inasmuch as the periscope of a submarine provided only limited means to identify ships. The nationality of a ship was not always clear through this system of small mirrors, especially since Britain exploited the practice of flying the American flag. Identification of passengers, crew, and cargo of a vessel was impossible. Visit and search would have been the answer, but as the German government pointed out, those rules worked better with cruisers than submarines, which would undergo great risks to surface and halt vessels on the sea. The first U-boats were flimsy craft, and well-placed shots from guns of merchant ships could sink them, or a surfaced submarine would be easy prey for an enemy cruiser if the halted vessel were able to summon one. Traditional rules would have deprived submarines of the important element of surprise, and the Ger-

[13] Note by C. J. B. Hurst. Feb. 22, 1915, F. O. 382/185.

man government was not going to surrender that advantage unless forced to do so. Perhaps Wilson would attempt it, but how far
he would press the issue, exactly what he meant by "strict accountability," the Germans could discover only through incidents
on the Atlantic.

Spring 1915 quickly produced cases to test the American attitude toward submarine policy. A torpedo on March 28 sent to the
bottom the *Falaba,* a British ship on which an American lost his
life. The following month a German airplane attacked the American vessel *Cushing,* and on May 1 a torpedo struck the *Gulflight,*
also an American vessel, with loss of American lives. Outrageous
though these acts appeared, they produced numerous and frequently novel questions, the answers to which would determine
Wilson's policy. What if a ship tried to escape and signaled for
help, as the Germans said of the *Falaba?*[14] Should the president
allow a single American citizen, pursuing only his interest, to
involve the nation in grave difficulty?[15] Was the *Gulflight* following British patrol boats and seemingly under convoy of these
vessels?[16] While Wilson had reason for deliberation, his slowness
led many individuals to wonder if he would be as firm as his
message to Germany had seemed. What would he do, they wondered, if some clearly atrocious incident occurred, such as the
sinking of a large passenger liner? "If a British liner full of
Americans be blown up," asked Walter Page on May 2, "what
will Uncle Sam do? That's what's going to happen."[17]

It happened at approximately 2:00 P.M., May 7, when the
Lusitania, over 30,000 tons, pride of the Cunard line, queen of
the Atlantic passenger service, a virtual floating city capable of
over 25 knots, took a torpedo in its starboard side and sank in less
than 20 minutes. Of the nearly 2,000 passengers and crew aboard,
almost 1,200 perished. Of these, 128 were Americans. With a
single exception it was the worst thing that could have happened
to German-American relations on the seas. Only if the ship had
been American would the crisis have been greater. Most Ameri-

[14] Ambassador Gerard to the secretary of state, April 14, 1915, ibid., 370.
[15] As Bryan asked Wilson, April 6, 1915, Wilson Papers.
[16] The secretary of state to Page, May 6, 1915, *For. Rels., 1915, Supp.,* 381.
[17] To Arthur Page, Page Papers.

cans were little impressed with the fact (which became public later) that the *Lusitania* did carry contraband, and through proper procedure, assuring the safety of the passengers, was eligible for sinking. They did ponder several other thoughts: death of so many innocent passengers; possibility that no vessel, merchantman, or liner, neutral or belligerent, would be safe on the Atlantic; the dreaded idea that the United States might be at war.

Americans in London and many Britons were as interested in these ideas as were the people in the United States. Centers of activity were the American embassy and Page's residence at Grosvenor Gardens, for from one of these places might come a hint of what the United States was going to do—perhaps, some Britons thought, news that the United Kingdom had a new ally. First report of the sinking, which reached the embassy about 4:00 P.M., failed to mention the huge loss of life, but by the time Page went home new facts gave some indication of the catastrophe. The Pages went on with the dinner planned for Colonel House that evening, although the usual joviality gave way to gloom and anticipation for detail. Page had the dubious honor of bearing the unhappy tidings to the small group as the evening went on. It was almost like a wake.[18]

While it would take months before Page recovered from the incident, by the following day he had enough control of himself to give thought to a proper course of action. The problem was clearly a matter of German-American relations and of no official concern to Page, but, feeling as he did, he could not stand by idly. House agreed that the United States should act even if it meant war, that he should urge action on the president. His first *Lusitania* message, which went out about noon, was full of war spirit: "The freely expressed unofficial feeling is that the United States must declare war or forfeit European respect. So far as I know this opinion is universal. If the United States comes in, the moral and physical effect will be to bring peace quickly and to give the United States a great influence in ending the war and in so reorganizing the world as to prevent its recurrence. If the United

[18] Hendrick, *Page,* 2: 1–2.

States submits to German disregard of her citizens' lives and of her property and of her neutral rights on the sea, the United States will have no voice or influence in settling the war nor in what follows for a long time to come. This, so far as I can ascertain, is the practically unanimous opinion here."[19] This telegram, which set the tone for communication to come, promised much for the United States if it would enter the conflict: end of the war, permanent peace, respect for American rights, end of German militarism, and a voice in reorganizing the world, all the things Page wanted for his country.

Satisfied with his report, the ambassador began with House an uneasy wait for Wilson's expected historic and face-saving response to Germany. Confidence in the president was widespread, but already a few individuals were expressing doubt, pointing out that Wilson had not protested the Falaba and Gulflight. The following day Page made the unpleasant journey to Euston Station, and the picture there deepened his conviction that something needed to be done. Back at the embassy, he talked further with House. Now deeply worried, the colonel had prepared a telegram for Wilson which he showed Page. In much the same tone as Page's message, it called for action, warned that the United States no longer could remain a spectator. That seemed good to Page, but the ambassador wished to go all out on this one, make it clear beyond question. He suggested the colonel say: "A very safe move now and war if necessary will make the Democratic Party and insure your election as nothing else could; a failure now to act will kill the party for a generation." For House that was too much: "I would lose an arm before I would allow the President to think I could be influenced, or thought he could be influenced in such a situation by a selfish motive for either self or party."[20] The colonel sent the original message. Page's suggestion was in poor taste, not typical of his usual idealism, and was simply poor

[19] Page to the secretary of state, May 8, 1915, For. Rels., 1915, Supp., 385–86.
[20] House Diary, May 9, 1915; for House's telegram May 9, 1913, see Seymour, Colonel House, 1: 433–34.

strategy. It did indicate the great effect of the *Lusitania* on Page, his desperation in attempting to arouse Wilson.

Another day or two passed without official word from Washington; worse yet, news came to London about a speech in Philadelphia in which the president uttered something about a nation being "too proud to fight." Destined to become one in the Wilsonian anthology of slogans, the phrase seemed rationalization why the president should not act, indication he would not. Page, House, other individuals at the embassy became angry, then depressed and almost embarrassed at their close identification with a government that would not stand up for its rights. A large number of Americans told Page they were ashamed of their government.[21] Grey, as usual, was tactful. "We do not want to discourage belligerent elements in the United States," he told colleagues in the Foreign Office, "but our [press?] should say as little as possible & not attack the President."[22] The press, however, was not always that patient. At first full of faith in Wilson and the United States, several newspapers and journals now became doubtful and even abusive. And for the moment, Britain's famous magazine of satire dropped humor in favor of a serious plea:

> In silence you have looked on felon blows,
> On butcher's work of which the waste lands reek;
> Now in God's name, from which your greatness flows,
> Sister, will you not speak?[23]

Unable to bear such criticism longer, Page again cabled the president. He warned that inaction would shut the United States out of British and European respect for a generation, alleging that British aristocrats expected, even welcomed American indecision to justify their distrust of democracy. "The best friends of America," he reported, hoped for at least a break in relations and convening of Congress to hear the voice of the nation.[24]

[21] House Diary, May 11, 1915, Seymour, *Colonel House,* 1: 438.

[22] Foreign Office note, May 11, 1915, F. O. 371/2586.

[23] *Punch* 148 (May 12, 1915) : 361; see also Page to Wilson, May 12, 1915, Hendrick, *Page,* 3: 244; *Times* (London) , May 11, 1915.

[24] Page to the secretary of state, May 11, 1915, *For. Rels., 1915, Supp.,* 391–92.

All the while Wilson was going his own way. Aware of the emotional reaction to the terrible deed, insistent upon placing himself above this emotion, obtaining facts, and acting for the honor and best interest of the nation, he resisted the temptation to fire off a threatening note. For some strange reason—perhaps mere accident, perhaps anger—he burned Page's first message, and commented to Bryan that it did not express Page's view but that of the British public.[25] That was not true and Wilson knew it, but apparently he felt it best to play Page's game and proceed with a note which he, and not House, Page, or the British, felt best.

Wilson was not immune from the feeling toward Germany which welled up in many Americans, including Page and House, upon hearing the *Lusitania*'s fate. But there were forces within the president's personality and environment which made his attitude necessarily different from his compatriots in London. There was Wilson's temperament and training, the scholar who wished to weigh alternatives carefully and if possible settle disputes by discussion. Second was the huge responsibility the president felt for the fate of the nation, and his reading of American opinion to mean that while Americans wanted firmness they did not want war.[26] The result of the president's deliberation was the first *Lusitania* note, a document that coursed between the views of his principal advisers at the time—Counselor Lansing, who felt much like Page and House, and Secretary Bryan who preferred a weaker message. A mixture of firmness and conciliation, the message of May 13 deplored sneak attacks on unarmed vessels, insisted the Germans revert to accepted rules of naval warfare, disavow sinking of the *Lusitania,* pay an indemnity, take measures to prevent such acts. That was the firm part; the note was conciliatory in what it left unsaid. It was no ultimatum, threat-

[25] May 10, 1915, *The Lansing Papers,* 1: 387.
[26] Wilson wrote Senator Robert L. Owen on May 20: "I shall school myself to such a course of action as will keep the country out of war if it is humanly possible to maintain our rights without it." Ray Stannard Baker, *Woodrow Wilson: Life and Letters,* 8 vols. (Garden City, N.Y., 1927–1939), 5: 348; see also Robert Lansing, *War Memoirs of Robert Lansing* (Indianapolis, Ind., 1935), 27–28.

ened no break in relations, and left ample room for discussion.[27]

After what seemed an unbearably long week of waiting, the word came to London. The president had moved decisively, the note seemed to say. Attitudes within and outside the embassy underwent a revolution. Newspapers said the most flattering things; politicians made similar comments; Americans who had expressed misgivings about their leader now confessed shame. Page cabled this commendation to Washington and added personal congratulations.[28] Probably he felt ashamed also at having doubted the president; Wilson's way was better inasmuch as it was deliberate, had full possession of facts, regarded legality and morality. He felt the result would be the same, since the German warlords, having no concern for orderly warfare except as it suited their purposes, no concern for innocent victims of war, would reject Wilson's note, continue their tactics, and bring about the break in relations.

To the dismay of Page and his British confreres the German-American break failed to materialize. Germany answered Wilson's first note with contention that the *Lusitania* carried contraband (which it did), Canadian troops, and was armed (which was not true). The Imperial Foreign Office blamed the incident on the British, who by starving Germany's population had forced retaliation. While the government expressed regret at the large loss of life, it would not admit the deed was wrong and could not promise there would be no recurrence.[29] Wilson wrote another note which repeated much of the first, stated that the United States contended for the rights of humanity, but contained no threat that Germany concede or face diplomatic rupture and possible war.[30] Hoping to persuade Germany to abandon unrestricted sub-

---

[27] The secretary of state to Ambassador Gerard, *For. Rels., 1915, Supp.,* 393–96. For the opinion of Bryan and Lansing see the counselor for the Department of State to the secretary of state, May 10, 1915, *The Lansing Papers,* 1: 391–92; the secretary of state to President Wilson (undated), ibid., 392–94.

[28] Page to the secretary of state, May 16, 1915, *For. Rels., 1915, Supp.,* 397.

[29] Ambassador Gerard to the secretary of state, May 29, 1915, ibid., 419–21.

[30] The secretary of state ad interim to Ambassador Gerard, June 9, 1915, ibid., 436–38.

marine warfare without hostilities, the president avoided any statement so blunt as to make peaceful settlement impossible. The summer was well into June, over a month after the great ship went down, and there was no settlement. What Page feared above all—an extended literary debate which would permit people to forget—appeared to be taking place.

The ambassador did find satisfaction in one aspect of the *Lusitania* controversy. Secretary of State Bryan had refused to sign the second *Lusitania* note out of fear it would lead to war. Bryan's refusal prefaced his resignation. If he had many shortcomings as secretary of state, one must credit him with steadfast desire to avoid war and treat belligerents equally. In the *Lusitania* crisis the secretary had felt that some points of the German argument were legitimate and that the British used American lives to protect ammunition transported across the Atlantic. The only way to protect American lives, he thought, was to keep them off belligerent ships in the war zone. And if the United States addressed a strong message to Germany, it should balance that effort with a note to Britain.[31] Many of his ideas lacked legal precedent and probably were unworkable, but of all members of the administration, the president included, Bryan surely was the most neutral in spirit. Resignation was a sad climax to a brief and in many ways unusual term as head of the State Department, during which he had failed to gain much respect from his colleagues. He had been a private topic of ridicule for supplementing his salary with public speeches, his belief that treaties could make war obsolete, his provincial mannerism in a cosmopolitan environment, even his dogmatic fundamentalist Protestantism. The Washington diplomatic corps never forgot Bryan's substitution of grape juice for wine at social functions. One of the diplomats who failed to take Bryan seriously was Spring-Rice, who had written in August 1914: "All the State Department are on our side except jelly fish Bryan who is incapable of forming a settled judgement on anything outside party politics."[32]

[31] The secretary of state to President Wilson, June 3, 1915 (two messages), June 7, 1915, *The Lansing Papers*, 1: 422–28, 445–49.
[32] To Grey, Aug. 25, 1914, Grey Papers.

Bryan's withdrawal from the government at a time when unity seemed essential restored to public mind criticism of almost a score of years—the hayseed who wanted to be president, destroyer of honest currency. To these the newspapers added many new barbs: "Billy Sunday in the wrong niche," said one; guilty of "unspeakable treachery," another.[33] Though not public, the unkindest cuts of all came from Walter Page who, having disliked Bryan at the beginning of service in the Wilson administration, disliked him even more two years later. And when the secretary became identified with a soft line toward Germany, the ambassador's explosion sounded almost the voice of hatred. Page's first comment, a letter to his son shortly before Bryan quit his post, gave a "cast-iron confidential" opinion of, among other pacifists, his boss in the State Department: "We're in danger of being feminized and fad-ridden—grape juice (God knows water's good enough: why grape juice?) ; pensions; Christian Science, peace cranks; efficiency—correspondence schools; aid-your-memory; women's clubs; co-this and co-t'other and coddling in general; Billy Sunday; petticoats where breeches ought to be and breeches where petticoats ought to be; white livers and soft heads and milk-and-water;—I don't want war: nobody knows its horrors or its degradations or its cost. But to get rid of hyphenated degenerates perhaps it's worth while, and to free us from 'isms and soft folk. That's the domestic view of it. As for being kicked by a sauerkraut caste—O Lord, give us backbone!" At the bottom Page cut a notch in the paper and wrote "This notch is the place to apply a match to this letter."[34]

Delighted at Bryan's absence, infuriated at the manner of departure, Page sent Wilson congratulations for being a fine "executioner," went on and on about the former secretary: "One American newspaper says truly: 'There always was a yellow streak in him, and now in this crisis he shows a white liver.' Why didn't he

[33] The quotations from the Syracuse *Post* and New York *World* are in the New York *Times,* June 14, 1915.

[34] To Arthur Page, June 6, 1915, Page Papers; most of the letter is in Hendrick, *Page,* 2: 10.

resign and silently go off at [*sic*] sit down? The excitement of the platform will not let him rest. Conscience he has about little things—grape juice, cigarettes, peace treaties, etc—but about a big situation, such as embarrassing a President, he is fundamentally immoral. Well, cranks always do you a bad turn, sooner or later. Avoid 'em son, avoid 'em!"[35]

Bryan did anything but go off and sit down. In speeches and on the pages of his periodical *The Commoner* he campaigned for peace and "neutrality toward both." In summer 1915 he talked about a mission to Europe to see if he could help end the war. Despite consistent opposition to peace talk and aspirants to mediation (Page felt the war had to continue until Germany lost), the ambassador felt no distress at the thought of Bryan visiting London. "Send him over here if you wish to get rid of him," he wrote House. "He'll cut no more figure than a tar-baby at a Negro camp-meeting. If he had come while he was secretary, I should have jumped off London Bridge and the country would have had one ambassador less."[36] Page refused to take him seriously and believed the leaders of Europe did not either.

Bryan's resignation meant that the top cabinet post was vacant and, surprising as it seems, Page was among those persons mentioned as a possible new secretary of state. Lansing later expressed the opinion that Wilson would have selected Page had it not been for his "lack, or apparent lack, of conformity with the President's policy of preserving a neutral attitude toward all the belligerents."[37] As it was, the scant records of Wilson's thoughts about a replacement for Bryan had little to do with Page. The president considered House, and except that the colonel was in poor health and that he did not want an official position, Wilson might have offered it to him. Lansing was a logical possibility, for he was an

---

[35] Page Diary, June 9, 1915; Page to Wilson, June 12, 1915, Wilson Papers. Another time Page wrote: "Nobody ever caught and tamed and managed him as the Great White Chief did: that was a work of art; for now he can do no serious harm. He's simply hanged himself. Adieu Willum J.!" To Arthur Page, June 23, 1915, Page Papers.

[36] Undated letter [probably August 1915], Hendrick, *Page*, 2: 13.

[37] *Memoirs*, 15–16.

experienced international lawyer and already interim secretary, but at first Wilson believed him unimaginative and not large enough for the secretaryship.[38] Apparently House, back from sharing the *Lusitania* crisis with Page, feeling, one can imagine, something like battlefield camaraderie, was Page's chief, perhaps his sole backer and at that the colonel suggested a number of other men, including Lansing, about whom he wrote Wilson: "the most important thing is to get a man with not too many ideas of his own and one that will be entirely guided by you without unnecessary argument, and this, it seems to me, you would find in Lansing."[39] This statement was probably what Wilson wanted to hear, for he liked to do things his way. The colonel had written differently to Page: "I suggested your name and McAdoo said that the President thought it would not do to take an ambassador from a belligerent nation and make him Secretary of State. I disagree with this conclusion and I shall again urge the desirability of you."[40] Later when House wrote Page of Lansing's appointment he reiterated preference for the ambassador, saying "it would have worked admirably in the general scheme of things."[41]

Opposition to Page came less from his position, as House mentioned, than his view. Considering the broad difference between Wilson and Page on the sinking of the *Lusitania*, it is impossible to imagine the president putting Page in charge of the nation's foreign relations. And one may doubt that House was as vigorous in the ambassador's support as he gave Page to believe. What likely happened was that House cautiously mentioned Page to the president, perhaps in passing, and when there was opposition dropped the idea immediately. It was a rare occasion when House persisted with advice toward which Wilson seemed disinclined. One reason for Lansing's selection, as the president told House, was that "Lansing would not be troublesome by obtruding or

[38] David F. Houston, *Eight Years with Wilson's Cabinet, 1913 to 1920*, 2 vols. (Garden City, N.Y., 1926), 1: 141.

[39] June 16, 1915, House Papers. House wrote another time that he "preferred Houston but . . . was afraid Houston would be very hard to work with." Diary, June 14, 1915.

[40] June 17, Page Papers.

[41] June 25, 1915, ibid.

injecting his own views."[42] If such was the type of person Wilson wanted for the job, the verbose, opinionated ambassador in London was not his man.

Page had no illusion about moving up in the administration. His only comment was a diary notation, surprising in view of past criticism of the "library lawyer": "Robert Lansing appointed Sec[retary of] State—very good; no jarring of the machinery while we cross this bridge."[43] In a short time the ambassador would have reason to retract that statement.

Meanwhile the *Lusitania* controversy dragged, futilely it seemed to Page, through June and into July. Germany's answer to the second *Lusitania* note had promised not to hinder "legitimate" American shipping and Americans traveling on "neutral" ships.[44] If interpreted properly this meant nothing at all. Encouraged by the United States's tolerant policy with Britain, Germany wished a similar attitude, and as Gerard wrote, "to keep the matter 'jollied along' until the American people get excited about baseball or a new scandal and forget."[45] Wilson refused to accept the German position, believing England's violation of property rights differed from violation of "the rights of humanity," but the American people seemed less than ever inclined toward war.[46]

The prolonged German-American discussion produced deep disappointment in London. There the view was that Wilson's admirable stand in the first note to Germany was contingent upon a German surrender, or if Germany did not yield to American demands, a stronger and perhaps final position in the second *Lusitania* note. Neither event had happened and it seemed that the affair was going exactly as Germany wanted. The English press either criticized the American government or by silence

[42] House Diary, June 24, 1915.

[43] June 23, 1915. One might add that Lansing also had approval of the British. The appointment, wrote Spring-Rice, "is a very good one. He is cool-headed. . . . He is friendly to us." To Grey, June 25, 1915, Grey Papers.

[44] Ambassador Gerard to the secretary of state, July 8, 1915, *For. Rels., 1915, Supp.*, 463–66.

[45] To House, June 1, 1915, Seymour, *Colonel House*, 1: 455.

[46] As he had written Bryan June 2, 1915, Bryan-Wilson Correspondence, National Archives.

inferred that the Americans were not worth writing about. Members of the government, most of them friends of Page, greeted the ambassador with a weak smile which seemed to say: "Sorry that your government has a weak spine, will not uphold the national honor." At least that is what Page believed they were thinking. "A considerable part of English opinion is already saying that we are very valiant with the pen and that we count on notes," he wrote his son in July. "Notes don't hurt Germans."[47] Mincing scarcely a word, the ambassador reported this criticism in letters and cables to Wilson and House. He could take no joy in such environment, for the ambassador was deeply distressed to have such things said about his old friend. To avoid hearing British criticism, and avoid having to defend American policy, Page kept social activity to a minimum. He would not permit subordinates to speak critically, and in their presence struggled—it must have been a struggle—to defend the president.[48]

The reticence of his friends would not have been so bad had Page not shared their belief that American policy was wrong in its premise that the nation could or should avoid war. "The clearer it becomes to me," he noted in June, "that it will be a great good fortune for the U. S. if we go to war with Germany." Page listed benefits of such action: "Internal or domestic gain—Emancipation from feminity and fads. Foreign gain: a lasting & close relation with England and France; a warning to Japan. General gain: the satisfaction of helping to put down a wild beast now loose in the world."[49] And war seemed almost a certainty. Germany's attitude in the *Lusitania* negotiations, the German "barbaric" temperament assured that submarines would sink more ships with innocent American passengers. Then Wilson's decision would be simple; the "jig would be up." In a letter to House, Page virtually hoped for an incident similar to the *Lusitania* which would force war.[50]

[47] To Arthur Page, July 25, 1915, Page Papers.
[48] Hendrick, *Page*, 2: 19–20. For examples of Page's messages see Page to House, July 21, 1915, ibid., 25–26; Page to Wilson, July 15, 1915, ibid., 3: 248–49.
[49] Page Diary, June 1915.
[50] Page wrote: "We've got to get in: they won't play the game in any other way. I have news direct from a high German source in Berlin which strongly

Another problem that troubled Page's harassed mind during those summer days of 1915 was the attitude of people in Washington he had been trying to impress. What disturbed him was the indifference of such men as Lansing and Wilson to his recommendations, official and unofficial. Correspondence between Washington and London concerned largely British-American relations and if not entirely satisfactory to Page it was regular, but from the State Department came not a word, not even acknowledgment of messages he had been sending about the *Lusitania* and German-American relations. The greatest disappointment was Wilson, who for months had written not a page to answer the ambassador's long letters.

There was in Washington a growing concern about the way the ambassador in Britain seemingly had gone over to the other side. Page's devotion to the British cause, evident since the controversy over the Declaration of London, had become clear in the ambassador's telegrams about the *Lusitania* which seemed to say that British public opinion should be a guiding principle of American foreign policy. The man most concerned was, of all people, Colonel House, now several weeks removed from the London atmosphere and back in the stream of American opinion. A good judge of trends, House knew from travel in administration circles—a caustic comment here, a revealing silence there— that Lansing and Wilson were not impressed with what the ambassador was doing, and the colonel himself had become weary of Page's persistent bias. "To read Page's letters one would think the Germans were just outside London and advancing rapidly westward upon New York," he wrote Wilson early in August. House thought it might be good for Page to spend thirty or forty days in the United States, since "the war has gotten on his nerves and he has no idea what the sentiment of the people in this country is in regard to it."[51] Already the colonel had set in motion a plan to get the ambassador to the United States for a vacation. On August 4 Page's only daughter, Katherine Alice, married Charles G. Loring of Boston,

---

confirms this. It's a curious thing to say. But the only solution that I see is another *Lusitania* outrage which would force war." July 21, 1915. Hendrick, *Page*, 2: 26; also Page to Arthur Page, July 25, 1915, Page Papers.

[51] Aug. 4, 1915, Seymour, *Colonel House*, 2: 62.

an occasion for which King George paid the ambassador the unique honor of offering the Royal Chapel in St. James's Palace. A friend of Loring, House saw the young man before he departed for London and asked him to insist that his future father-in-law take a vacation in the United States. As Loring relayed the message to Page, it sounded as if the vacation were only a pretext for top-level conferences between Page, Lansing, and Wilson about foreign policy.[52] Doing this without Wilson's knowledge, House hoped that Page would request a vacation, take a rest at home, learn the American view, and go back a reformed ambassador. Not understanding the message that way, Page notified the State Department he could come home immediately, and prepared to make a candid presentation of American shortcomings. A telegram from the secretary of state squelched the enthusiasm. The president did not want the visit, Lansing wrote. It might give appearance of a crisis.[53] About the same time Wilson made his position clearer to House: "With regard to Walter Page I have this feeling: he is undoubtedly too much affected by the English view of things and needs a bath in American opinion; but is it wise to send for him just now; and is it not after all, rather useful to have him give us the English view of things so straight?"[54]

Near the end of summer consideration of the submarine problem gave Wilson opportunity to hear from Page more of the straight English view. The president on July 21 had sent a third *Lusitania* note, a firm document which rejected almost all German contention and threatened that the United States would interpret repetition of the *Lusitania* (that is, sinking of another passenger ship) as "deliberately unfriendly." Not quite an ultimatum, the sort of message Page probably would have written in May, it was the strongest language Wilson had used and drew hearty applause in London.[55] Less than a month after Wilson's note, before Germany had answered, a torpedo struck the British

[52] Such was the way Page explained the misunderstanding to Wilson, Aug. 19, 1915, Wilson Papers.

[53] See Page Diary, Aug. 1, 1915; Hendrick, *Page*, 3: 246–47.

[54] Aug. 21, 1915, House Papers.

[55] The secretary of state to Ambassador Gerard, *For. Rels., 1915, Supp.*, 480–82; Page to the secretary of state, July 27, 1915, ibid., 489.

WALTER HINES PAGE
on his arrival in London, May 24, 1913

Photo by Paul Thompson
Courtesy of Houghton Library, Harvard University

PRESIDENT WOODROW WILSON AND
COLONEL EDWARD M. HOUSE

Courtesy of the National Archives

SIR EDWARD GREY

Courtesy of the National Archives

ARTHUR BALFOUR

Courtesy of the National Archives

liner *Arabic*. Bound westward from England, the *Arabic* could not have been carrying contraband. Although loss of life—two Americans died—was nothing compared to the loss of life on the *Lusitania,* the sinking was the expected supplement to the submarine controversy which placed the United States almost at a point of no return.

Page had good reason to believe that the attack on the *Arabic* was the deliberately unfriendly act. Out of town when the incident occurred, he rushed back to the embassy expecting to hear about the break with Germany. Days passed and nothing happened; Wilson was gathering facts, newspapers said. It almost seemed the *Lusitania* over again. The facts are clear, Page cabled; a submarine sank the ship deliberately, without provocation. And the ambassador added another gloomy statement about British opinion: "conservative-minded, non-political, thoughtful Englishmen . . . express the friendly grave fear lest delay in action should deepen the impression throughout Europe that the United States is seeking to maintain peace at the price of humiliation in the face of repeated offenses."[56]

It is astonishing that Page expected to influence the president with messages which little more than paraphrased British editorials. To be sure, he always clothed reports with explanation that he was giving British opinion, not his own, but there was little doubt that Britain's attitude guided Page's thoughts. Doubtless the British did want the United States to take action against Germany; they stood to benefit. Yet Page reported, and with his thoughts so confined perhaps believed that Britain wanted American action not so much for benefit, as from desire to see the United States maintain its national honor.[57] Such unselfishness was difficult to believe, and to say it was true strengthened the

[56] Page to the secretary of state, Aug. 24, 1915, ibid., 524–25; see also Hendrick, *Page,* 2: 26.

[57] Page to House, June 8, 1915, Page Papers; Page to Wilson, Oct. 5, 1915, Hendrick, *Page,* 2: 42. When in London House had received a different impression from at least one Briton. Kitchener had remarked that "nobody but a damn fool would think it could not be of benefit to us, and I am surprised that any Englishman would question it." House Diary, May 12, 1915.

impression that Page could say nothing objective about his friends in London. As the president waded those murky waters in 1915, balancing the thought of Americans dying in the Atlantic with the thought of war, Page's telegrams would arrive which suggested nothing new and placed such great importance on pleasing the British. True or not, they were irritating. So it was with Page's dispatch about the *Arabic*. "It is a little provoking to have Page do this kind of thing," Wilson scribbled on the message. "Of course, that is the view over there, but we know how crazy they are to have us follow them. This makes one wish to order P. to visit his native land."[58]

While Wilson could not let the *Arabic* incident pass unchallenged, he was anything but "crazy" to follow the British into the World War. The problem was that the *Lusitania* notes had said almost all he could say short of an ultimatum, and if the president sent a message about the *Arabic* it would have to be a threat to break relations. Rather than force the Germans to a public showdown, he permitted Lansing to convey orally his serious thought to the German ambassador, Count Johann von Bernstorff. Impressed with Lansing's performance, anxious to stave off rupture, Bernstorff pleaded with his government to grant concession. Partly on his own initiative, the ambassador on September 1 told the secretary of state that submarines no longer would sink liners "without warning and without safety of the lives of noncombatants provided that the liners do not try to escape or offer resistance."[59] If the message made no specific reference to the *Lusitania* or *Arabic* and left several questions unanswered, it did grant the promise for which Wilson prayed.

American officials scarcely had settled back to enjoy their first victory over the Germans when a new crisis erupted with the Teutonic powers. Less than a week after Bernstorff's concession the United States learned that the Austro-Hungarian ambassador to the United States, Constantin Dumba, was engaged in spy activity. Page was involved in the matter, inasmuch as he trans-

[58] Cited in Arthur S. Link, *Wilson: The Struggle for Neutrality, 1914–1915* (Princeton, N.J., 1960), 568–69.
[59] *For. Rels., 1915, Supp.*, 530–31.

mitted to Washington Dumba's letter, seized by the British, which described plans to provoke strikes in American munitions factories.[60] The American government demanded Dumba's recall. Then the British liner *Hesperian* received an apparent torpedo hit about dusk September 3, although nobody saw submarine or torpedo. Germany said the vessel probably struck a mine. Page did what he could to jostle the matter, sending a reputed torpedo fragment which had landed on the deck of the *Hesperian,* along with another report about British opinion. The ambassador explained that because the United States accepted a German promise which was vague and did not mention the *Lusitania,* because the incident of the *Hesperian* showed the promise not genuine, the British thought Americans hopeless, a "loose aggregation of different nationalities without national unity, national aims or definite moral qualities."[61]

In midst of the difficulty with Germany, nerves frayed by hot weather and the almost constant threat of war, Wilson wrote Page. A short missive that said almost nothing about American policy, the letter brought the news Page hoped the president would write. Wilson said it would be "jolly" to see Page and "it would refresh you to get into the freer and cooler mental atmosphere of this country of ours." He assured Page that his letters were valuable, asked for more, and blamed lack of reciprocity on his inability to think of anything interesting to say. Even though the letter's brevity seemed to say that foreign policy was no fit topic for discussion, it was friendly and encouraging.[62]

It is difficult to understand why the president chose this troubled time to write a man he had ignored for months, why he left an impession so incompatible with recent private remarks about

[60] Page to the secretary of state, Sept. 1, 3, 1915, ibid., 932, 936–41.

[61] Page to the secretary of state, Sept. 8, 1915, ibid., 537–38; Hendrick, *Page,* 2: 40. Lansing referred Page's telegram to Wilson and asked how he should answer it. The president replied that no answer was necessary, that while it was useful to know opinion on the other side of the Atlantic, "after while even Englishmen will begin to understand (I wonder if they really ever will?) that what we are guided by is our sense of what is just and right and not our sensibilities as regards what other nations think about us." *The Lansing Papers,* 1: 476–77.

[62] Sept. 10, 1915, Page Papers.

Page. Perhaps it simply was a belated touch of courtesy, an attempt to quiet the ambassador's puzzlement about his standing at the White House. Perhaps the recent trouble with Germany took some of the unpleasantry from Page's barbed messages, for however critical the English, Wilson feared he might have to join them. Whatever the reason, the letter was a disservice in that it encouraged the sort of report that would drive the ambassador farther apart from Wilson, to the point eventually where the president gave serious thought to replacing him.

The crisis that might have determined the tone of Wilson's letter passed with more ease than had been felt possible. Facts were unobtainable about the *Hesperian,* and the United States could not press that issue. There still was the *Arabic* and the general impression that Germany had reneged on Bernstorff's pledge. Again avoiding public discussion, the president sent Lansing to private talks with Bernstorff, and Lansing, during what must have been his most successful month as secretary of state, worried Bernstorff to the point of exasperation. The ambassador, again stretching his instruction, virtually allowed Lansing to write his message of October 5 which disavowed the sinking of the *Arabic,* promised indemnity for American lives lost and stated: "The orders issued by his Majesty the Emperor to the Commanders of German submarines . . . have been made so stringent that the recurrence of incidents similar to the *Arabic* case is considered out of the question."[63] Here was a withdrawal, a diplomatic victory for the secretary and president. It conceded all the United States had asked on the *Arabic* incident, delighted the Wilson administration and most of the American people, temporarily settled the most pressing features of the submarine controversy and permitted the war danger to pass.

There was little joy in London upon hearing that Germany and the United States had patched up their differences. The British believed that Wilson did not understand the Germans, that barbarians do not keep promises; and Page felt the same way. The trouble with Bernstorff's message, said the ambassador, was

[63] *For. Rels., 1915, Supp.,* 560. For Lansing's memorandum of the interview of Oct. 5, see *The Lansing Papers,* 1: 485–86.

that it failed to mention the *Lusitania,* and that omission negated the sincerity of the German pledge. "We shall not get credit in English opinion for a decisive diplomatic victory over Germany until the *Lusitania* case is satisfactorily closed," he wrote the president. If Americans had forgotten that outrage, the British had not. "Remember the *Lusitania*" had been a successful recruiting circular and, more than once, the battle cry of British forces in France.[64] After October Page worried more about relations with Britain than Germany, but when he did mention the Germans he talked about the huge Cunarder now rusting off Old Head Kinsdale, a large hole in her side.

[64] Oct. 16, 1915, Hendrick, *Page,* 3: 262–63.

Chapter Six

Harassing the British Again

WHILE PAGE WAS devoting such great energy to the problem of the submarine, events would not allow him to forget, wish though he might, that the United States continued to have difficulty with Great Britain. In fact, German-American relations were for Page's position secondary to the diplomacy between Britain and the United States. The year 1915 saw the Western Allies establish the so-called blockade of Germany, justification for which they found in Germany's use of the submarine. In the controversy that followed, Page with increased vigor acted his self-appointed role of guardian of Anglo-American friendship, dedicating himself to smoothing issues that might disturb this friendship. If Page's suggestions for allaying incidents involved American concession and seemed to be contrary to immediate American aims, to the ambassador it was merely a means of promoting the "long view."

The proclamation on March 1 of the Allied intent to curtail all foreign intercourse with Germany, supplemented a few days later with an order-in-council, had curious features. Britain and France never called the system a blockade, although that was what they had in mind. As one British official described the strategy: "the action contemplated would have to be in the nature of (a) a departure from the 2nd rule of the Declaration of Paris, which confers immunity on enemy goods under the neutral flag; (b) the establishment in fact—although the actual word might be avoided —of a blockade under conditions which render practically impossible some of the ordinary rules of blockade hitherto held to be essential."[1] Traditional rules held that to be legal a blockade had to be effective, which Britain and France in March 1915 could not guarantee. They discarded the accepted method of stationing ships outside blockaded ports in favor of a cordon of vessels cruising farther out to sea and covering a larger distance.[2] A blockade is an act of war and a blockading force legally cannot seal off ports of neutral nations. Yet because of the neutrals' propensity to ship excess imports to Germany, this was what the Allies proposed to do. The United States had provided something of a precedent for such procedure during the Civil War when Union warships cruised Caribbean shores to prevent arms and munitions reaching the Confederacy. The Allies, especially Great Britain, expanded the policy in 1915 by covering a larger area and excluding not only armaments but any product they chose. Argument depended upon point of view, and seeing the situation as a neutral the United States had ground for protest and, if it chose, stronger action.

The Allies had little more than announced the new policy when Page set out to ward off a response which the British might regard as unfriendly. Feeling the measure justified by submarine warfare—"an obvious necessity," he told Grey—he thought the United States should offer no challenge, and so prepared a message which he showed House.[3] "He had," the colonel noted, "a lot of things in it which I advised eliminating. It was the strongest sort of pro-British argument, and I knew it would weaken his

[1] Memorandum by Sir Eyre Crowe, Feb. 13, 1915, F. O. 382/185.
[2] As Page explained to the secretary of state, March 21, 1915, *For. Rels.*, *1915, Supp.*, 146–47. For the text of the order-in-council see Page to the secretary of state, March 15, 1915, ibid., 143–45.
[3] The foreign secretary to Ambassador Spring-Rice, March 1, 1915, F. O. 382/185.

influence both with the State Department and with the President. He reluctantly cut it down to a short statement."[4] If House influenced Page to weaken his message one wonders how the original read, for the telegram of March 3 was emphatic: "In view of the decisive effect of the British reprisals which brings the war into its final state, in view of the unparalleled power with which the British will be left when peace comes, and in view of this government's courteous regard for us and for our rights, and in view of British public opinion which is more thoroughly aroused and firmly united than ever before in English history, I most urgently recommend the following: That we content ourselves for the present with a friendly inquiry how the proposed reprisal will be carried out and with giving renewed notice that we hold ourselves free to take up all cases of damage to our commerce and all unlawful acts on their merits as they occur. This will enable us to accomplish all that we can accomplish by any sort of note or protest."[5] On instruction of his government, Page asked Grey for clarification and pointed out what was obvious, that while the proclamation sounded like a blockade, the Allies had announced no such policy. Grey in his soothing manner explained that the purpose of the order-in-council was to grant power to certain crown officials, the extent and severity of which was up to orders of the government and decisions of authorities. He promised that subject to restriction of German trade, the first object would be to minimize inconvenience to neutral commerce.[6] It was an altogether vague response which did nothing to remove uncertainty about a blockade or provide a clear idea as to standards the British expected to follow. But Page expected no more and a few days later he sent the State Department a message stronger than the first one, perhaps reinserting the passages to which House had objected. He now said that the United States should not worry about trade with the Continent, since British purchases would make up for these losses, that the Allies would do as they wished

[4] March 4, 1915, Seymour, *Colonel House*, 1: 456.
[5] Cited in Arthur S. Link, *Wilson: The Struggle for Neutrality, 1914–1915* (Princeton, N.J., 1960), 338.
[6] Page to Grey, March 8, 1915, Grey to Page, March 15, 1915, F. O. 382/185.

regardless of what the United States said, that unofficial attitude toward American communications was to "smile at our love of letter writing as at Fourth of July orations . . . , laugh at our . . . lawyer's disquisitions . . . , receive them with courtesy, pay no more attention to them."[7]

Page had good reason to rejoice when the American message came, for it was little stronger than what he had recommended. Page had Wilson to thank for this, since the president overruled Lansing's long and legal approach in favor of a placid, optimistic document. It was less the friendly inquiry the ambassador suggested than an assumption that the Allies would consider American rights. After conceding several changes in international warfare, the note reiterated these rights, cautioned that the blockade provided opportunity for extreme violation, and assumed that the Entente Powers would adjust accordingly—in effect, that the Allies would not do what they said. Although the message was not quite what Page had advised, its failure to contest the blockade delighted the ambassador who must have been all smiles as he, after correcting certain "errors and omissions," delivered the dispatch to Grey.[8] The note's one objectionable feature, he wrote Lansing, was its timing, since it came before the Easter holiday which the English "take seriously." He looked with optimism on relations with Britain, "never better at any period since the war began."[9]

Despite the friendly tone of the American message the British were not certain where they stood. From Spring-Rice came new words of caution, a reminder about the possibility of an embargo on shipments of contraband to the Allies. While that policy seemed unlikely to the Foreign Office, one puzzled official, who found it difficult "to define what the U.S. gov't are [sic] driving

---

[7] Page to the secretary of state, March 21, 1915, *For. Rels., 1915, Supp.,* 147.

[8] Page to Grey, April 2, 1915, Page to Prime Minister Asquith, April 2, 1915, F. O. 382/186. For another copy of the note see the secretary of state to Page, March 30, 1915, *For. Rels., 1915, Supp.,* 152–55. For interdepartment discussion, see the counselor for the Department of State to the secretary of state, March 22, 1915, the president to the secretary of state, March 24, 1915, *The Lansing Papers,* 1: 281–85, 288–89.

[9] April 8, 1915, *The Lansing Papers,* 1: 700–701.

at," thought it would take "some skillful fencing to parry their attack which is 'all over the place.' " Sir Eyre Crowe, the assistant undersecretary, felt the British should not bother to answer the American note. He wanted to hold firm and see if the United States would not accept Britain's view. To Grey and other persons such a stand seemed discourteous; what they decided to do was to begin work on an answer to the note, all the while applying the blockade as strenuously as the United States would tolerate.[10]

Hence Anglo-American relations did not continue far along the straight and smooth road they seemed headed in spring 1915. A large number of American ships continued to point their bows past the British Isles to Rotterdam or other neutral ports; a few optimistic captains even sailed for Bremerhaven or Hamburg. Repeatedly the same thing happened: one of His Majesty's cruisers appeared, drew closer, signaled the vessel to stop, announced politely that a search party would have to come aboard; after a brief look about, an officer stated (still politely) that the ship would have to go into port. In port one of several things might happen. Sometimes the British allowed the ship to continue, or they might purchase the cargo; frequently a prize court condemned the produce on the following grounds: (1) since the goods had been headed to a neutral country already in excess of normal consumption of that product, the court presumed the goods would find their way into Germany; (2) because Germany was in a high state of military organization, with little distinction between civil and military population, the court presumed that German military forces would use the goods, making them contraband, subject to confiscation; (3) if American shippers could not prove that the goods would not reach the German military, the aforementioned presumptions would prevail (the burden of proof was on the Americans, not the British).[11]

---

[10] Spring-Rice to Grey, April 1, 1915, Grey Papers; notes by Hurst, Grey, and Crowe accompanying Page's letter to Grey, April 2, 1915, F. O. 382/186. Grey wrote Spring-Rice on April 13, 1915, that Page had told him the note should be answered; at the same time the ambassador expressed belief that the note's purpose was to keep the record straight about international law; ibid.

[11] As summarized by Messrs. Henry Veeder *et al.* (counsel for American

In the United States, people were not of mind to admit such reasoning. Shippers protested to the State Department; newspapers began to snipe at the British; congressmen took up the campaign for their constituents' demands. Finally, as one member complained to House, the cabinet began to feel that things were not right in American-British relations: "You would be interested, I think, in hearing some of the discussion around the Cabinet table. There isn't a man in the Cabinet who has a drop of German blood in his veins, I guess. Two of us were born under the British flag. I have two cousins in the British army and Mrs. Lane has three. The most of us are Scotch in our ancestry, and yet each day that we meet we boil over somewhat, at the foolish manner in which England acts. Can it be that she is trying to take advantage of the war to hamper our trade? If Congress were in session we would be actively debating an embargo resolution today."[12] Also perturbed at Britain's behavior, the president wrote House that because of "this intense irritation" the nation was thinking about curtailing shipments of arms and war supplies.[13] As Wilson appeared ready to address a new note to Britain, the *Lusitania* affair turned attention to the German problem. Even that dramatic incident did little to relieve British relations and for some time Wilson considered a note to Britain like the one he had sent to Germany in May. He urged House in London to induce the British to grant concessions.[14]

For a few days House thought he might have what the president had ordered. Conversation with Grey led him to believe that Britain might entertain the compromise the United States had suggested three months earlier—that Germany revise submarine policy if Britain permitted foodstuffs to Germany.[15] Page would have no more to do with the plan than before, fearing, as he did

meatpackers) to the secretary of state, Oct. 6, 1915, *For. Rels., 1915, Supp.,* 561–64.

[12] Franklin K. Lane (secretary of the interior) to House, May 5, 1915, Seymour, *Colonel House,* 1: 458–59.

[13] May 4, 1915, House Papers.

[14] May 18, 1915, ibid.

[15] Page to the secretary of state, May 19, 1915, "Rush for the President" [signed Edward M. House], *For. Rels., 1915, Supp.,* 400–401.

earlier, that if Germany approved and Britain refused, it would present the English unfavorably to the world. He promised House to arrange a conference with Grey, then decided the proposition was useless. House went anyway and received what he considered a favorable response on condition that Germany also avoid using poison gas.[16] As the colonel might have known, this agreement provided not enough for the Germans, who previously had insisted that raw material be allowed into Germany. When Gerard repeated the German position, House dropped the scheme. Knowing Britain would never meet that condition, feeling war with Germany imminent (the *Lusitania* crisis had begun), the colonel prepared to sail home.[17]

Page must have been glad to see House go. The ambassador had regarded him a friend, sympathetic with his view of the war, but he could not understand or concur in the colonel's attempts to end hostilities. He thought House's scurrying here and there, proposing this peace settlement, that agreement between the belligerents, left a bad impression with British leaders and showed inability to understand fundamental issues.[18] Besides, Page could not fail to resent House's authority to "go over his head," acting, which the colonel did, as liaison between the president and British leaders. Careful not to hurt the ambassador, House also withheld information. "He has not the faintest conception of the people I have met and what I have done," the colonel wrote Wilson. "I enlightened him but little for it seems best not to endanger our very warm and cordial relations by telling him of my activities in which he has not participated." House had a simple but private code he used when corresponding with Wilson. "White" referred to Sir Edward Grey, after decoding; "Zenobia" meant England. The trouble with Page, House continued, was

---

[16] House to Wilson, May 20, 1915, Seymour, *Colonel House*, 1: 446–47; see also House Diary, May 19, 1915.

[17] Diary notation, May 30, 1915, Seymour, *Colonel House*, 1:453–54. House quoted Gerard's telegram in a message to Wilson, May 25, 1915, ibid., 452.

[18] "Whatever may be said or thought of this English opinion," Page wrote on March 6, 1915, "it is clear that the British regard this move on our part as well-intentioned meddling, and it lessens their respect for our judgment." *For. Rels., 1915, Supp.*, 134; Page to Wilson, March 10, 1915, Wilson Papers.

that "he is so frank and honest that he believes everybody is as much so."[19]

House came home to endure with the president and American people a long, hot summer of uncertainty and crises. Most pressing, of course, was the trouble with Germany, the *Lusitania,* and submarine, which appeared ready any day to explode in rupture if not hostilities. Almost as irritating, if less dangerous, were Britain's mishandling of American shipping and seeming blasé attitude about American dispatches. Wilson continued to feel pressure for another note; Lansing had drafted such a message, but the president decided against sending it because with the German controversy at hand he believed it no good time to press Britain.[20] Although the next note did not come until October, almost seven months since the last, it was not because the British treated American commerce kindly. Only the Germans saved them.

Ironically, these feelings developed among men strongly inclined in Britain's favor. With Bryan absent, anglophiles monopolized the executive branch. Individuals who had the most influence in American foreign policy—Wilson, House, and Lansing—each preferred a purely formal debate with Britain, and not a strong one at that. Lansing, for example, wrote House, "In no event should we take a course that would seriously endanger our friendly relations with Great Britain, France or Russia, for as you say, our friendship with Germany is a thing of the past."[21] House admitted to Wilson that the United States could press hard before Britain came to the breaking point, but in so doing "we would gain their eternal resentment for having taken advantage of their position and our action would rise to haunt us." Wilson constantly sought a pleasant way to compromise difficulty with Britain.[22]

The British thus had great advantage in dealing with the

---

[19] March 9, 1915, Wilson Papers.
[20] President Wilson to the secretary of state, May 20, 1915, *The Lansing Papers,* 1: 411. For Lansing's draft, May 15, 1915, see ibid., 297–99.
[21] July 30, 1915, House Papers.
[22] July 22, 1915, Wilson to House, July 27, 1915, ibid.

United States, and they exploited this advantage to the hilt, confident, it appeared in Washington, that the Americans would forebear anything they chose to do. The sympathetic American attitude steadily turned into perplexity. However friendly, the administration could not openly acquiesce in the blockade. Congress and the people would not permit it, and there was feeling that a stand regarding Britain might influence Germany to ease its policy, hence diminishing the possibility of war. It was irritating to have a note, submitted with however much reluctance, ignored in practice. It was irritating to have in a foreign capital an ambassador who showed no sympathy for his government's position, seemingly had gone over to the other side.

For Page the summer of 1915, if not hot, was as long and difficult as for people in Washington. Katherine departed to live in the United States after her marriage in August, and while Page approved his daughter's spouse, her absence was "devilish hard on the old man."[23] The ambassador tried to escape the London pressure with journeys into the country, working in an occasional bad round of golf (he should play golf with howitzers, he once confessed), but with diplomatic problems what they were, he could not go far or stay long. Nor could he avoid the London newspapers, their ridicule of his president and country. English friends fluctuated with the tone of American messages to Germany, and since most of the time the tone was unsatisfactory, friends were at best wary. Grey was the most consistent of the lot; he could not avoid Page, as some others chose to do. Grey would not have shunned Page anyway. He was a true friend, but since his problems were greater than Page's could provide little cheerfulness.

Grey's room in the Foreign Office must have appeared as a second home to the ambassador, he spent so much time there. It was already the scene of some of Page's most satisfying and depressing moments. His visits if anything increased in 1915. Each time an inquiry came from Washington, each time a shipper protested to the State Department, Page had a new case or question to confront Grey. When they discussed ships—why is this

[23] Page to Wilson, Aug. 19, 1915, Hendrick, *Page*, 3: 257.

ship detained? how long? what will happen to cargo?—rarely was there tension. The familiar story of one confrontation reveals the atmosphere in such meetings: among mementos in Grey's office was a canceled check Britain had paid the United States for the *Alabama* claims. The British framed the check and displayed it to remind all who entered the room of Britain's fair dealing. One day, when discussing a detained ship, Page glanced at the check and exclaimed: "If you don't stop these seizures, Sir Edward, some day you will have your entire room papered with things like that." Grey replied: "That may be so, but we will pay every cent."[24] Page felt this procedure safe. As long as he could keep debate on individual cases, seeking to hasten procedure or obtain damages, the ambassador was satisfied and did a respectable job presenting the American argument.[25] (Even so he later came to feel that cases were picayune points among problems of much greater importance.)

If discussion advanced beyond mere cases, perhaps to the blockade, Page's aggressiveness dwindled almost to embarrassment that he had to mention such subjects. Such a day was July 19, when the ambassador journeyed to the Foreign Office to deliver a message from Lansing, not an inquiry about a ship this time but a short statement of irritation and need for change in British procedure. The mood was different that day. When Grey heard the dispatch "he became," Page wrote, "sadder than I had ever seen him," which in view of Grey's frequent depression was saying a great deal. The foreign secretary replied: "Well, will we have to throw up the sponge then?" Grey went on to plead the case Page knew so well: if he permitted unrestricted American trade with European neutrals it would destroy British efforts at economic pressure on Germany, prolong the war, put the ultimate issue in doubt. The foreign secretary might have intimated to Page, and also at one

[24] Ibid., 1: 390; Joseph P. Tumulty [Wilson's secretary], *Woodrow Wilson as I Know Him* (Garden City, N.Y., 1921), 230–31.

[25] Indeed, Page so pestered the Foreign Office that Sir Eyre Crowe, a person much less patient than Grey, became deeply disturbed. Protesting to a colleague, Crowe called the complaints "a gross impertinence . . . , baseless . . . , deliberate bad faith." Page to Lord Crewe, June 11, 1915, Sir Eyre Crowe to Arthur Nicolson, June 11, 1915, F. O. 382/12.

time to House, what he confessed after the war, namely, that he would have surrendered the blockade rather than risk rupture with the United States and a loss of the American warehouse. If he did so he spoke in such grave manner that the ambassador pledged himself to prevent that catastrophe. "Now I'm for stiffening Uncle Sam's backbone against anybody who does wrong," Page wrote House after the interview of July 19, "especially who does us wrong. But there are big views of big subjects and there are little views of big subjects. You may mention this subject to only *one* man. And you may burn this note. But remember—*we shall be at war with one side and not at peace with the other.*"[26]

Grey did have reason for depression in the summer of 1915. The United States by that time had given notice that it did not intend to accept broad application of the blockade. Most immediately threatening were cries from the southern states where cotton interests feared that the British navy, acting within the broad authority of the order-in-council, would destroy the entire Central European market. The cotton traffic always had been a difficult problem, for while the British felt it essential to keep that produce out of German hands, they knew the great trouble an arbitrary policy would create in the United States—as an economic hardship on the cotton states and as representative of stringent trade restriction. For that reason Britain had not placed cotton on the contraband list and had attempted to pay for much of the cotton seized. But this treatment had not been fully satisfactory; it had produced haggling, delay, many dissatisfied shippers and cotton growers. And with harvest approaching for the crop of 1915, southerners feared that continued British restriction would so reduce the price of cotton as to create depression.

Grey was so concerned about the cotton problem and the general state of Anglo-American relations that he gave serious thought to abandoning the order-in-council. He had confided to Lord Crewe in June that it might be better, instead of prohibiting

[26] July 20, 1915, Page Papers (the italics are Page's) ; Page to the secretary of state, July 19, 1915, *For. Rels., 1915, Supp.*, 478–79. For Lansing's message, July 16, 1915, see ibid., 473–74. For Grey's account of the interview see the foreign secretary to Ambassador Spring-Rice, July 19, 1915, F. O. 382/12.

import of all foodstuffs into Germany, to fall back on traditional rules of conditional contraband, and by these means assure that friction between the United States and Germany would not pass to Britain.[27] On July 22 the foreign secretary sent the cabinet a memorandum which set down likely alternatives for dealing with the United States. One course of action would be to continue the present policy of blockade and risk serious difficulty with the most important supplier. Or Britain could abandon the order-in-council and rely on international law respecting contraband and continuous voyage as applied by the United States during the Civil War. Such procedure probably would help stop imports to Germany and reduce friction with neutrals. "But," Grey continued, "we should abandon at a stroke all restrictions upon the export trade of Germany to neutral ports." Finally, Britain could say to the American government what is the truth: that commercial interests in the United States would object to any course the Allies chose, "that what those who protest against our policy really desire is that, in a crisis of our national fate, we should give up all attempt to exert economic pressure on our enemy." Grey suggested approaching the Washington government in the following manner: explain that Britain does not believe the United States wished to place the Allies in "such an unprecedented position of inferiority, while Germany acts with unprecedented barbarity," and then offer to withdraw the order-in-council on clear understanding that the United States recognize certain measures as justified.[28] Britain never made this offer to the United States; it did not abandon the blockade, but in August 1915 it did devise a scheme for purchase of huge supplies of cotton to help maintain a decent market price. And then on August 19, with American opinion aroused about the sinking of the *Arabic,* Britain placed cotton on the contraband list.[29] The arrangement, which did much to quiet protests from the cotton growers, allowed the

[27] Grey to Lord Crewe, June 14, 1915, Grey Papers.
[28] Grey's memorandum, July 22, 1915, "Printed for the use of the Cabinet," F. O. 382/12.
[29] For a discussion of the cotton-purchase arrangement see Link, *The Struggle for Neutrality,* 605–16.

Foreign Office to evade a possible crisis; but numerous other problems remained and Britain did not face clear sailing in relations with the United States, not even in 1915.

Most irritating of all American complaints was the implication that Britain restricted American trade so that English merchants could gain these markets for themselves. The consul general in London, Robert Skinner, sent reports to show how British trade had increased with neutral countries in several goods restricted to American shippers. The Foreign Office became upset at the charge, feeling the Americans accused it of bad faith, and when in autumn it seemed trouble might occur between the two governments the State Department rushed Skinner to the United States for consultation.[30] While the department never found evidence to press the case, it sounded peculiar. Page would not believe it an instant. He had investigated and found no proof; besides he could not believe the British capable of so base a deed, certainly not his friend Edward Grey.[31]

The ambassador continued to find Grey compelling. Having assumed the battle for civilization, what Grey attempted to do was to cast a small share of that burden on Page, and through Page the United States. His clear if unspoken logic reasoned that if the British and French did the fighting, suffered all the casualties, the United States surely could make a small contribution by tolerating minor excesses of the Allies. Thinking it a modest contribution, probably embarrassed it was so small, Page took on his shoulders the obligation his country refused to admit. He sought ways whereby the British could accomplish the most regulation while causing the least irritation, consequently the least danger with the United States. He advised Grey to use a method other than the order-in-council to announce restrictions, for this term historically had created ill feeling. Grey was unable to accept this advice; it was merely the British way. Page did not participate in the arrangement to purchase American cotton, but he had suggested broader use of the contraband list and doubtless

[30] Page to the secretary of state, Sept. 27, 1915, *For. Rels., 1915, Supp.*, 557–58; Counselor Polk to Wilson, Oct. 1, 1915, Polk to Lansing, Oct. 1, 1915, the Papers of Frank L. Polk, Yale University Library.

[31] Page to House, Sept. 21, 1915, Hendrick, *Page,* 2: 38–39.

was happy to see the list expanded in a way that would not arouse new hostility. On several occasions Page urged the foreign secretary to answer the last American note, but this advice conflicted with information Spring-Rice sent from Washington, and so the reply, completed by May 28, did not go out until the end of July. Sir Edward, in his often-quoted description of one encounter with the ambassador, told how Page remarked after reading a dispatch contesting Britain's stopping ships going to neutral ports: "I have read the dispatch, but I do not agree with it; let us consider how it should be answered."[32] It might be meaningful to note that House, sometimes with Wilson's knowledge, also collaborated with British officials.[33] Even so, with Wilson and Lansing irked at the ambassador's unsympathetic attitude toward what the United States attempted to do, it is inconceivable that the president would have retained Page in the British capital had he possessed full knowledge of the ambassador's maneuvers.

The ambassador believed he was acting not merely for the United States, but for all humanity, and the longer the war lasted, the more Page felt that the world needed Anglo-American cooperation. While he was no systematic diary-keeper, he liked to jot down occasional thoughts; and these scribblings reveal the workings of his mind. One idea was to form a club of "clear-thinking" men in the United States to promote Anglo-Saxon unity after he left his post. Possible members were Joseph Choate, "if he be not too old," Arthur Page, Plimpton, Wilson "after he's out of office, Taft? T. R.?—(no 'cranks') , Eliot, D. F. Houston."[34] Though not a racist of the extreme sort, Page was in some respects a social Dar-

[32] Grey, *Twenty-five Years, 1892–1916*, 2 vols. (New York, 1925) , 2: 110–11. Because Grey rarely left a record of his conversations with Page, about the only source for this discussion is information the foreign secretary saw fit to send Spring-Rice. For example, Grey wrote on June 10, 1915, that Page urged him to answer the note. Lord Crewe's memorandum of June 2 reported the same advice. Spring-Rice replied on June 11 that delay was imperative, that Page was acting without instructions. All these messages are in Grey's Papers. See also the foreign secretary to Ambassador Spring-Rice, July 19, 1915, F. O. 382/12.

[33] For example, House on July 8, 1915, suggested to Grey that France take greater responsibility for stopping ships, as the case of the *Dacia*. Seymour, *Colonel House*, 2: 56–57.

[34] Aug. 1, 1915.

winist with feelings of racial superiority. He believed the Anglo-Saxons were examples for the world in individual liberty and democracy and, if Britain and the United States worked together, could lead in military power, prevent war, and democratize the world. One diary entry even hinted desire to preserve racial purity: "Immigration to the U.S.—it must be regulated. The right principles are (1) Exclude racially unassimilable races, such as Negroes and Jews, and (2) politically unassimilable people, such as Germans."[35]

Neither the dozens of cases nor disgust at the United States's apparent inability to understand the war took a toll on the quantity or quality of the ambassador's letters to friends in the United States. He spent many a late night hour at the writing desk composing in his capable hand letters of often fifteen or twenty pages, typical Page missives, in language sophisticated and vernacular, saturated with praise of the British, criticism of Germany, pride in American democracy, advice about American policy. Occasionally he mustered a touch of humor, such as the story about an American living in Britain—"a half-expatriated loafer who talks 'art' . . . , the intellectually affected and degenerate type"—who told the ambassador he was ashamed of his country. "I remarked," wrote Page, "that I felt sure the feeling was mutual."[36] When he wrote about American policy he could be neither humorous nor pleasant, for he saw the administration stumbling into momentous mistakes. To House he complained that "the lawyer-way in which the Department goes on in its dealings with Great Britain is losing us the only great international friendship that we have any chance of keeping or that is worth having."[37] One wonders how Page found time to do this writing when the response was so unencouraging. Wilson almost never replied, and when he did write he sent a paragraph or two that told why he had not written. House generally answered but in a manner increasingly unsympathetic.

Looking back to House's stay in London one could see how

much his attitude had changed. The colonel also had found the British attitude compelling, especially after what one might describe as the Grey treatment. The foreign secretary had been friendly and cooperative in almost every way, setting aside a special hour at which House could come any day he wished. Grey would take him into the study and talk intimately about Anglo-American relations, the war, the future of the world, as he had done with Page. Then the two men might fall to discussing other matters, important things of life such as "nature, solitude, Wordsworth."[38] House usually left with feeling of greatest friendship, the immensely flattering belief that Grey trusted him with secrets of highest importance. Grey's attributes were easily transferable to the British cause, making both seem above reproach. House had noted in April: "His [Grey's] mind and mine run nearly parallel, and we seldom disagree. . . . It is . . . my good fortune that Fate has given me two such good friends as Woodrow Wilson and Edward Grey."[39] About that time he noted: "I like Page. He is direct and without guile."[40]

In fairness to House and Page, one must say that Grey was magnetic, and in fairness to Grey one must say he was not dishonest. The foreign secretary was every bit a gentleman wedded to the principle of Anglo-American friendship. He also was convinced of the need for an English victory in the war and was not above using his talents—dramatism, a depressed mood now and then, perhaps withholding a fact—to make the British cause appear faultless. Merely being himself and adding an occasional touch of color, the foreign secretary struck a great blow for Britain in the mind of the president's friend, and there is little reason to believe that if House had been the American ambassador he would have behaved any different than Page.

Unlike Page, the colonel did not stay long in the British capital and after a few weeks in the United States could manage more

[38] House Diary, Feb. 13, 1915, Seymour, *Colonel House*, 1: 371; House to Wilson, Feb. 9, 1915, ibid., 362; see also Grey, *Twenty-five Years*, 2: 123–24.
[39] April 30, 1915, Seymour, *Colonel House*, 1: 428.
[40] March 5, 1915, ibid., 389. As House left in June for the United States Page asked that the colonel give a good account of him in Washington. "Which, of course, I shall do," noted House. Diary, June 3, 1915.

objectivity. This is not to say that he abandoned his desire for British victory and Anglo-American friendship, but he was able to understand once again the American view and the reason for American policy. Now Page was a "blue funk," and so was Sir Edward. Understanding better than anyone the value of a change of environment, House advised Wilson to bring Page back to the United States for a rest.[41] To the ambassador he wrote: "Sir Edward and you cannot know the true situation here. I did not know it myself until I returned and began to plumb it. Ninety percent of our people do not want the President to involve us in war."[42] Later he explained: "I can understand quite well the inadvisability of what you term a 'nagging policy' and the futility of it. I think the view here is that something of the kind is demanded and that if it were not done it would arouse a suspicion of favoritism. I doubt whether anything we could do, short of intervention, would satisfy the Allies now that the fortune of war seems to be going against them; and even should they win, the loss of men and treasure will be laid at our door."[43]

One can understand the difficulty under which Page labored; the London atmosphere was so captivating it would have taken a large man, or an individual with no ideas or capacity for feeling, to resist it. And one can sympathize with Page's tiresome and irritating chores of arguing points of law, such minor questions as inconveniences of a Chicago meatpacker, while Grey worried about battles in France and the disastrous Gallipoli campaign. The ambassador's duties easily could appear to him what Prime Minister Asquith once remarked about House's peace talks: "the twittering of a sparrow in a tumult that shakes the world."[44]

Nonetheless, as Page easily forgot, there was an American view which seemed sound and sensible in 1915. To uphold this view, maintain an appearance of neutrality, and obtain respect for American rights, the State Department could not avoid pressing the Foreign Office. Page's approach was not satisfactory; he fa-

[41] House to Wilson, Aug. 4, 1915, Seymour, *Colonel House*, 2: 62.
[42] Aug. 4, 1915, ibid., 60–61.
[43] Aug. 19, 1915, ibid., 63.
[44] Page Diary, March 11, 1915.

vored nothing that would force Britain to alter its policy and show respect for American neutral rights—little less than placing American commerce under British control. If it would hinder the enemy, and if they could do it safely, why would the British not push the United States as far as possible? Grey later admitted that such was the object of British diplomacy.[45]

Even if the administration could have disregarded American opinion and national honor, Page's policy was objectionable from another point of view. In the background was the German danger, the possibility of an indiscriminate onslaught against ships in the war zone; and had American policy been so clearly in favor of the Allies it is difficult to imagine Germany exercising the restraint it showed for large portions of two years. Within the Second Reich a struggle raged for months between those individuals who wished to avoid war with the United States and the faction which wanted to use the submarine without restriction, at risk of provoking the Americans. While we can never know what the Germans would have done in a different situation, we do know that the "peace faction" won out for two years, which it might not have done had America's British policy been weaker.

One would have to base the wisdom of Page's recommendations involving policy with Britain or Germany on presumption that the president, Congress, and American people were ready and willing to enter the war in 1915 and that American participation would have served the best interest of the nation. While it is impossible to determine what the course of the world and the United States would have been had that nation entered the war earlier, one can say that America was not ready for belligerency in 1915.

If the American attitude—at least the attitude of Americans toward their position in the war—had changed little since the conflict began, Page had adjusted his thoughts to find good in what seemed a useless and wasteful struggle. The war now fitted into the ambassador's scheme because it could (he hoped) destroy the old political order, force Anglo-American cooperation, do in a few years what might have taken generations. Fulfillment de-

---

[45] *Twenty-five Years,* 2: 107.

pended on two factors: that Britain not lose (if there were no independent British nation, there hardly could be Anglo-American leadership) , and that the United States not follow policy such as meekness toward Germany, premature peace efforts, harassment of Britain, which would destroy British respect and desire for cooperation. The way the United States acted in 1915 it seemed to Page that either or both might happen. Unwillingness to force the submarine issue continued to stimulate British ridicule. He wrote Wilson in September: "Unless some explanation be made or some action taken, I am sorry to report that we shall be regarded with slight respect by English opinion for a long time to come."[46] And the government made the additional error of pestering the Foreign Office and threatened to go farther.

It was no secret that the American government was not satisfied with British relations in the fall of 1915. Bogged down with the German problem, the administration had sent no public note since the gentle message of March 30, but dispatches from Washington indicated that the Americans did not intend to let the Royal Navy have its way on the sea. In July, after a long and, to the State Department, insulting wait, Britain answered the American note of March 30. The reply was polite as usual, and as usual gave no substantial concession.[47] The event that made a new American note virtually inevitable was German concession on the *Arabic*, for it gave the administration both temporary relief in the submarine crisis and inspiration to make publicly clear that it pressed its rights with both groups of belligerents.

Page summoned his best efforts to prevent another public protest, explaining to House and Wilson that at such critical stage of the war a note would be useless and have a bad effect. His pleas were in vain; the note still was coming. "England won't read it," he retorted in the diary, "till there comes a lull in the fighting or in the breathless diplomatic struggle with the Balkans. . . . What is the vital thing—the killing of fifty people last night by a Zeppelin within sight of St. Paul's on one side and Westminster Abbey on the other, or is it making representations to Sir Edward

[46] Sept. 9, 1915, Wilson Papers.
[47] Page to the secretary of state, July 24, 1915, *For. Rels., 1915, Supp.,* 168–71.

Grey, who has hardly slept for a week?"[48] The ambassador's final appeal, a short telegram, explained that because of tragic events in the Gallipoli campaign, feeling was tense in Britain, like "Northern opinion . . . the week after Bull Run or after Lee crossed the Potomac on his way to Gettysburg." There might be a political crisis. Page would make no recommendation but did say that "it is certain that the note will receive no serious attention by the Government till the present tension is relaxed, and its presentation at this moment is likely to result in a public reception that may tend to defeat its purpose."[49]

The warning had no effect. Wilson read the dispatch, fumed a little, asked House if it should change anything. Ignore it, the colonel advised, and added (with some exaggeration) that when in London he differed so much with Page that it was not possible to carry on a discussion with him.[50] Wilson had the State Department send the note on October 21. It had many pages and sections, a tediously long message that presented a critical review of the entire British maritime system. If many of the charges were old, especially the section concerning commerce with neutral nations, compared with the American note of March 30, the new note showed how the American position had changed. The first message apparently accepted the blockade, assuming that most neutral commerce was safe. The note of October 21 protested the illegality and ineffectiveness of the blockade, listed ships detained in Britain, insisted on a change. There still was no threat of punitive action, but it made clear that the United States did not wish to acquiesce in the British system.[51]

Page did not have to read a word before his heart sank. The message must have looked like a volume to the frustrated diplomat. Pouring over the words and figures, he found little to relieve his disgust: the language sounded bad and he would have to smooth it in places; the note contested the blockade. One paragraph was especially alarming. Section thirteen had to do with

[48] Hendrick, *Page*, 2: 66; Page to Wilson, Sept. 26, 1915, ibid., 94–102; Sept. 9, 1915, Wilson Papers.
[49] Page to the secretary of state, Oct. 15, 1915, *The Lansing Papers*, 1: 303.
[50] Wilson to House, Oct. 18, 1915, House Papers; House to Wilson, Oct. 19, 1915, ibid.
[51] *For. Rels., 1915, Supp.*, 578–601.

British commerce, pointing out that British trade had increased with the same neutral countries with which the United States wished to deal. In doing so Britons were helping create a situation the government used to justify interception of American goods for these countries, a "manifest injustice," the note said.[52] Are they, Page undoubtedly asked himself, repeating Skinner's foolish, insulting charge, accusing the British of bad faith? He dashed off a telegram requesting explanation of the paragraph and to ascertain that it should stay in the note. Lansing replied almost abruptly that the paragraph should stand, that it was clear enough and had nothing to do with British policy in regard to increasing British trade.[53] As he delivered the message to Grey on November 5, Page tried to make the pill as sweet as possible. He pointed to section thirteen and assured the foreign secretary it did not mean what it might seem to mean. He explained, almost apologetically, that the note was not as long as it appeared, for much of it was appendixes. Accepting the document, Grey said it probably would take some time to prepare a reply. That was reasonable, said Page.[54]

While the long note was on its way to Britain, American newspapers had circulated a rumor that Page would resign. The source of the rumor is not known; Page said it was "partly because of the newspaper itch to find mare's nests, partly because of House's pussy-cat way of slipping about and of purring at the wrong times and in the wrong tones."[55] The rumor concerned Wilson enough that he had Lansing ask and receive Page's assurance it was false. The secretary followed with a note of gratification for the ambassador's service.[56] It was not a truthful statement, certainly not for Lansing and not for the President either, unless Page's reports of British opinion were important enough to obscure his failing in

[52] Ibid., 581–82.
[53] Both messages Nov. 4, 1915, ibid., 609–10.
[54] The foreign secretary to Ambassador Spring-Rice, Nov. 5, 1915, F. O. 382/12. After delivering the message, Page sent Grey letters Nov. 5 and Nov. 6 to clear up "ambiguous" and impolite phrases; ibid.
[55] Diary, Dec. 28, 1915.
[56] The secretary of state to Page, Oct. 25, 29, 1915, The Lansing Papers, 1: 702.

other areas. Wilson evidently thought that even if the ambassador did little for the American case in London, he did no harm, and the president was in no mood to treat the problems—appearance of an Anglo-American crisis, the task of finding a replacement— which Page's exodus would create.

The ambassador wrote a large number of letters in winter 1915, most of them concerning the note and Anglo-American relations. Letters to Wilson, polite and respectful, tolled the destruction of American prestige in Britain. The outstanding effort was an eloquent, unrestrained twenty-five page letter to House, which called the note "an uncourteous monster of 35 heads and 3 appendices." "There is not a courteous word," he wrote, "nor a friendly phrase, nor a kindly turn in it, not an allusion even to an old acquaintance, to say nothing of an old friendship, not a word of thanks for courtesies or favors done us, not a hint of sympathy in the difficulties of the time. There is nothing in its tone to show that it came from an American to an Englishman: it might have been from a Hottentot to a Fiji-islander." Page thought he should have seen a draft of the note. After all, he explained, Anglo-American relations were his business; he had learned something about diplomacy and the way friendly governments address one another: "I should have suggested a courteous short note saying that we are obliged to set forth such and such views about maritime law and rights of neutrals, to his Majesty's Government; and that the contention of the United States Government was herewith sent— etc., etc." Grey obviously was Page's example, and a good one, for the foreign secretary politely had exercised control over much of America's commerce with Europe. "If it be done courteously," Page continued, "we can accuse them of stealing sheep and of dyeing the skins to conceal the theft without provoking the slightest bad feeling."

The ambassador then explained to the president's envoy how best to assure peace: "There's no further good in having venerable children build houses of sand at the Hague; there's no further good in peace organizations or protective leagues to enforce peace. We had as well get down to facts. So far as ensuring peace is concerned the biggest fact in the world is the British fleet. The next biggest fact is the American fleet, because of itself and still more because of the vast reserve power of the United States which it implies. If these two fleets perfectly understand one another about the undesirability of wars of aggression, there'll be no more big wars as long as this understanding continues. Such an understanding calls for no treaty—it calls for only courtesy."[57]

For all Page's blustering about the note, the Foreign Office came to the conclusion that it was not a cause for alarm. From several important sources emerged the idea that the motive behind the American government's action was to impress national opinion and not promote drastic change in British-American relations. The American embassy in London was one of these sources. Lord Robert Cecil, undersecretary of state for foreign affairs, reported a discussion with the embassy's counselor, who expressed "dismay at . . . our passion for abandoning our aims and claims at the mere sound of American criticism." Page, who privately called the note "ineffective humbug, written for home-consumption," hinted to Cecil the same idea.[58] Even Spring-Rice, a person usually obsessed with need for concession to the United States, wrote Grey that "it would be a pity to take [the] words too seriously. The Germans have not, and they have not suffered."[59] The most convincing information came from a private source, a letter to Lord Cecil from Frederick Dixon, a respected newspaperman of the Boston *Monitor*, which told of a recent discussion with the secretary of state. Lansing had said that the note was "a political safety valve, that not much was expected from it, as it would certainly not be pressed." Dixon suggested that Britain "stand like a rock on essentials, & give everything away that has no value." This advice seemed sound to Cecil and other officials.[60]

[57] Nov. 12, 1915, Hendrick, *Page*, 2: 69–79. Page also was frank with the president. Writing Wilson on Nov. 19, 1915, he called the note a "long, legal, de-humanized document." Wilson Papers.

[58] Foreign Office notes by Lord Cecil, Nov. 21, 1915, concerning discussion with the embassy's counselor, and Nov. 19, 1915, concerning discussion with Page, F. O. 382/12.

[59] Oct. 28, 1915, Grey Papers.

[60] Frederick Dixon to Lord Robert Cecil, undated (stamped Nov. 10, 1915), notes by Lord Cecil. Nov. 18, 19, F. O. 382/12.

As Crewe in November summarized the British position, "It being certain that we do not intend to abandon our policy of strangling German trade, import or exports, the question with the U. S. becomes one of tactics, not of principle."[61]

Within a few days the Foreign Office had the opportunity to apply, or make preparation for applying, the much discussed rigidity in relations with the United States. His old self again, Spring-Rice sent new reports of irritation so intense as to recreate the danger of embargo. On December 26 he warned that Congress might remove the question from Wilson's hands by attaching an embargo rider to a defense bill which the president could not veto.[62] Britain's response was not—as it had been in July—to consider removing the blockade, but was a movement toward retaliation. On the final day of 1915 the Foreign Office cabled Spring-Rice that the Allies would reply to an embargo by cutting off all shipments of raw material to the United States, and on the same day asked France, Russia, and Italy to stand together in this firm policy.[63]

Even though Page did not know about the goings-on in the Foreign Office, he found enough in American foreign relations at the end of the year to be in an attitude of gloom and dissatisfaction. In November a submarine had sunk another ship, the *Ancona*, with Americans aboard. The submarine had borne an Austro-Hungarian ensign, and because that empire was not party to Germany's submarine pledge, negotiation began anew. The settlement was satisfactory to the United States, but it was another case of torpedoing, which the president met with note-writing. While the *Lusitania* controversy lay, where it had been for six months, submerged beneath German procrastination and Wilsonian pacifism, newspapers reported that more notes would come to Britain about the blockade. The ambassador by now had

[61] Attached to a dispatch from Ambassador Spring-Rice to the foreign secretary, Nov. 21, 1915, ibid.

[62] Ambassador Spring-Rice to the foreign secretary, Nov. 21 and Dec. 26, 1915, ibid.

[63] The foreign secretary to Ambassador Spring-Rice, Dec. 31, 1915, the foreign secretary to ambassadors in France, Russia, and Italy, Dec. 31, 1915, ibid.

lost almost all confidence in Wilson. "This job was botched," he confessed to House.[64] Page felt that problems between Britain and the United States would have been even more serious had it not been for the efforts of Edward Grey and himself, for he did have, as he wrote his daughter, "some sense of the inevitable destiny of the great English-speaking race—so that, when we have come to sharp corners in the road, I have known that whatever happens we must travel in the right general direction—that no temporary difference must be allowed to assume a permanent quality." Page nonetheless believed there was greater chance of trouble than anyone expected.[65] And to make matters worse, rumor had it that House was coming again to talk peace.

[64] Nov. 12, 1915, Hendrick, *Page,* 2: 79.
[65] To Mrs. Charles G. Loring, Dec. 7, 1915, ibid., 118–19.

Chapter Seven

The Worst Year

As THE OLD year ended and the new one began, Page found good reason for believing that one way or another, a decisive time had come. Newspapers and letters from House reported that the United States government again was pressing the *Lusitania* case. It even had appeared for a short time that the ambassador might get all he wished out of that issue. House had written that the United States was much nearer a break with the Central Powers and suggested that Page tell "our friends in England . . . that the lower their fortunes seem the more ready we are to help."[1] The ambassador was delighted to transmit that information, but as time passed the United States produced pitifully little evidence that it was true. On December 30 the British passenger liner *Persia* was torpedoed in the Mediterranean with loss of two American lives. Page seized that opportunity to hasten the move House said was possible. "We now have come to the parting of ways," he cabled on January 3, and went on to describe the passing of American prestige in Britain: "Ridicule of the administration runs through the programs of the theaters; it inspires hundreds of cartoons; it is a staple of conversation at private dinners and in the clubs. . . . There is even talk of spheres of German influence in the United States as in China." The way to escape this terrible predicament, he explained, was to sever relations.[2] But no one saw the submarine which hit the *Persia;* Austria-Hungary and Germany disclaimed responsibility; nothing came of the incident.[3] And January was so full of events and rumors of events—House coming to London in quest of peace; the United States and Germany to close the *Lusitania* case peacefully; Wilson to send a strong note to Britain; Lansing proposing that Britain stop arming merchant ships—that Page could see it was going to be a busy year. Little did he expect it was going to be the most perplexing year of his ambassadorship.

Among the first and certainly not the least of Page's problems was the visit of the wily, quietly deceptive little colonel. To the ambassador, House had become almost synonymous with mediation, which he knew to be a most unwelcome word in London. But this visit was to have nothing to do with peace, so the newspapers said; House was coming to advise American ambassadors in Europe and not to talk peace. Lansing had cabled the same idea.[4] So had House on December 1, and two weeks later the colonel had written: "There is [*sic*] absolutely no peace plans in my visit and I would be glad if you let this be known."[5] This story might have convinced some persons but not Page, who noted on Lansing's message: "Why lie to me about it?"

Commonly called the "second peace mission," it would be as accurate to describe the journey as House's "first war mission," for the colonel's plan might have been means for bringing the United States into war on the side of the Allies. Dissatisfied that the United States was stumbling from one crisis to another, fearful that events might force the nation into action, House chose to try to end the war by mediation or participation. His now well-known scheme, devised in the final weeks of 1915, was to tell

---

[1] Dec. 12, 1915, Page Papers.

[2] Page to the secretary of state, Jan. 3, 1916, *The Lansing Papers,* 1: 703–704.

[3] Ambassador Gerard to the secretary of state, Jan. 17, 1916, Ambassador Penfield to the secretary of state, Jan. 22, 1916, *Papers Relating to the Foreign Relations of the United States, 1916, Supplement* (Washington, D.C., 1929), 145, 148–49.

[4] Dec. 23, Page Papers.

[5] House to Page, Dec. 1, 1915, ibid.; see also House Diary, Dec. 15, 1916, *Times* (London), Dec. 23, 1915, Spring-Rice to Grey, Dec. 23, 1915, Grey Papers.

British leaders that the president wished to mediate, and obtain understanding that the British would be favorable to Wilson's terms. He would continue his journey to Berlin, tell German leaders the president wanted to end the war, intimate that the Allies probably would reject the proposal. If Germany accepted, assuming Britain already was of mind to do so, Wilson could strike a giant blow for peace. If Germany refused, which was likely, the United States would enter the war on the side of the Allies. House thought his idea that of a master diplomat, but when one considers his behavior in Europe, it seems more the work of an anglophile.[6]

Anxious for an honorable way out of a complex and dangerous situation, Wilson gave his blessing to House's trip, but he was not certain about committing the United States to war. To the colonel's proposition that the United States would become a belligerent if Germany refused the terms, the president, of course, inserted the word "probably."[7]

The colonel arrived at Falmouth on January 5 and the red carpet was rolled out. Most passengers had to remain on board another twenty-four hours for inspection. Not so with the House party. The British arranged for the baggage, engaged taxicabs, sleeping-car accommodations, everything possible to make the trip to London comfortable.[8] The mission seemed started in grand fashion, that is, until House arrived and ran into Walter Page. "Mr. House is here again," the ambassador almost wearily wrote Grey. "Let us instruct . . . [him] at whichever time suits you best."[9]

While the foreign secretary was showing House his customary, if at times vague, tact and friendliness, Page in his own blunt manner began the instruction. For the ambassador's reaction to the mission and American policy in general, let the colonel's diary tell the story:

[6] House outlined his plan in his diary, Oct. 8, 1915, Seymour, *Colonel House,* 2: 84–85.

[7] In House's letter to Grey, Oct. 17, 1915, ibid., 91; also Wilson to House, Oct. 18, 1915, Ray Stannard Baker, *Woodrow Wilson: Life and Letters,* 8 vols. (Garden City, N.Y., 1927–1939), 6: 128.

[8] House Diary, Jan. 5, 1916, Seymour, *Colonel House,* 2: 115–16.

[9] Jan. 5, 1916, Grey Papers.

January 7	Page lunched with me. He was full of the growing unpopularity of the President and the United States in Britain.
January 12	He criticized both Lansing and the President severely because of their sending notes to him to present to the Foreign Office, and making demands they did not mean to have fulfilled. . . . I wish he could go home for a while.
January 19	Page took me to lunch and was as pessimistic as ever. It has become a punishment for me to be with him because he is so critical of the President, Lansing, and our people generally. Page is a man of high character and I am fond of him, but he is so antagonistic to American policy that I have a feeling he will retard rather than help in this matter.

After preliminary conversation in England, House on January 20 left for a few days in Germany, where he found the attitude sufficiently unyielding for him to proceed. When he returned, through France, Page again was ready to pounce:

February 9	The Ambassador called at the Ritz Hotel a half hour after our arrival. He was as pessimistic as ever. . . . Everything the President was doing was wrong. . . . In reply I literally flayed him and I was surprised afterward that he took it so kindly. The man hinders me in my work because he tries to discourage me, and would totally do so if I were of a different temperament.
February 10	My entire evening was spent in listening to denunciation of the President and Lansing, and of the Administra-

tion in general. He thought the State Department should be cleaned out from top to bottom. . . . I did not argue with him. One might as well argue with a petulant woman. "The President has no policy. He has lost the respect of Great Britain and the world. Lansing insults every one of his notes, etc., etc."

February 14   It was as much as I could do to contain myself. I sat still and quiet looking into the fire until he had relieved his mind. Grey views the situation much as I do, and I find in him a colleague far more sympathetic than Page.

Page need not have been so disturbed, for the colonel came bearing not ill will but a program of assistance for the British. It would be difficult to state one's position more clearly than did House in conference with Page and British leaders. The ambassador had begun by saying he had been asked what the United States wished Britain to do; to which House replied: "The United States would like Great Britain to do those things which would enable the United States to help Great Britain win the war." That statement made faces beam all round the table, and Page's was brightest of all. "You have answered the question with more cleverness than I had the wit to do," the ambassador replied. But then House started talking about trade difficulty and faces became serious again.[10]

As the colonel's diary has shown, Page saw no reason for House's being in London, doing work which fell within his own domain. Hence the colonel became a vent for the emotions Page had stored up the past several months. Page directed his sharpest blows at House's scheme for ending the war. "This purely academic nonsensical stuff, House thinks is good sense," he noted privately. "Of course the fatal moral weakness of the foregoing

[10] House Diary, Jan. 11, 1916, Seymour, *Colonel House*, 2: 124; Page Diary, Jan. 12, 1916.

scheme is that we should plunge into the war, not on the merits of the cause, but by a carefully sprung trick. . . . Of course such a morally weak, indirect scheme is doomed to failure—is wrong in fact."[11] If the United States wished to help the British, Page had a simple method: send Bernstorff home; stop all ships to Germany; fight the Huns if necessary. Why this pussyfooting it to Germany and back; why this silly talk about mediation which, if made public, would cause an uproar such as House never had seen?[12]

House insisted he had to do things his way, the president's way, and after returning from Germany, he gathered British leaders to outline the plan. He invited Page, not because he needed the ambassador's collaboration but because he feared that Page otherwise would feel insulted. Page declined: "House told me that we'd have a meeting . . . Asquith, Grey, Reading, George, he & I. No we won't. He doesn't yet see that no member of the Gov't can afford to discuss any such subject, nor does he see that not one of them has any confidence in the strength of the President for action. I told House that I couldn't go with him into any such conference, and I wouldn't."[13] House went ahead and set forth his plan for intervention or mediation, which Grey incorporated into the famous memorandum. The colonel left the meeting encouraged, with a vague understanding that the British would choose the time for Wilson to act. The United States would be "in the thick of it" very soon, "perhaps within 30 days," he assured an English friend as he returned home to await the word from London.[14]

The British never sent the word and repeated urgings would not budge them. The Foreign Office reasoned that it could not propose a conference while the Germans were winning, and when

[11] Page Diary, Feb. 9, 1916.
[12] These thoughts Page set down partly in his Diary, Feb. 12, 1916, and partly in a message to the State Department, Feb. 17, 1916, *The Lansing Papers*, 1: 705–706.
[13] Memorandum, Feb. 9, 1916, Page Papers; Hendrick, *Page*, 3: 281–82.
[14] Diary notation, Feb. 23, 1916, the Diary of Horace Plunkett, microfilm copy in Princeton University Library. The memorandum is reproduced in Grey, *Twenty-five Years, 1892–1916*, 2 vols. (New York, 1925), 2: 127–28; copies of the document are in various places; for example, Page Papers, House Papers, Grey Papers.

the Allies gained the advantage they felt encouraged to go on to victory. As Page had said, the British lacked confidence in Wilson's willingness to involve the United States in war. Nor could Britain talk peace without concurrence of the Allies, particularly the French; and with an alignment of allies they might never have again, the French wished to regain the provinces lost in the war of 1870–1871 and eliminate the German menace. In 1916 a negotiated peace seemed to the Paris government out of the question.[15] It is not likely that Britain's leaders ever intended to invite American mediation. They tolerated House, knowing it was bad business to shun the president's representative.

If Page's attitude was realistic, it hardly was diplomatic. Admittedly he opposed House's scheme on moral grounds, that it was a deceitful way of entering the war, and that position would have been honorable if the ambassador had not justified intervention on grounds equally dubious. Refusing to cooperate, he violated no instructions, since there were none, but had he put in a good word for the plan, or at least kept silent, he might have improved his standing in Washington. He could not do that, however, because Grey then might think that no American understood the war. He chose to disassociate himself from the plan, wait for inevitable failure, and set to repairing the damage. Small wonder that for Page the happiest day of the colonel's visit was the time House went home. "Last night House left London for Falmouth to sail for N. Y. on Friday," the ambassador noted. "He cannot come again—or I go."[16]

Page had not waited for House's departure to try to put the administration on the right track. While the colonel was moving about London, to the Continent and back, the ambassador began his own campaign to induce a turn in American foreign policy.

[15] The French in July restated their position as follows: "The complex questions which will be raised by the conclusion of peace cannot be approached without inconvenience until victory has been assured." The British ambassador in France (Bertie) to the foreign secretary, July 1, 1916, F. O. 800/2803; Grey, *Twenty-five Years*, 2: 128–29. For correspondence between House and Grey see Seymour, *Colonel House*, 2: 275–92.

[16] Feb. 24, 1916. Another time Page wrote: "House is doing a lot of harm here, wh. I must somehow turn to good—eg., make it accentuate the crisis as soon as he is gone." Diary, Feb. 13, 1916.

Still searching for a means of accommodation with Britain's maritime system, on January 15 he sounded the secretary of state on the American attitude if, instead of the confusing order-in-council, the British declared a simple and strict blockade of the enemy.[17] Lansing answered that while he would favor return to rules of blockade and contraband, he could make no statement of the American attitude concerning such a "hypothetical case."[18] Encouraged by this vague response, Page replied with a long, impassioned message which had a new reason for the United States not pressing Britain. The ambassador pointed to alarming conditions in Asia where the Japanese, having already made severe demands on China, apparently intended to dominate the entire Pacific area. If the war ended in an inconclusive peace, Britain would have to devote its major attention to Europe, leaving for the United States not only an unsatisfactory European situation but also necessity of facing Japanese expansion alone. An Allied victory, wrote Page, would eliminate all these dangers, for it would stabilize Europe, allow Britain to cooperate with the United States in the Far East and in general world settlement. The key to victory in Europe was Britain's strangling of German trade, possible only if the United States refrained from challenging a stringent naval policy. There followed a warning that Britain soon would declare an absolute blockade of Germany, that American acceptance of this policy was the final opportunity to assure Anglo-American friendship and cooperation. "This seems the critical moment of the war for us," Page concluded, "a moment that demands a constructive and decisive suggestion. If you have such a suggestion, however tentative, that I may privately use it may secure a permanent peace . . . and change the course of history for a century."[19]

[17] *The Lansing Papers*, 1: 305.
[18] Jan. 20, 1916, ibid., 305–306.
[19] Page to the secretary of state, Jan. 22, 1916, ibid., 306–307. It might be meaningful to explain the change about which Page wrote. The order-in-council of March 11, 1915, proclaimed that the Allies felt themselves free to stop all goods entering or leaving Germany, directly or indirectly. The order did not proclaim a blockade because the Allies could not meet the legal specifications—that the blockade be effective—and it was legally impossible to

Page apparently took this action on his initiative, for there is no indication that Grey had put him up to it or that Britain planned to change the tactics it had used the past several months. Talk in the Foreign Office of retaliation against the United States, so common a few weeks earlier, had died down because there seemed no need for it. Spring-Rice was on the rampage again, shouting trouble in almost every message. But the ambassador did not always make good sense; while he told of cries of protest from various American groups, he was not clear what they meant or what to do about them. The message of January 13, for example, stated that though the situation was "somewhat alarming," the United States was not likely to take "united" action against Britain; another dispatch, written a week later, warned of irritation so intense as to warrant Britain's making preparation for producing munitions in Canada.[20] Like his American counterpart in London, Spring-Rice had weakened his influence, leaving superiors bewildered and unresponsive. "It becomes increasingly difficult to know what practical value to attach to these daily varying estimates of the parliamentary situation in America," grumbled Crowe. "I confess that I do not share Sir C. Spring Rice's feelings

---

blockade the neutral countries which siphoned so much trade to Germany. Neutral ships could attempt to enter neutral ports, or even German ports, but in doing so they bore risk of being captured by the Royal Navy. Page in his message warned that the Allies in January 1916 planned to declare—although they never did—an absolute blockade of Germany, under which conditions neutral ships were not even to attempt to enter or leave German ports. Page hoped that Britain could solve the problem of trade with the neutral countries by expanding on American precedents of the Civil War, applying the doctrine of continuous voyage, namely, that the nature of goods was determined by the ultimate, not immediate, destination. What the ambassador wished of his government was advance notice that it would accept without protest, or with protest merely for the record, the blockade as effective and allow its application stretched to include neutral ports. He gave the United States two ways to rationalize a passive attitude: 1) the legal ground that the blockade now, and not in March 1915, was effective; 2) the practical fact that any other attitude would present in the future great danger for the United States. Page would have been delighted to have his government accept either line of reasoning.

[20] Spring-Rice to Grey, Jan. 13, 1916, Grey Papers; Ambassador Spring-Rice to the foreign secretary, Jan. 18, 1916, F. O. 382/1099; other messages include the ones sent Jan. 13, 1916, ibid., and Jan. 29, 1916, Grey Papers.

of alarm."[21] Most officials in the Foreign Office agreed with this judgment and Lord Eustace Percy, calling the United States an undisciplined and disunified democracy, offered the opinion that "we can . . . so far as America is concerned, adopt any naval policy that we please."[22] Ever cautious about American opinion, Grey would not go that far. The foreign secretary, pressed by associates in the Foreign Office and also by his French ally, was not willing to weaken policy, nor did he see profit in changing the structure. A variation of the blockade might soothe some irritation, but it would create other difficulties, particularly, as Grey cabled Spring-Rice, the problem of enemy exports on neutral ships. Troublesome as the order-in-council was, Grey seemed content to muddle through with it.[23]

While the foreign secretary doubtless at some time had made the ambassador aware of obstacles to a change in the blockade, Page chose to act not because of Grey's urging, but because of his estimate of the world situation at the time.[24] The first weeks of

[21] "I confess I share Sir E. Crowe's bewilderment," wrote Robert Cecil. Both notes accompanied Spring-Rice's dispatch of Jan. 18, 1916, F. O. 382/1099.

[22] Memorandum by Lord Percy, "The U.S.A. and the Blockade," Jan. 24, 1916, Grey Papers. "I think," wrote another official (Hurst), "that we can disregard the attitude of the U.S.A. altogether. The racial cleavage would make them uncertain of the support of the masses, whichever side they took." This note and others by Crowe and Cecil accompanied Spring-Rice's message of Jan. 12, 1916, F. O. 382/1099.

[23] The foreign secretary to Ambassador Spring-Rice, Feb. 3, 1916, F. O. 382/1099. Hurst added on January 27, 1916, his opinion that Britain could not change the blockade because the United States would not recognize the doctrine of continuous voyage; ibid. As to French opinion, the French premier (Aristide Briand) expressed hope at a meeting of the Allied War Council on January 19, 1916, that the blockade could be tightened. Grey replied that the matter "was a very delicate one, owing to the resentment amongst neutrals, which was very strong." The foreign secretary added that he would welcome French suggestion of how to strengthen the system. "Minutes of the Allied War Council," Jan. 19, 1916 [author unknown], F. O. 371/2804.

[24] Indeed, Page, Grey, and Lansing did not seem to be thinking about the same system. The ambassador wrote of an absolute blockade, which technically made contraband lists superfluous. All goods would have been contraband. Yet Lansing spoke of returning to rules of contraband, and Grey in his message to Spring-Rice mentioned the same thing. It also is difficult to understand how the foreign secretary's major point of concern—goods of

1916 did seem a decisive stage of the war and American policy. Early in January the British had to evacuate Gallipoli and abandon that disastrous campaign. Messages from the Continent reported German troops massing, and in February would begin the ferocious battle of Verdun. English opinion was restive, with many individuals feeling the nation was not getting the most from its seapower, that instead of piecemeal measures the government should impose a strict blockade and let the United States be damned.[25] From House, Page learned that American policy was in flux; but if mediation was to be the change, it was the wrong kind. What service he could be to Britain, the United States, and the world, Page must have thought, if he could channel the change properly, secure American acquiescence to a true blockade, and remove the only obstacle to that policy.

The administration would not allow Page that satisfaction, although there was some interest in the ambassador's cable. Garbled in transmission, Lansing had some difficulty making out the sentences, but the meaning was clear. The secretary told Wilson that he gave the telegram more weight because with House in Europe it might have contained the colonel's feeling. "I think it is all Page," the president replied, and while he thought the argument forceful, Wilson preferred to wait for House's communication.[26] They never mentioned the dispatch again.

If Page could not give Grey any pleasant news, the foreign secretary had a message for the ambassador upon summoning him on January 25. There is no verbatim record of the conversation, but it probably began with a statement by Grey, such as "What do you think of the American proposal about disarming merchant ships?" "What?" Page perhaps replied, puzzled. "Lansing's plan that British merchantmen remove their guns," Grey repeated. "Do you mean that you do not know about it?" When the ambas-

---

enemy origin traveling in neutral ships—could have been a problem under conditions of true blockade.

[25] See, for example, *Times* (London), Jan. 19, 20, 22, 1916.

[26] Both messages Jan. 24, 1916, *The Lansing Papers*, 1: 307–308. Still hoping he could make his plan work, House wrote Wilson on January 16 that at the moment there should be no change in policy with Germany or Britain. House Papers.

sador had to confess he did not, the foreign secretary handed him a dispatch from Spring-Rice, and in this manner Page learned the administration's latest plan for preserving neutrality and halting the submarine threat.[27]

Lansing's logic was simple enough: For some time he had sympathized with the German contention that a submarine could not emerge and halt an enemy merchantman if there was danger of the vessel's firing on the submarine. And recent facts—information that the *Persia* carried a deck gun, and that there was an armed Italian liner in New York—convinced the secretary that the Allies customarily outfitted ships for offensive action. He reasoned that if submarines were safe from hostile action by their victims, the commanders would not object to stopping a ship according to international law, that the Allies would be happy to disarm noncombat vessels in return for assurance against deadly sneak attacks. If the belligerents accepted his *modus vivendi*—the Allies disarm merchant ships, the Central Powers abide by rules of visit and search—the greatest threat to American neutrality would vanish.[28]

International law favored the seafaring nation, inasmuch as traditional rules had permitted defensive arming of merchant vessels for the purpose, long since obsolete, of warding off pirates. Because the plan required that the Allies accept a change of rule, Lansing after receiving Wilson's hearty approval had sent it to Britain, France, and Italy on January 18.[29]

The secretary had chosen to act, not through Page as was customary, but through the British ambassador in Washington, and had failed to inform Page. By the time the news reached the ambassador it was a week old. When Grey learned of Page's ignorance, he seemed disposed to say little, only that the State

[27] The scene is improvised from Page's report of the meeting. Page to the secretary of state, Jan. 25, 1916, *For. Rels., 1916, Supp.*, 151–52.
[28] The secretary of state to President Wilson, Jan. 2, 7, 1916, *The Lansing Papers*, 1: 332–35.
[29] The secretary of state to the British ambassador, *For. Rels., 1916, Supp.*, 146–48; President Wilson to the secretary of state, Jan. 10, 17, 1916, *The Lansing Papers*, 1: 335–36; Ambassador Spring-Rice to the foreign secretary, Jan. 21, 1916, F. O. 382/929.

Department had not foreseen how fully the measure favored the Germans, speaking, Page reported, "as one speaks of a great calamity." The ambassador was considerably more verbose, repeating the old theme that if the administration persisted it would destroy the confidence and good will of the Allies, and that Britain might halt its large purchases in the United States and trade elsewhere. He called the proposal a mistake comparable to the blunder with the Declaration of London, advised treating it as the United States did the Declaration, and suggested the administration reread his message of January 22.[30]

Although the matter dangled for several weeks, the American government had to do exactly as Page suggested. Lansing and Wilson had failed to foresee the effect of the plan; certainly they had mistaken the attitude of the British, who showed extreme distaste if not contempt for the proposal. Spring-Rice for several weeks had warned that Germany and the United States might strike a bargain over the *Lusitania* dispute, and now Lansing's plan seemed undeniable proof the deal had taken place.[31] It is "tantamount to a complete capitulation to the German view of submarine warfare," wrote one disgusted official.[32] Even Grey, who usually tried to keep his colleagues' comments from leaving the Foreign Office, asked Spring-Rice to pass along feelings of "disappointment and dismay."[33] The ambassador expressed these thoughts to Lansing on January 26, at the same time suggesting the plan was part of a general agreement with Germany. The secretary of state denied the charge, saying he had made the decision independently; but no one believed him. "It is amazing to what depths the U. S. Gov't will stoop in order to save their faces," one official noted on Spring-Rice's report.[34] As the British

[30] Page to the secretary of state, Jan. 25, 28, 1916, *For. Rels., 1916, Supp.,* 151–53; Page to Wilson, Feb. 4, 1916, Wilson Papers.
[31] Ambassador Spring-Rice to the foreign secretary, Jan. 10, 13, 1916, F. O. 382/1099, and Jan. 24, 1916, F. O. 382/929.
[32] Note by Hurst accompanying Spring-Rice's dispatch of Jan. 21, 1916, F. O. 382/929.
[33] The foreign secretary to Ambassador Spring-Rice, Jan. 25, 1916, ibid.
[34] Ambassador Spring-Rice to the foreign secretary, Jan. 27, 1916, note by Sir W. Langley, Jan. 28, 1916, ibid.

saw it, the outcome of the *Lusitania* outrage and the inhumane, illegal submarine campaign was to be, not punishment for the offenders, but a major Allied concession. Lansing's plan if accepted would grant official recognition of submarine warfare and deny Allied merchantmen legitimate means of protection.[35] Of course there was a side to the argument unmentioned in correspondence between London and Washington: Britain certainly did not wish to help the United States reach a solution on the submarine question. The U-boat remained the most likely means for embroiling Germany and the United States and the British had no desire to lose this instrument. And so, with Britain so uncompromisingly opposed, with the United States unwilling to force a change of rules, there seemed no alternative to dropping the idea. It served only to arouse the British, weaken House's position in London, and help inspire a new submarine campaign.

The administration might have avoided some difficulty had the State Department and London embassy enjoyed better relations. Lansing could have instructed Page to probe Grey's feeling about the matter and upon learning the foreign secretary's opposition, abandon the scheme. Or if the ambassador had established a reputation for sound, objective evaluation, he might have intercepted the plan before it reached Grey. As it was, Lansing completely bypassed Page, the ambassador virtually ridiculed the proposal, and relations between the two men remained a weak spot in the conduct of American foreign policy.

The armed-ship controversy did not discontinue Page's efforts to change American policy. Lansing's plan merely added new evidence that the administration sought alternatives to the old course of neutrality. But what alternatives it chose! House had come back from Germany full of the idea of American intervention, and with Lansing's scheme still in the air American policy seemed going in two directions. The colonel had the important conference with high British officials on February 14 and spent most of that evening listening to Page's denunciation of American policy. The following day the ambassador prepared a new mes-

[35] The foreign secretary to Ambassador Spring-Rice, Jan. 25, Feb. 2, 1916, ibid.

sage for the president which suggested still another plan. It was a bold dispatch, and Page justified its frankness with explanation that "my loyalty to you . . . would not be absolute if I shrank from respectfully sending my solemn conviction of our duty and opportunity." What was Page's explanation of America's duty and opportunity? "Immediately refuse without further parley to yield a jot or tittle of your original *Lusitania* notes, . . . at once sever diplomatic relations with Germany and follow this action by a rigid embargo against the Central Powers." Results of this policy, Page felt, would be astounding: Germany would surrender gracefully; it would save lives and money; the United States would command absolute loyalty of the British fleet and Empire; Wilson would become immortal; finally (with an eye to the coming presidential election) the administration would win the sympathy of the American people. He offered all this at almost no cost; the United States could end the war, secure the peace, and "we should not have to fire a gun or risk a man."[36]

While the message was confidential, "for the President," Page made little effort to keep the contents secret in London. He showed House the dispatch, and a few days later when Horace Plunkett, an Irish friend, active in British propaganda, dropped by the embassy, the ambassador proudly brought out a copy. Plunkett took the dispatch to Arthur Balfour, another friend of Page and the man who soon would replace Grey as foreign secretary. Balfour was amazed, remarking that "he had never seen any such communication [from] an Ambassador to his master," and asked for a copy.[37] Within a few days, one must suspect, Page's urgent message had circulated among all members of the government.

The strategy was simple: assure Wilson that by breaking relations he would have all the benefits of victory while avoiding participation, which the president feared most. Knowing as well as anyone the improbability of having one without the other, the

[36] Page to the secretary of state, Feb. 17, 1916, *The Lansing Papers,* 1: 705–706. While Page did not send the message until February 17, the diaries of Page and House indicate it was written February 15.

[37] Plunkett Diary, Feb. 25, 1916.

ambassador noted privately what he expected to follow: "If then, they sink one of our ships or a ship with American passengers, we sh^d declare an embargo against Germany and begin economic war. This would lead to actual war."[38] In weeks to come Page would promise the president several times he could break with Germany and avoid hostilities. It is a rare occasion when one can accuse Page of dishonesty, but in this instance it seems clear that with false assurances he tried to promote a situation which would force war upon Wilson.[39]

In view of so much diplomatic activity during the first two months of 1916, it is remarkable that American policy changed so little. Allied merchantmen kept their guns (those vessels that had them) ; House did not connive the United States into war, or trick the belligerents to peace. In six weeks since the beginning of the year Page had tried three times to promote a drastic turn in foreign policy, and to each plea his government had replied with silence. But there was one unwelcome event after Lansing's plan, namely, the German announcement on February 10 of a new submarine campaign against armed merchant ships.

It is hardly fair to give the secretary of state full responsibility for this act, because the Germans long had contemplated such a move. The tactical struggle continued within the Second Reich between the civil government, represented much of the period by Chancellor von Bethmann Hollweg, and the naval faction which contended that victory would come only through unrestricted use of submarines. In the era of neutrality each concession Germany tendered the United States on submarine warfare marked temporary victory of the civil party, but victory never was complete and after a concession such as the *Arabic* pledge there was new pressure for the use of the U-boat fleet. The government in 1916 was

[38] Diary, Feb. 12, 1916.

[39] Another time Page wrote: "The only effective thing to do is to create a situation—or to recognize a situation and fall in with it. Suppose the President doesn't like it? I recall the Tammany-boss's remark about Cleveland: 'Damit: what can you do with a man who don't want nothin?' " Ibid., Feb. 17, 1916. For other messages which promised that a break in relations would not lead to war, see Page to the secretary of state, March 26, May 6, 1916, *The Lansing Papers*, 1: 706–707.

under pressure so compelling that it seemed impossible to deny. Then Lansing made a proposal against armed merchant ships, and in a careless moment the secretary of state had encouraged the Central Powers to the same view.[40] Seizing the opportunity, the Germans announced their intent to regard armed merchantmen in the same category as cruisers, not subject to visit and search. Susceptibility of a merchant ship to sudden sinking rested upon the ability of a submarine commander to determine if it was armed.[41] A new incident seemed likely, and it came on March 24 with torpedoing of the unarmed French channel steamer *Sussex* on which eighty persons, among them Americans, were killed or injured.

The *Sussex* attack aroused emotions Americans had experienced intermittently for almost a year. To Page this meant new hope that the United States at last would move against Germany. Unfortunately he could do nothing himself; even his power to influence through messages largely was gone; the dispatch of February 17 had been so dramatic that it left him little to say. His first *Sussex* cable was a brief, restrained restatement that severance of relations would bring an early peace, "save perhaps a million lives," and not lead to war.[42] This time the ambassador had some powerful allies, for House favored the same act and Lansing, who felt "the time for writing notes [had] passed," drafted a message to break relations with Germany.[43]

The president still hesitated. "He was afraid," House noted, "if we broke off relations, the war would go on indefinitely and there would be no one to lead the way out."[44] Wilson took the one step that remained, short of a diplomatic breach. He threatened to

[40] Memorandum by the secretary of state of a conversation with the Austro-Hungarian Chargé (Zwiedinek), Feb. 9, 1916, *The Lansing Papers*, 1: 341–42.

[41] Ambassador Gerard to the secretary of state, Feb. 10, 1916, *For. Rels., 1916, Supp.*, 163–66.

[42] Page to the secretary of state, March 26, 1916, *The Lansing Papers*, 1: 706–707; Page to Wilson, March 30, 1916, Wilson Papers.

[43] House Diary, March 30, 1916, Seymour, *Colonel House*, 2: 227–28; the secretary of state to President Wilson, March 27, 1916, *The Lansing Papers*, 1: 538. For Lansing's draft, see ibid., 540–42.

[44] Diary, March 30, 1916, Seymour, *Colonel House*, 1: 228.

break relations if Germany would not conduct submarine warfare according to international law. Not quite an ultimatum, the message gave the Germans another chance.[45]

For the final time, exponents of peace with the United States had the upper hand in Germany. The German government announced on May 4 that hereafter submarines would confront merchant vessels only according to rules of cruiser warfare, with qualification that the United States compel Britain to observe international law. Otherwise Germany reserved "complete liberty of decision."[46] The final sentence was, of course, a hole through which the Germans might crawl, anytime they chose, but for several months they chose not to use it.

Page accepted this turn of events with remarkable resignation. He was disappointed that Germany and the United States again had reached agreement, that Wilson had allowed another atrocity on the seas. A "real lack of leadership," he called the situation privately, and reiterated his conviction that "Americans would follow gladly if the President were to hold up his hand & say 'come on!' "[47] But he no longer entertained the high expectation of a year earlier when the *Lusitania* went down, and if the *Sussex* crisis failed to bring war it did produce a threat to break relations, more than ever before and surely only a step from hostilities. "He [Wilson] and Good Luck may yet save us," Page wrote his son. "If he buck up at last—if he really act at all—we'll be drawn into this war (even tho' too late for the best)."[48] And when Wilson insisted on the last word with Germany, refusing to make German policy contingent upon relations with Britain, Page thought it a master stroke.[49] Settlement of the *Sussex* affair provided him the first breathing spell in months. Availing himself of the lull, the ambassador took to the English hills for his first vacation since the war began.

The administration considered the *Sussex* settlement not a lull,

[45] The secretary of state to Ambassador Gerard, April 18, 1916, *For. Rels., 1916, Supp.*, 232–37.

[46] Ambassador Gerard to the secretary of state, ibid., 257–60.

[47] Diary, May 8, 1916.

[48] To Arthur Page, May 8, 1916, Page Papers.

[49] Page to House, May 23, 1916, Hendrick, *Page*, 2: 156.

but reason to change the emphasis in American diplomacy. This is not to say that Wilson conceded privately what his message to Germany had denied—that German concession depended upon reciprocal action from the British—but Germany's backdown inevitably accentuated the controversy with Britain, and coupled with unwillingness of the Foreign Office to yield on important points of dispute, it made the British appear as hardened, though not the vicious criminals their enemies were. Wilson might have pressed the Allies sooner had not House's plan, Lansing's proposal, and then the *Sussex* incident caused a suspension of the debate about trade difficulty. With the agenda clear (or almost clear) of these issues, with the president dissatisfied over what he described as "the altogether indefensible course" of Great Britain, Wilson felt the time had come for readjustment of Anglo-American relations. As the president saw it he could take one of two courses: either Britain would cooperate with the United States in a move for peace, along the line House had suggested, or he would have to insist upon American neutral rights "with the same plain speaking and firmness" used against Germany.[50] A choice was no great difficulty; peace easily was preferable, if only the British would cooperate. House had had a new exchange with Grey and the foreign secretary offered not a word of encouragement. For two years, wrote the dejected colonel, "he has been telling me that the solution of the problem of international well-being depended upon the United States being willing to take her part in world affairs. Now that we indicate a willingness to do so, he halts, stammers and questions."[51]

Grey's attitude was the major obstacle to a new peace movement, but House knew also that a campaign for mediation would arouse Page. During the colonel's last visit to London, the ambassador had expressed himself forcefully about Wilson and Lansing, and while Page had not criticized House he had ridiculed his ideas, leaving the colonel to feel that Page resented his presence there. In the United States, House began to hear reports which corroborated this suspicion. Hugh Wallace had returned from

[50] Wilson to House, May 16, 1916, House Papers.
[51] Diary, May 13, 1916.

London early in May with news about a lively discussion with Page. House understood Wallace's first report to mean that if he went to London again the ambassador might resign. That news greatly irritated the colonel who felt he was responsible for Page's receiving the London post, that the ambassador was "under real obligations" to him. "One would think," House noted, "if he could not accept the situation, he would quietly get out upon some pretext or other than the real one." Wallace came back the next day and clarified matters. Page might not resign, the story now went, but if House planned another trip the ambassador wished to know about it so that he might protest to the president. Wallace said the entire London embassy was "a nest of disloyalty to the President." House cooled off with this new information. He thought it proper that the ambassador express his dissatisfaction to Wilson, well aware that Page could not challenge him for the president's favor.[52]

Thereafter House had scarcely a good word about the ambassador. He wrote Wilson on May 10: "We have in Page a cog that refuses to work smoothly in the machinery you have set in motion to bring about peace and a reconstruction of international law," and reopened the campaign to get the ambassador back to the United States. House alleged that Page was of no service in London, that the war had warped his mind, and explained to the president that two months in America might straighten him out, but if Page wished to resign and remain at home, Wilson should not discourage it.[53]

No one knew of the House-Page disagreement, except for Wilson, some State Department officials, and a few mutual friends. If Page suspected what House was doing, his letters did not show it. Correspondence between the two men lessened only slightly, if at all, and it was generally friendly. The State Department was delighted to hear that Page had angered House, for Lansing, Polk, and Chandler Anderson hoped the colonel now might do what they had been unable to accomplish—get Page home for a rest, or permanently.[54]

[52] Ibid., May 4–5, 1916.
[53] House to Wilson, May 10, 18, 1916, House Papers.
[54] House Diary, May 17, 18, 1916.

The president was not ready to make that move until he had made one more attempt at mediation. Tired of waiting for a signal from Britain, he went before the League to Enforce Peace on May 27 to hint that he would like to help end the conflict. While the speech was an important pronouncement in Wilson's foreign policy, with some admirable words about America's willingness to depart from tradition and take part in preserving peace, it had a ring of lofty impartiality. With the war's "causes and objects," the president said, "we are not concerned."[55]

Most Britons received Wilson's words with disappointment and dismay. The purpose, cabled Spring-Rice, was "plainly to gain German sympathy during elections and to detach Pacifists from [the] Republican Party."[56] To talk peace was bad enough, and to suggest that there were no differences between the belligerents, that the Allies were as bad as the Central Powers, was disgusting —"another too-proud-to-fight, as the English view it," Page wrote House.[57] The ambassador did believe that the British quoted passages out of context and overlooked the best parts of the speech, but he did little to impress these ideas upon his friends in the Foreign Office. "From this point of observation, the less said about peace, at least till some new and decisive event happens, the better," he wrote.[58] With reaction no better from other belligerent nations, the movement for mediation, needless to say, stopped and for the time being the president dropped the question.

Wilson could not set aside as easily the question of British-American relations and the growing list of Britain's abusive practices. Present were most of the old acts of irritation—trade restriction and censorship of American mail—and in 1916 the British added some new ones. The government's harsh suppression of the Easter Rebellion in Dublin aroused indignation, and feeling reached a high point in the summer with the death sentence passed on Sir Roger Casement, who with German aid had tried to land arms for Irish nationalists. The most persistent irritant was

[55] See Baker, *Wilson*, 6: 220.
[56] Ambassador Spring-Rice to the foreign secretary, May 29, 1916, F. O. 371/2794.
[57] June 2, 1916, Seymour, *Colonel House*, 2: 302.
[58] To Wilson, June 1, 1916, Hendrick, *Page*, 3: 299.

the blockade, which despite Page's warning never became official. The Foreign Office had gone its leisurely way in treating American protests, and not until April 24, after approximately six months, did the department receive an answer to its note of October 21, 1915, rejecting American claims, although it promised to make restrictions as unburdensome as possible.[59] Finally, the Allies abandoned all attempts to abide by a modified Declaration of London, as promised in the first months of war. The Declaration, they said with remarkable honesty, did not "provide belligerents with the most effective means of exercising their admitted rights," and modification "exposed the purpose of the Allies to misconstruction."[60] The Allies returned to older rules of international warfare, except when new conditions justified new measures, which they, of course, felt free to determine.

In those painful months the government of Great Britain interpreted international law with convenient liberality. Nothing explained the grasp of Allied economic warfare more clearly than a letter from the ambassador in Washington to his chief. Wrote Spring-Rice: "the facts are that American trade is in a way under British control. In order to avoid Prize Courts, everything that passes across the Atlantic goes under a pass signed by a British Officer. In order to prevent Germany receiving intelligence by the mails, every letter going from America to the continent is subject to inspection. In order to prevent Allied subjects trading with the enemy, the operations of American commerce are subject to a general power of control, and American citizens may be ruined at any moment by being put on a blacklist in Paris and London. . . . It is astonishing that there is not more friction than there is. The mere statement of what is being done in the way of restriction would astonish the world."[61] In part a warning that the British should steer a cautious course on the sea, Spring-Rice's letter expressed hope that the Foreign Office could find ways to grant concession to the United States.

[59] The British ambassador to the secretary of state, *For. Rels., 1916, Supp.*, 368–82.

[60] Page to the secretary of state, July 10, 1916, ibid., 413–15; Ambassador Sharp to the secretary of state, July 8, 1916, ibid., 408.

[61] Spring-Rice to Grey, Aug. 10, 1916, Spring-Rice Papers; also in Grey Papers.

The British ambassador had a better idea of the American attitude and the danger in ignoring this attitude than did his counterpart in London. On rare cases such as the *China,* Page exerted his best efforts for the American argument,[62] but when a problem involved Britain's war machinery, he reported that Grey, "so exceedingly considerate of the United States," became "more and more rigid," and the ambassador thought it best not to press the issue. The longer the war lasted, the bloodier it became, the more Page valued long, quiet chats with Grey before the fireplace, at which times the two men discussed political philosophy, British-American relations, "the future of the English-speaking peoples, Wordsworth, fishing—any sort of thing that is big and interesting."[63] The ambassador continued to write long letters to Wilson which always were respectful and full of advice. Not fully recovered from House's last visit, he advised that the colonel should not come again, citing, by way of illustration, an incident in the House of Commons when a questioner had asked Grey if he planned to send a special envoy to the United States. "No," the foreign secretary answered, "His Majesty's Government has complete confidence in its Ambassador to the United States." "Thus," added Page, "this English mood smites everybody on every side."[64] Letters to House were less polite and respectful, reiterating vexation at the "nagging" policy of the State Department, warning that Britain could not relax the blockade.[65] To all correspondents Page expounded anglicized Americanism, drew bright pictures for the world if the two countries cooperated, and to his former publishing partner wrote: "I play the game with these fellows

[62] The *China* was a sort of *Trent* case in reverse, in which the Royal Navy stopped an American vessel and illegally removed German nationals. While Page urged and secured release of these individuals, Grey came to regret the decision to grant concession. The foreign secretary explained to colleagues that he promised to release the men, believing they were not of military age or character—information he later learned to be false. Grey said he would keep his promise, but had he known the truth, he never would have made it. Memorandum, July 25, 1916, Grey Papers. For diplomatic correspondence about the *China* see *For. Rels., 1916, Supp.,* 632–62.

[63] To Wilson, July 21, 1916, Hendrick, *Page,* 3: 302.

[64] June 1, 1916, ibid., 299.

[65] For example, Page to House, June 16, 1916, Page Papers; Seymour, *Colonel House,* 2: 311.

squarely, sometimes I fear indiscreetly. But what is discretion? That's the hardest question of all. We have regular meetings. I tell 'em everything I can—always on the condition that I'm kept out of the papers. If they'll never mention me, I'll do everything possible for them. . . . Yet I'm immensely proud that I have had the chance to do some good—to keep our record straight—as far as I can, and to be of what service I can to these heroic people."[66]

Meanwhile in Washington, the problem of Page had become a common topic within the inner circles of the administration. When House, Lansing, and Polk discussed the ambassador, their solution always was the same: get him home.[67] With careful scrutiny Page might have surmised that his performance was under review back home, but it is doubtful that he caught the hints. If he noticed a slightly slackened pace of cases coming to the embassy, he probably did not guess that it was because Lansing, having abandoned faith in the ambassador, now sent many complaints through the consul general in London, Robert Skinner. Nor did House's advice that Page read American newspapers arouse suspicion.[68] Wilson now discussed Page with House, and while the president showed much indecision he considered replacing the ambassador: a safe way to do so might be the old procedure of "kicking him upstairs," perhaps to the post of secretary of agriculture, but before doing that he would have to find a place for Houston. House began suggesting people for the London post. One time he mentioned Wilson's wealthy friend Cleveland Dodge, another time the minister to Belgium, Brand Whitlock.[69]

Page eventually came home for a rest, but not until American opinion of the Allies had reached a nadir. The low point came in summer and autumn 1916 with publication of the British blacklist. It is ironic that this measure should have aroused such discontent in the United States, for unlike many British practices it was

[66] To Frank N. Doubleday and others, May 29, 1916, Hendrick, *Page*, 2: 138–39.
[67] For example, Polk to House, June 19, 1916, Polk Papers.
[68] House to Page, June 20, 1916, Page Papers.
[69] Wilson to House, July 2, 1916, House Papers; House to Wilson, May 14, 1916, ibid.

altogether legal. Viewed from the western side of the Atlantic the blacklist—a list of American firms with which British subjects were forbidden to deal because of their commercial relations with enemies of the Allies—was an arbitrary measure to discriminate against Americans. Besides British business, the designated firms stood to lose the patronage of many American companies which feared Britain might blacklist them. Carelessly timed, the action inspired a storm of protest. In the opinion of a normally pro-Ally newspaper, it was "the most tactless, foolish and unnecessary act of the British Government during the war."[70] Angry as never before, Wilson wrote House he was at the end of his patience. "This blacklist business," he said, "is the last straw. I am seriously considering asking Congress to authorize me to prohibit loans and restrict exportations to the Allies." The president said that he and Polk were drawing up a note which he might "feel obligated to make . . . as sharp and final as the one to Germany on the submarine."[71]

In the same letter Wilson told House he had called Page to the United States. Delighted, the colonel wrote Polk his wish that the ambassador would go west and "get a complete bath of American opinion."[72] It was not Page's attitude on the blacklist that inspired the move; he thought the measure a gross mistake, and evidently told the British so.[73] The blacklist brought to a boil matters which had been simmering for some time, and Page's behavior was one of the matters. The unsuspecting ambassador, believing the visit was for a "personal conference" to discuss matters of great importance, was happy to return home.[74]

The day Page set sail, Britain was astir with news that the Irish rebel Casement was going to the gallows, thus bringing to a climax the controversial aftermath of the Easter Rebellion. The English felt they had reason to crush the Irish uprising with all

[70] New York *Times*, July 20, 1916; for the proclamation see Page to the secretary of state, July 10, 1916, *For. Rels., 1916, Supp.*, 413–15.

[71] July 23, 1916, House Papers.

[72] July 25, 1916, Polk Papers.

[73] Page to the secretary of state, July 22, 1916, *For. Rels., 1916, Supp.*, 412–13.

[74] Page to Wilson, July 21, 1916, Hendrick, *Page*, 3: 308.

expediency, but their acts infuriated Irish-Americans and seemed
unduly harsh to many other individuals in the United States.
Page did not share the emotion of his compatriots. If he felt
England had mismanaged the Irish problem—"a fundamental
English stupidity"—he could muster little sympathy for the insur-
gents. "Any man may become a martyr who is willing to rise &
plot against England and to cry out 'I die for my country'—if he
be an Irishman," he wrote aboard ship. "In other words, Irish
martyrdom is perhaps the cheapest thing in the world to achieve.
How they can look in a mirror and keep a straight face is astounding; and why people of other races humor and indulge them—
proves the discipline strength of the Catholic Church."[75] The
Casement affair would do nothing to ease Page's tasks in the
United States.

From the day the ambassador set foot in New York, everything
seemed to go wrong. He arrived on an August evening in a nation
excited about the presidential election and threatened with a
serious railroad strike. On hand to greet him, besides the family,
were the third assistant secretary of state, William Phillips, and
reporters who tried in vain to pry out information. Have Britain
and the United States settled the blacklist question? "You must
ask the State Department about that matter." Will the present
Allied offensive bring peace by the end of the year? "You might as
well ask me about the millennium." Relatives then drew him
aside and gave the sad news that his son's young bride of only two
months was seriously ill with infantile paralysis. The following
day the Page family began to mourn the death of Mrs. Frank
Page.[76] But the ambassador would not allow even that tragic
event to deter him long from the primary task of his mission, and
shortly after the funeral, he left for Washington to set the administration straight.

The administration hardly had planned a grand reception.
"The Ambassador has arrived and they tell me he is in excellent
form," Polk wrote House and prepared to go on a short vacation.[77] Summering in New Hampshire, the colonel himself felt

[75] Diary, Aug. 3, 1916.
[76] New York *Times*, Aug. 12, 13, 1916.
[77] Aug. 18, 1916, Polk Papers.

safely out of Page's reach. Anxious as everyone seemed to get him home, no one wished to talk to him after he arrived, or if they had to see Page they were not disposed to talk about the war. In Washington the attitude seemed to be that Page could go wherever he wished and do what he wanted, as long as he did not talk diplomacy. For the ambassador, who did not know he needed rehabilitation, it was a dreadful experience, and from almost any point of view it was a cruel performance by the president and his advisers.

Thus Page's first two weeks in Washington produced little beyond frustration and irritation. Shortly after arrival he lunched with the president. The conversation was general: doubtless Wilson extended condolence over the death of Page's daughter-in-law; perhaps he made some trite comment about the London weather; there was "not a word about England, not a word about foreign policy or foreign relations." Page wanted a conference. The president told him to rest and come back. Two weeks later, he had another lunch with Wilson, and still there was nothing about foreign affairs.[78] The ambassador wanted to see House, but the colonel, Page complained, had "got off and hid." House did write to explain his absence and to advise that Page spend in the United States the full sixty days allotted by department regulations.[79] With Polk gone, that left only Lansing. "The Secretary," Page noted after meeting him several times, "betrayed not the slightest curiosity about our relations with Great Britain. The only remark he made was that I'd find a different atmosphere in Washington from the atmosphere in London. Truly. All the rest of his talk was about 'cases.' " And other members of the administration were little better. Page and the American ambassador to France lunched one day with some cabinet members: "Sharp and I might have come from Bungtown and Jonesville and not from France and England. We were not encouraged to talk—the local personal joke held the time and conversation."[80] Perhaps the most respect shown Page came from Polk after the counselor returned to Washington. Although Polk was "as bad as the Prest.," and

---

[78] Memorandum, Aug. 1916, Page Papers; Hendrick, *Page,* 2: 171–72.
[79] Page to House, Aug. 26, 1916, House to Page, Aug. 30, 1916, Page Papers.
[80] Memorandum, Aug. 1916, ibid., Hendrick, *Page,* 2: 174–76.

could not "get it out of his mind that Eng. is insulting us," he did discuss the problems.[81] Indeed the persons happiest to have Page in Washington were not American officials but British, and Spring-Rice kept his government informed of the good service the ambassador was doing. As one dispatch explained: "Page has spoken up for us most valiantly and has been of very great use in presenting before the eyes of the Cabinet here the state of affairs in England. He understands."[82]

If Page had to hold his tongue those first two weeks, he privately gave rein to his thoughts. Criticism of Wilson flowed from his pen: "the President suppressed free thought and free speech when he insisted upon personal neutrality. On this cushion of nonresponsibility the great masses fell back at their intellectual and moral ease—softened, isolated, bullied. That wasn't leadership in a democracy, right here is the President's failure."[83] The largest blast Page reserved for Lansing, a man he had known only through correspondence. Meeting the secretary had confirmed Page's worst suspicions: "a mere routine—clerk, law-book-precedent man; no grasp, no imagination, no constructive tendency or ability—measuring Armageddon, if he tries to measure it at all—with a six inch rule. And yet, I find, the public thinks him equal to the task. He writes Notes—big-sounding Notes—to England & publishes them. O God! what a crime and what a shame to have this manikin in that place now!"[84]

August gave way to September, the sun over Washington had the glow that warned of autumn, the time for Page's return rapidly approached, and he had accomplished nothing. Before the ambassador's eyes, the attitude toward Britain continued the worsening trend. Wilson had sent a note protesting the blacklist, and the British had not answered. They waited three months. In what seemed to many anglophiles a shocking move, Congress passed a law empowering the president to retaliate against coun-

[81] Page Diary (undated).
[82] Spring-Rice to Grey, Sept. 15, 1916, Grey Papers. See also Spring-Rice's letter, Sept. 4, 1916, ibid., and his dispatches Sept. 16, 17, 1916, F. O. 371/2795.
[83] Memorandum, Aug. 1916, Page Papers.
[84] Memorandum, Aug. 30, 1916, ibid.

tries which restricted American trade, and voted a huge naval appropriation. Page trudged about Washington, more depressed each day. He had further discussion with Lansing and Polk. Although the counselor failed to grasp the significance of the war he was decent and agreed to correspond after the ambassador returned to London. Lansing was impossible—still obsessed with cases.

While it would be inaccurate to say that the secretary of state deliberately provoked Page, Lansing's attitude, which was indeed provoking, was something designed specially for the occasion and not representative of the secretary's true thoughts. Page would have stared in disbelief had he seen what Lansing wrote privately at almost the same time as his discussion with the ambassador. "I only hope," noted the secretary in a diary, "that the President will adopt the true policy which is 'Join the Allies as soon as possible and crush the German autocrats.' "[85] As Lansing explained in his *Memoirs,* published after the death of both men, the concern for small and seemingly picayune points of law was the secretary's way of avoiding essential issues and keeping relations with Britain safe. Long notes were part of the plan. Short notes were dangerous.[86] In the pressing controversy over the retaliatory legislation Lansing maneuvered, apparently without Wilson's knowledge, to ensure that the problem did not create a diplomatic impasse. News of Congress's action had aroused in London feeling of shock and anger, both of which emotions Grey expressed to Spring-Rice on September 15. The foreign secretary pointed out that since June 1, 1916, submarines had sunk 258 merchant vessels, often without warning. Tell this to the State Department, Grey instructed, "and warn them privately," that if the United States resorted to action the Allies would draw "a most invidious contrast" between this action and the willingness to allow submarine warfare without protest.[87] Hearing this information from Spring-Rice, Lansing promised that Wilson would exercise the

[85] Memorandum, Sept. 1916, "The President's Attitude toward Great Britain and Its Dangers," the Papers of Robert Lansing, Library of Congress; Lansing, *War Memoirs of Robert Lansing* (Indianapolis, Ind., 1935), 171–72.
[86] *Memoirs,* 171–72.
[87] F. O. 371/2795.

new power only as a last resort. He explained that the legislation was a result of the election, that the president had asked for the law to calm American opinion and forestall passage of more serious measures.[88] Even though Lansing's words did not represent Wilson's opinion, it would have been soothing for Page if the secretary had said these things to him.

Annoying as Lansing was, Page might have overlooked him had he been able to communicate with the man who was the author of American foreign policy. Wilson maintained stony silence. The ambassador was persistent. He sent several requests for a conference, stating that he had an urgent message from the British. "I'm not going back to London," he wrote Laughlin, "until the President has said something to me or at least till I have said something to him. I am now going down to Garden City and New York till the President send [sic] for me; or if he do [sic] not send for me, I'm going to his house and sit on the steps till he come [sic] out."[89]

After a wait of five weeks Page received an invitation to spend a night at the president's summer house at Shadow Lawn on the coast of New Jersey. Wilson evidently decided that he might as well hear out the ambassador and get it over with. For a time it seemed that fate was going to strike from Page that hard-won invitation. A freight wreck at South Amboy held up his train and the ambassador did not arrive until 10:00 in the evening. Wilson was to make a campaign speech the following day; and if the two men talked that night it must have been about such lesser matters as the railroad strike, the election and the recent death of Wilson's sister. The following morning Page finally had his hour. It must have been a dramatic discussion for these men who, separated by the war, at one time had had much in common. Both had keen minds, schooled in logic and expression, sincere and eloquent. Because of different responsibilities and different views of the war, the rhetoric of both was useless.

There is no record of Page's argument, but there is little diffi-

[88] Ambassador Spring-Rice to the foreign secretary, Sept. 23, 1916, F. O. 382/1100.
[89] Hendrick, *Page*, 2: 179; see Page to Wilson, Sept. 16, 20, 1916, Wilson Papers.

culty guessing what he said. With frank, respectful words he probably told Wilson of Britain's anxiety for American friendship, how exigencies of war called for extraordinary, perhaps in some cases illegal, measures which the British hoped the United States would recognize and accept, that the future of the world depended on Anglo-American friendship, and whatever the technical problems with Britain, the United States should not lose sight of that fact. The ambassador handed Wilson a German medal which commemorated the sinking of the *Lusitania,* and virtually smothered the president with data about Anglo-American relations and conversations he recently had had with British cabinet members. Wilson handled the German medal, but seemed unimpressed; he listened respectfully.

Page recorded Wilson's response in a small notebook, approximately four by six inches, turned upside down, begun at the back. He wrote with such scarce legibility, which was unusual for the ambassador, that it is reasonable to assume he wrote on his lap as he returned by train from Shadow Lawn. "The P. said," Page began, "he started out as heartily in sympathy w[ith the] Allies as any man c^d be. But England had gone on doing everything she wished regardless of rights of others & Amer[ican] pride (his pride) was hurt." "The P. said," Page continued, "tell those gentlemen for me—and there followed a homily about damage done to any Am[erican] citizen is a damage to himself. He described the war as a result of many causes—some of long origin. He spoke of England's having the earth, of Germany's wanting it. Of course the German system is directly opposed to everything American. But this didn't seem to him to carry any very great reprehensibility."

Wilson told the ambassador that because of the election he would not do anything with the retaliatory acts, but if provocation continued after the election (if he were elected) he would. He complained that British delay in answering American notes showed contempt. When Page told of Britain's hope (and this apparently was the urgent message) that if Germany asked him to propose an armistice, the president would decline, Wilson answered that he would refuse to urge a purely military armistice, but if it were an armistice looking toward peace, "yes, I shall be glad." Page's scribbling concluded with Wilson's remark that at first everyone he met favored the Allies, but now he "came across nobody who was not vexed with England."[90]

The conference lasted an entire morning; and if Page's notes contain only a portion of what was said, they covered the important issues. There seems to have been no hedging, nor is there evidence that either individual induced any change in the other. Certainly the discussion produced nothing encouraging for the ambassador. Wilson gave him reason to worry about the future, leaving as possibilities almost every line of policy Page dreaded. Nonetheless the meeting had been a touching experience for both men and perhaps each recalled happier days when they had agreed about such topics as the South, progressivism, literature. Wilson's eyes moistened as Page clasped his hand in farewell.[91]

Not long afterward Page finally met with House. As a matter of fact, as the ambassador was leaving Shadow Lawn he saw the colonel coming in, and they arranged to meet. House had abandoned the idea of avoiding Page and was anxious to see if his plan of reeducation had worked. He was disappointed. "He is," the colonel noted, "as pro-British as ever and cannot see the American point of view." On September 25 the two men reviewed the issues covered at Shadow Lawn, but the tone differed. No longer addressing a superior official, Page unleashed his emotion, delved into personalities in a scathing attack on American policy. House responded (as the colonel recorded it) in much the same manner. Page's opening remarks, critical of Lansing, showed profound regard for Wilson, "a feeling," House noted, "I am afraid he exaggerates." For some unknown reason the ambassador turned on Spring-Rice, and remarked with satisfaction that Lansing believed the British ambassador was unfit for his post. House commented: "Page does not know that Lansing's opinion of the British Ambassador is perhaps a shade higher than his opinion of Page himself." The ambassador admitted that Britain would have

[90] The notebook is in Page's Papers; reproduced (with correction) in Hendrick, *Page*, 2: 185–86.
[91] Hendrick, *Page*, 2: 188.

fought alongside France had the French (and not the Germans) violated Belgian neutrality (in contradiction to the moral and legal argument that Britain went to war to protect Belgium's territorial integrity and to honor the pact assuring Belgian neutrality), but complained that poor relations with Britain were due largely to the United States, that no administration official understood the war.

House responded with an argument more critical of Britain than any he delivered during the period of neutrality. He accused Britain of hypocrisy on Belgium and mentioned American friendship and partiality for the Allies, despite which relations had worsened. He charged that if the United States entered the war "we would be applauded for a few weeks and then they would demand money. If the money was forthcoming, they would be satisfied for a period, but later would demand an unlimited number of men. If we did it all, they would finally accuse us of trying to force them to give better terms to Germany than were warranted."[92]

House had not intended to say those things, but the ambassador had provoked him. Indeed it is remarkable the way Page could induce anti-British comment from men basically pro-British. Moreover the ambassador's attitude influenced the administration to discount what otherwise might have been suggestions worth consideration. Page had advised that a general and an admiral go to Britain to study military prosecution of the war; another idea which seemed sensible was that an eminent legal mind (Polk was acceptable to Page) go to England and discuss technical differences between the two countries. A third suggestion, that Page receive greater power of negotiation, was, as Lansing put it, "folly."[93]

Page did do his government one good service before leaving the United States. After seeing Wilson and House he dropped by the British embassy to take a parting shot at the blacklist. His visit,

[92] House Diary, Seymour, *Colonel House*, 2: 319–20.

[93] *Memoirs*, 160; see Page's memorandum, Hendrick, *Page*, 2: 177–78, and his "Notes toward an Explanation of the British Feeling toward the United States," Sept. 25, 1916, *The Lansing Papers*, 1: 708–13.

the ambassador told British officials, "had only confirmed tenfold his opinion . . . that the publication of the blacklist was a blunder; without it there would have been no retaliatory clauses." Page insisted that Britain must find a way to remove from the list names of all American firms.[94]

After these conferences Page sailed back to London. No one, incidentally, had suggested he do anything else. How different this trip from that first voyage some three and one-half years earlier, when with great enthusiasm he had embarked upon a new and exciting assignment. No reason for optimism this time. Relations with Britain were bad, and Wilson had intimated that by proposing mediation again or by curtailing shipments to Britain, he might make them worse. Page did manage to obtain a promise that House would warn him if the president planned retaliation against Britain, but he knew that if Wilson so decided, he could not prevent something terrible happening.[95] The ambassador surely pondered how intelligent men like Wilson and House could not understand the war, why, with international leadership thrust upon the United States, Wilson would not take it. "Now when democracy and free opinion are at stake as they have not been before," he wrote, "we take a 'neutral' stand—we throw away our very birthright. We may talk of 'humanity' all we like: we have missed the largest chance that ever came to help the large cause that bro't us into being as a nation."[96] Then he thought back to those insulting days in Washington, when the administration had treated him like an outcast. That treatment was more than any self-respecting man could allow, and he would tolerate it no more. "There's nothing . . . [in Washington] that I w^d for the world be mixed up with," he had written his wife a month earlier; and that position still stood. He would serve the few remaining months of the presidential term, and when it ended, would resign and return home "March 4 at Midnight."[97]

[94] Ambassador Spring-Rice to the foreign secretary, Sept. 28, 1916, Grey Papers.
[95] House Diary, Sept. 30, 1916.
[96] Memorandum, Sept. 1916, Page Papers.
[97] Aug. 26, 1916, ibid.

Chapter Eight

War at Last

WHEN PAGE RETURNED to the London embassy in October 1916 there was little indication that within six months the United States would be at war with Germany. To be sure, the ambassador had felt since the *Lusitania* went down that hostilities were possible at almost any time, but with Germany—to Wilson's satisfaction at least—honoring the *Sussex* pledge, and with feeling what it was in Washington, it seemed in autumn 1916 that the chance of war with Germany was less than it had been in many months. Many people in the United States would have preferred to fight Britain. Having no way of knowing the future, Page suffered as much the final months of neutrality as the months before. He was so out of touch with the administration that he never knew what the United States was going to do. If Wilson never retaliated against Britain, Page feared he might, and the president took other moves in diplomacy—notably the long campaign for mediation—which were anything but popular with Page's friends in the Foreign Office or with British public opinion. Matters did take a better turn in February 1917, when Wilson severed relations with Germany, but that act produced disappointing results, inasmuch as the president struggled two additional months to prevent what seemed to Page an unavoidable conclusion. Despite dissatisfaction with almost everything his government did, Page was no lameduck ambassador during the last phase of neutrality; he was concerned as ever about American policy, and ever trying to change it.

What Page did not know is that while he was home on leave the British government was giving thorough reevaluation to its standing with the United States. Inspiration for this study was the retaliatory legislation passed in September, which produced temporary fear in London that Wilson soon would act to interfere with the munitions traffic.[1] Contemplating a response to such a move, British officials raised the possibility of reprisal, presumably, as considered a year earlier, curtailment of shipments of raw material to the United States. Before deciding upon any policy the Foreign Office felt it necessary to determine the extent of Britain's economic dependence on the United States.[2] Even though new reports from Spring-Rice, especially the account of a conference with Lansing on September 22, which pointed to domestic political reasons for the legislation, seemed to lessen danger of quick American action, the government went ahead with the study and arranged an interdepartment conference for October 3, 1916.[3] Persons attending that meeting saw with devastating clarity what a few individuals had suspected for months. As Lord Percy wrote in his minutes: "it developed at once . . . that there was really nothing to deliberate about because our dependence was so vital and complete in every possible respect that it was folly even to consider reprisals. In munitions . . . all previous estimates of our being able to fill our own needs by a certain time have been entirely destroyed. . . . In steel . . . we have been obliged to buy up the whole of the United States' steel output; in

[1] See Spring-Rice's messages to Grey, Sept. 11, 12, 1916, the second of which contained a memorandum by Sir Richard Crawford, trade advisor to the embassy in Washington. Crawford took a very "serious view" of the retaliatory measures. F. O. 371/2795.

[2] The foreign secretary to the Admiralty, Treasury, War Office, Munitions Office, Board of Trade, Agriculture Office, Colonial Office, Sept. 13, 1916, ibid.; see also minutes by various officials, Sept. 14, 1916, ibid.

[3] Ambassador Spring-Rice to the foreign secretary, Sept. 23, 1916, F. O. 382/1100.

foodstuffs and especially in wheat . . . , in all industrial raw materials and above all in cotton and lubricants American supplies are so necessary to us that reprisals, while they would produce tremendous distress in America, would also practically stop the war."[4] A few days later John Maynard Keynes of the Treasury Department described the similarly sorry state of Britain's finances. He reported that of the 5,000,000 pounds sterling needed daily to prosecute the war, 2,000,000 had to come from North America, a figure which would get much larger. "It is hardly an exaggeration to say," continued Keynes, "that in a few months time the American executive and the American public will be in a position to dictate to this country on matters that affect us more nearly than them. It is, therefore, the view of the Treasury, having regard to their special responsibilities, that the policy of this country towards the U.S.A. should be so directed as not only to avoid any form of reprisal or active irritation, but also to conciliate and to please."[5] Or as Lord Percy earlier had put it: "our job is not merely to maintain decently friendly relations with the United States, but to keep sentiment in America so sweet that it will lend us practically unlimited money."[6]

In keeping this news from Page, British officials in fact were doing him a favor, for the ambassador would have experienced sadness almost beyond description to learn how his government with a few simple moves could have brought about collapse of the British nation, at least could have compelled Britain to sue for an inconclusive peace. But Page knew enough to worry. The visit to Washington had been an eye-opening experience and it inevitably affected his tasks in resuming the duties as ambassador. On at least one important issue Page showed himself to be a vigorously loyal diplomat. Shortly after his return to London he called on Grey to speak "with the greatest emphasis and feeling" about

[4] "Minutes of the Interdepartmental Committee on the Dependence of the British Empire on the United States," Oct. 4, 1916, F. O. 371/2795.

[5] "The Financial Dependence of the United Kingdom on the United States of America," Oct. 10, 1916, "Printed for the use of the War Committee of the Cabinet, November 1916," F. O. 371/2796.

[6] "Minutes of the Interdepartmental Committee . . . ," Oct. 4, 1916, F. O. 371/2795.

resentment among "our best friends in America" as a result of the blacklist. Page said the measure was damaging, needless, and, wrote the foreign secretary, "he pleaded most earnestly for some modification."[7] Grey as usual was friendly and understanding, carefully explaining the purpose of the measure and that Britain had not meant to alarm the United States. The ambassador did his best with the blacklist, and while he could not persuade the British to abandon that policy, he did obtain Grey's promise to "whittle the list down to the smallest number of names possible."[8]

There is little indication the ambassador was as zealous with the blockade and older problems of Anglo-American relations. The blacklist was a new policy, to Page a clear mistake and a measure that had no substantial effect on the stifling of German trade. Facing the tested methods of sea warfare, the ambassador found himself torn more painfully than ever between the need for pleasing his government and not jamming Britain's war machinery. Hence he sent back an inconsistent description of his attitude. Writing to Polk a few weeks after return, he left the impression he was a changed man: "I argue, I protest, I ridicule, I abuse them. 'The Scriptures,' I tell them, 'lay down in ten commandments rules for the conduct of the whole of life. It requires nineteen rules for you to try to regulate our ships with which you have nothing to do.' "[9] On the other hand he reiterated to Wilson the old theme that Britain would not and could not change the blockade, that it was useless to try. If Page sought a change in British policy, it was a superficial change, one that would calm American opinion while having no practical effect. He continued to complain that the State Department was too blustering, that with courteous dealing the two governments could smooth out most problems, and again tried to get Polk to visit London.[10]

Despite Page's efforts, British-American relations did not im-

[7] The foreign secretary to Ambassador Spring-Rice, Oct. 10, 1916, F. O. 382/1100.

[8] Page to the secretary of state, Nov. 16, 1916, *For. Rels., 1916, Supp.,* 484. For other correspondence about the blacklist see ibid., 455–95.

[9] Jan. 11, 1917, Polk Papers.

[10] Page to Wilson, Dec. 30, 1916, Hendrick, *Page,* 3: 310; Page to the secretary of state, Nov. 27, 1916, *For. Rels., 1916, Supp.,* 486–87.

prove during the final weeks of 1916. Lord Percy's comment to the contrary, the British made little effort to sweeten relations with the United States. The Foreign Office decided that instead of granting superficial concession, it should keep a watchful eye on American opinion, especially business and financial interests, to assure a favorable lending public. Of course Britain also had to keep touch with Wilson's policy and stand prepared to head off a drastic change.[11] As it turned out the British never had to make that move, partly because, as Grey surmised, the American weapons were too large, too potentially damaging to the United States, to use, but more important because the president in weeks to come focused attention on another course for American diplomacy. Even so, there occurred in the fall and winter 1916 a number of small issues which, while individually not critical, contributed to a generally poor state of diplomatic relations between the two states. Besides the blacklist and blockade, the Admiralty introduced a new "bunkering" policy of withholding coal to captains of American ships unless they would give assurance of their vessels' friendly destination.[12] The armed merchantmen problem returned to arouse tempers when Lansing suspected that the British vessels used the guns offensively.[13] In October the case of the *U-53* had made temperamental Britons again indignant at the American government: this ship, one of Germany's new long-range submarines, stopped for a brief time at a New England port; putting to sea, she sank several Allied ships not far off the American coast. There was nothing the United States could do, since the sinkings took place outside American jurisdiction, but they created a feeling in Britain that Americans would ignore any inhumanity, no matter how close.[14] "I hate to feel that the two great democratic countries are drifting apart," Polk wrote Page, "but . . . I cannot persuade myself that the fault is entirely

---

[11] Grey's memorandum, Oct. 20, 1916, cited in Arthur S. Link, *Wilson: Campaigns for Progressivism and Peace, 1916–1917* (Princeton, N.J., 1965), 180–82.

[12] See *For. Rels., 1916, Supp.*, 455–89.

[13] For this issue see Lansing's memorandum of a fiery interview with Spring-Rice, Jan. 18, 1917, the Papers of Robert Lansing.

[14] For correspondence on the *U-53* see *For. Rels., 1916, Supp.*, 773–83.

ours, or even half ours."[15] Bad as they were, Anglo-American relations might have been worse had not the presidential election made Wilson unwilling to strike out on a new course.

Wilson's reelection in November meant that he would have to make important decisions in foreign policy. One was what to do with Walter Page, for late in the month the ambassador raised the question of his replacement. The thought came at the end of another fine literary effort, a sort of farewell message which philosophized on democracy and Anglo-American friendship and promised again that a break in relations with Germany would not involve the United States in war. Page had cooled off since the visit to Washington, for if his message was stronger than the formal statement which officials customarily send the president at the end of an administration, it was not a clearly final resignation. He explained his wish to come home in March, but said he would stay longer if necessary and asked Wilson's opinion.[16]

The letter arrived when the president was engrossed in another problem. The election had been close, victory due partly to the unauthorized slogan "he kept us out of war"; it was a clear mandate, thought Wilson, for nonintervention. The president believed the only certain way to assure peace for the United States was to bring peace to the world, that is, to make another attempt at mediation. The German government for some time had been hinting that Wilson should make a peace move, implying that if he did not, the navy might begin unrestricted submarine warfare. While Bethmann had been vague about Wilson's part in peace negotiation, and many individuals in the administration suspected German sincerity, the president did not feel that he could ignore these overtures. Wilson called in House on November 14 to discuss the way to proceed, explaining that otherwise the United States would "inevitably drift into war with Germany upon the submarine issue." The president wondered if it might be best for House to return to Europe.

House shuddered at the thought of another visit to Britain and told Wilson that among other things such a journey would mean

[15] Nov. 23, 1916, Polk Papers.
[16] Page to Wilson, Nov. 24, 1916, Hendrick, *Page,* 2: 190–95.

a showdown with Page. The two men then engaged in a long discussion about the ambassador. House told the president about Page's belief that Wilson was an able man and of service to the United States, but like Jefferson would not fight under any circumstances. Wilson was not pleased to hear this opinion of himself and talked about what to do with Page, to the extent of recalling him if he interfered with peace plans. "He declared," House noted, "no man must stand in the way." The colonel cautioned that removing Page would require replacing the entire staff at the London embassy, for all the ambassador's subordinates shared his view. Both men thought Page honest in his belief that an alliance between the United States and Britain was the best thing that could happen to humanity, but obsession with this idea made it impossible for him to consider any other.[17] As the president's mediation plans progressed, Wilson expressed increasing indifference to Page's attitude and even on one occasion suggested that House tell Grey that the ambassador did not represent the view in the United States.[18]

Such was the feeling in the White House when Page wrote to say that he would like to return home in March 1917. Wilson no longer read Page's letters; usually he saved them for House; this one he gave Mrs. Wilson who remarked that Page probably expected to have the resignation rejected.[19] Wilson let the matter ride and somewhat discourteously declined to answer the letter. Poor Page remained in London, confused about his future. There were matters to arrange, depending on the president's decision. He had engaged the servants until March. The lease on his house would soon expire and he wondered if he should renew it. A month passed and nothing happened. Again he wrote Wilson. When the new year began and still no answer had arrived, Page appealed to Lansing.[20]

The president had not forgotten Page, but neither he nor

[17] House Diary, Nov. 14, 1916.
[18] Wilson to House, Nov. 24, 1916, House Papers.
[19] House Diary, Dec. 4, 1916.
[20] Page to Wilson, Dec. 30, 1916, Hendrick, *Page,* 3: 310–11. An undated draft of the letter to Lansing is in Page's Papers.

House could decide. The colonel had seen a letter Page sent Hugh Wallace which struck at Wilson cruelly. The ambassador had written that Wilson should discard half to two-thirds of the people about him, which, noted House, "I suppose includes me."[21] Needless to say, the colonel was little inclined to rush to Page's defense. The president spoke to House several times about his intent to accept the resignation, and looked for a replacement, but weeks dragged on without a move and without a word to London.[22] Page did not receive an answer for over two months, in February 1917, when circumstances had changed drastically. The United States had broken relations with Germany, and Britain loomed as a probable ally, no time to provoke the British.[23]

Meanwhile the ambassador was witnessing some exciting events. The long-rumored shakeup in the British government came in December, bringing to power a new coalition cabinet headed by David Lloyd George, a dynamic Welshman dedicated to crushing the enemy. Arthur Balfour, a Conservative, nearly 70 years old, replaced Grey as foreign secretary, partly, Page said, because Grey was timid in applying the blockade (partly, one must add, because Grey was going blind). In view of Page's fear for the day of Grey's exodus, the transition brought little change in diplomacy. If the ambassador never attained with Balfour the intimacy he had with Sir Edward (now Viscount Grey of Fallodon), Page always could speak to the new foreign secretary on a frank basis, and above all, Balfour agreed that Britain and the United States should be friends.

One difference the change might have brought is in the attitude toward American mediation. Even though Grey had been the

---

[21] Diary, Dec. 17, 1916.

[22] House noted in his diary Jan. 3, 1917, that Wilson intended to accept Page's resignation. President and Mrs. Wilson suggested that House replace Page. On that date Wilson read a confidential dispatch from Page to be deciphered by the president and not the State Department. Wilson thought it a foolish proceeding "since the dispatch, from his viewpoint was unimportant." Page began the dispatch "at midnight." "I suggested," noted House, "that perhaps we were going to have a Sherlock Holmes recital, but it merely told about conversation with Lloyd George being anxious to work in harmony. It should be answered but I doubt whether he does so." House on January 12 again noted that Wilson intended to accept the resignation.

[23] The secretary of state to Page, Feb. 5, 1917, *The Lansing Papers*, 1: 716.

government's spokesman in rejecting the House plan and other mediation suggestions, the foreign secretary had begun to change his mind by the time of his departure from office. In a memorandum written for the cabinet on December 9, he suggested that perhaps the time had come to reconsider the proposal House had offered in February 1916. Pointing to Britain's desperate economic condition, Grey warned that if the British had to withdraw financial support to their Allies, one or another nation probably would attempt to end the war on the best terms possible; and if France or Russia did so, the other likely would follow. "Defeat of Germany is and will continue to be the only satisfactory end of the war," Grey concluded. "But we cannot force the Great Allies to continue the war against their will or beyond their strength. And if their action makes peace inevitable before Germany is defeated, then I would submit that the intervention of President Wilson (if it is still available in the spirit described) should be seriously considered."[24] This is not to say that Grey, had he remained in office, would have been able to persuade colleagues to accept his view. It is to say that Grey's retirement meant that Page had to deal with individuals less inclined toward mediation than the former foreign secretary would have been.

Balfour and his associates had been in office only a few days when Page brought first tidings of the peace movement. The news came as no surprise to the Foreign Office, for Spring-Rice had kept his government so fully informed that he virtually could tell the contents of the note.[25] Since the proposal was a German offer to the Allies transmitted through American offices, Page conducted this mission as, in a sense, the German ambassador. Despite the source and Page's opposition to negotiation, the transaction was not unpleasant, for the State Department had armed the ambassador with assurance that the United States had no part in it.[26] Lord Robert Cecil, who ran the Foreign Office during the illness of Balfour, said in accepting the note that the Allies would

[24] Memorandum, Dec. 9, 1916, Grey Papers.
[25] Ambassador Spring-Rice to the foreign secretary, Dec. 14, 15, 1916, F. O. 371/2805.
[26] The secretary of state to representatives in the Allied Countries, Dec. 16, 1916, *For. Rels., 1916, Supp.*, 94–95; a copy is in F. O. 371/2805.

reply jointly and, since there were no specific proposals, probably refuse to deal. Page replied that he "quite understood" and suggested, wrote Lord Cecil, "that we should . . . reply that it was an offer 'to buy a pig in a poke,' which we were not prepared to accept. He said he thought his government would expect such reply, and he himself obviously approved it." Cecil then asked if Page knew the type of proposal Wilson was going to make. The ambassador said no: "he did not think . . . it would be much more than a pious aspiration for peace; since that was the only thing that was equally applicable to the Germans and to us."[27]

Two days after Page had delivered the German offer and suggested that the British decline it, he had to deliver the American dispatch, pointed toward the same general end, and urge that Britain comply with its provisions. Wilson's message was not a list of conditions or a suggestion of mediation, but an attempt to provide an atmosphere for negotiation. It stated that while neither group of belligerents had been explicit as to their objects in the war, in general terms both seemed to fight for the same ends. The president proposed that all belligerents state their war aims, implying that with facts on the table (assuming they were similar) it might be possible to meet them peacefully.[28] Handing the dispatch to Lord Cecil on December 20, Page read the covering telegram which urged that he press the note "with the utmost earnestness," and contained the phrase: "it would be hard for the Government of the United States to understand a negative reply." Asked by Cecil for personal comment, the ambassador could say only "that the President . . . was an idealist by temperament, and this move . . . wise or not, was certainly dictated by the purest sentiment of humanity."[29]

This sincere and seemingly innocent proposal landed like a bomb in England, where the public and members of government alike uttered distress at Wilson's suggestion that war aims were

[27] The acting foreign secretary to Ambassador Spring-Rice, Dec. 18, 19, 1916, F. O. 371/2805.

[28] The secretary of state to the Ambassadors and Ministers in Belligerent Countries, Dec. 18, 1916, *For. Rels., 1916, Supp.*, 97–99.

[29] The acting foreign secretary to Ambassador Spring-Rice, Dec. 20, 1916, F. O. 371/2805.

similar; they were distressed at his inability to see that Britain was fighting a holy war. "The people are as mad as hell," a prominent publisher told Page. "Don't talk to me about it. It is most disheartening," was Asquith's comment, and King George V, perhaps most disheartened of all, broke down and wept.[30] Besides being angry, British officials were somewhat befuddled at the message and subsequent events. Wilson seemed to be feeling for peace, but he also had expressed fear that "the situation of neutrals, now exceedingly hard to endure," would become "altogether intolerable," which could appear a threat to take action against one or another belligerent. Then the secretary of state issued a statement on December 21 which suggested that the United States was not seeking peace after all. Lansing said that because the United States was nearing war, it wished to know what the belligerents sought in order to regulate conduct accordingly.[31] The secretary of state privately expressed the same ideas to Spring-Rice, adding that the government would have to take a firm stand to assert its rights—perhaps, it was possible to believe, a hint that Wilson was going to act against Germany.[32] If Lansing's behavior aroused hope in the Foreign Office, it quickly was squelched by Wilson, who compelled Lansing to issue what amounted to a retraction of his earlier statement, and by reports from Spring-Rice.[33] The British ambassador cabled that while German agents had maneuvered the peace note, Wilson was in the hands of no group; and the president, who wanted a Nobel Peace Prize, was indeed seeking peace. Spring-Rice suggested that although the British could not invite Wilson's mediation, it would be unwise, by sending a categorical refusal, to arouse the president.[34]

In midst of this confused but generally unsatisfactory atmosphere, Page participated in one of his most uncomfortable conferences since coming to London. Calling at Whitehall on December

[30] Page to the secretary of state, Dec. 22, 1916, *For. Rels., 1916, Supp.*, 108–109.
[31] New York *Times,* Dec. 22, 1916.
[32] Ambassador Spring-Rice to the foreign secretary, Dec. 21, 1916, F. O. 371/2805.
[33] New York *Times,* Dec. 22, 1916.
[34] Ambassador Spring-Rice to the foreign secretary, Dec. 22, 24, 27, 1916, F. O. 371/2805, 2806, 2796.

26, he listened to Lord Cecil reiterate the bad impression Wilson's message had left. Cecil pointed to the passage which appeared to put Britain on the same level with Germany and another sentence which he said sounded almost like a threat. Even though the ambassador insisted such was not the case—explaining as he understood the note, the term "intolerable state of affairs," referred to submarine warfare—he could not change the British diplomat's mood; and when Cecil remarked that recent American policy had a pro-German twist, Page could not reply. The acting foreign secretary went on to say that if a threat was intended, Britain would disregard it and that the Allies "were determined to carry on the war to a victorious conclusion so long as we were physically able to do so." He added deep regret for the "apparent check in the cordiality of our relations," and expressed hope that time would come when the two nations could cooperate to prevent future wars. "The Ambassador warmly agreed," Cecil wrote of the interview. "He said that it had been a shock to him, when he was in the United States recently, to find that, though his countrymen were fully aware of the facts of the war, they did not seem to appreciate what the German really was, or that Prussian militarism was, as he put it 'an organized crime.' Somehow or other, though the facts crossed the Atlantic the spirit of war did not; and he gave me an illustration drawn from his own experience at a private dinner party where, until he had explained at great length what was really going on on this side, his hearers, though men of the highest education and knowledge, had never really understood what was happening." In that apologetic tone Page ended the conference.[35] It was not the sort of talk which would hasten the president's movement toward mediation, but, of course, Page had not the slightest intent of doing that.

The meeting with Lord Cecil merely confirmed what Page already knew: the British had no desire to have Wilson mediate the conflict. To officials in the Foreign Office the question was not to discourage or encourage the president but how to phrase a discouraging response. Crowe opposed anything but a blunt refusal, afraid that otherwise Britain might find itself maneuvered

[35] The acting foreign secretary to Ambassador Spring-Rice, F. O. 371/2806.

into a position where Wilson would be a party to negotiation. In such case, wrote the assistant undersecretary, the American president would support some British demands and give to others, such as the restoration of Russian Poland, cession of Constantinople to Russia, and loss of German colonies, a lukewarm response. And there would be German demands, that is, the independence of Ireland and freedom of the seas, "which is the German and American equivalent of the abolition of British sea power," that Britain could not consider and would have Wilson's support. The ideal arrangement, Crowe continued, was to discuss peace only with the enemy, after the Allies had mastered them. He favored an answer which said: if the war aims are the same, take those of the Allies and ask how Germany proposed to meet them; and send the same reply to Wilson and the Germans. Lord Cecil disagreed with this approach. While he did not want Wilson to participate in a negotiated peace, he thought the Allies should treat the president's message tactfully and send a firm but careful statement of aims. "Like all discussions it has to be made between opposing evils," Cecil wrote in response to Crowe's comment. "If we take your line we help the German militarists, we disgruntle all the pacifists & semi-pacifists in our own countries & we offend Wilson & a good part of neutral opinion. If we take my line we perhaps help forward the idea of American eventual mediation though I am not much afraid of that resulting in those things Sir E. Crowe believes the Americans would support."[36] Of course, the Allied reply had to receive approval from high British and French officials, but once devised it followed much the line Cecil suggested.[37]

While Page did his utmost to discourage continuation of the American peace movement, he could not dissuade the president; and by the time the ambassador's messages arrived in Washington, Wilson had begun the next step in the campaign.[38] The Germans

[36] Minutes by Crowe and Lord Cecil, Dec. 26, 1916, ibid.
[37] For discussion between British and French officials, see Link, *Campaigns for Progressivism and Peace*, 237–39.
[38] One dispatch warned that the president's message would "for a long time cause a deep, even if silent resentment." Page to the secretary of state, Dec. 22, 26, 1916, *For. Rels., 1916, Supp.*, 115–16.

had refused to comply with the war aims request, stating they would supply them at a council of belligerents in which the president would have no part.[39] For a long time the Allies said nothing. When they did respond, they made their war aims unacceptably severe, and reemphasized that a decision would come on the battlefield, not at a peace conference.[40] Even so, Wilson believed the belligerents not as inflexible as they seemed. Accustomed to appealing directly to the American people, he decided to try the same tactic on the people of the world: go over the heads of government, clarify the American position, inspire a popular movement for peace. Speaking to the Senate on January 22, 1917, he seemed to say to the Germans: if you desire peace by a council of belligerents, you may have it; the United States will take no part in negotiation and will help preserve the settlement, if it is just. Addressing himself to all countries at war, the president outlined what he regarded as a fair peace; it should be, in summary, a "peace without victory."[41]

Page had a copy of the speech before delivery (the State Department sent copies abroad so that foreign newspapers could publish the message at an appropriate time), and the offensive phrase caught his eye. It seemed that Wilson was committing the same blunder again, saying that since all belligerents were the same, none should win. Lloyd George recently had said there could be no peace without victory, and from all indication most of the British people agreed. The ambassador cabled to suggest that the president substitute "peace without conquest" or some other phrase.[42] Lansing thought Page's advice wise and told Wilson that perhaps his language was ill chosen. The best the president would do was to tell his secretary of state, "I'll consider it."[43]

[39] Ambassador Gerard to the secretary of state, Dec. 26, 1916, ibid., 117–18.

[40] Ambassador Sharp to the secretary of state, Jan. 10, 1917, *Papers Relating to the Foreign Relations of the United States, 1917, Supplement 1* (Washington, D.C., 1931), 6–9.

[41] For the speech see ibid., 24–29. A good discussion of the background to the speech is in Link, *Campaigns for Progressivism and Peace,* 249–65.

[42] Page to the secretary of state, Jan. 20, 1917, *The Lansing Papers,* 1: 715–16.

[43] Lansing, *War Memoirs of Robert Lansing* (Indianapolis, Ind., 1935), 195.

"Peace without victory" subsequently became one of the most controversial if in retrospect one of the most enlightened slogans of Wilsonism. While the British government offered no comment, and while the speech drew applause from some liberal groups, most Britons expressed irritation at the president's desire to strike victory from their hands. It is difficult to see how Wilson could have avoided criticism if he was going to talk peace at all. Page's suggestion, elimination of the word "victory," might have lessened the furor, but it would not have carried the thought Wilson wished, and would have made mediation no more acceptable. One cannot avoid a feeling of sympathy as he observes the president in this last effort to stop the fighting in Europe. He understood that peace was the only way to keep the United States out of the slaughter, that a dictated settlement would sow the seeds of a future war; but the powers simply were not interested in a moderate settlement. Futile though the effort, the motive was high, and the alternative was to allow the war to grind on in barbaric fashion to the point where the United States became involved.

Page was willing, indeed anxious, to accept that alternative, hence his great dissatisfaction with the peace movement. It was not that Wilson saw no difference between the belligerents—Page knew he did—but that the president was so afraid of war that he stumbled into awkward and dishonest positions. "The President cannot be made to lift a finger for war—until the Germans should actually bombard one of our ports," he noted the final day of 1916. "It's cowardice or pacifism . . . Jeffersonianism."[44] The worst part of the campaign was Wilson's effort for peace without victory. The ambassador's epilogue came after the United States had entered the war, when Americans were fighting to achieve the victory Wilson had attempted to prevent. The president's phrase was a "remote, academic deliverance while G't [Britain] & France were fighting for their very lives." It "made a profoundly dejected feeling, & made my place more uncomfortable than ever. 'Peace without victory' brought us to the very depths of European disfavor."[45]

[44] Memorandum "for myself," Hendrick, *Page,* 3: 315–16.
[45] Undated memorandum, Page Papers; Hendrick, *Page,* 2: 214.

Page's days of fretting about peace and mediation were numbered, because the Germans, even before Wilson had spoken, had made the decision which would mean the end of American neutrality. The military had grown so influential in the Second Reich that by January 1917 the government could not make an important decision without consulting the High Command, at the time principally Field Marshal Paul von Hindenburg and Quartermaster General Erich Ludendorff. Bethmann remained chancellor and continued to urge peace with the United States, but the more the kaiser relied upon the generals the less he listened to the civil officials. Hindenburg and Ludendorff wanted a blockade of the British Isles, and the naval command promised that the recently strengthened U-boat fleet could starve England in six months, before America could affect Allied military strength. "Looked at from the military standpoint," one cocksure naval official stated, "I consider that the assistance which will result from the entrance of the United States into the war on the side of our enemies will amount to nothing."[46] The fateful decision emerged from a conference at the kaiser's residence at Pless on January 9, 1917. Bethmann doubted to the end that his country could withstand American military and economic pressure, but he had little chance against the impressive array of officers which favored the risky but potentially more rewarding submarine warfare. Unwittingly, the kaiser that morning made the decision which would lead to destruction of the German war effort, the Second Reich, and the Hohenzollern throne. On January 31 Bernstorff notified the secretary of state that Germany the following month would begin to sink all ships within the war zone.[47]

Perhaps the person most distressed at this news was the president. His *Sussex* message virtually demanded a break in relations; Lansing urged it; House urged it; the cabinet unanimously fa-

---

[46] Cited in Ray Stannard Baker, *Woodrow Wilson: Life and Letters,* 8 vols. (Garden City, N.Y., 1927–1939), 6: 249. The official was Admiral von Capelle.

[47] *For. Rels., 1917, Supp. 1,* 97–102. A summary of events in Germany appears in Ernest R. May, *The World War and American Isolation, 1914–1917* (Cambridge, Mass., 1959), 405–15, and Link, *Wilson: Campaigns for Progressivism and Peace,* 239–48.

vored the move. The step was inevitable, yet it was with agonizing reluctance that Wilson asked Lansing to draft the note. The decision became public February 3.[48]

For Page that day would have been a time of celebration had it not so much resembled the days following the *Lusitania,* the *Arabic,* the *Hesperian,* the *Sussex,* and other disappointing occasions. The ambassador had good reason to expect news that the United States had broken with Germany, and indeed he did, but experience would not allow him to discharge the frightening thought that Wilson, invoking some heavenly principle, might evade the German challenge. Page sat the day waiting for news with a small group of friends. At 9:00 P.M. the head of British naval intelligence rushed over to read a brief message from the naval attaché in Washington: "Bernstorff has just been given his passports. I shall probably get drunk tonight."[49] To Page the news must have appeared a finale to a long, painful effort, and to improvise the scene, one can see the ambassador that evening after the visitors had left, sinking into a deep-cushioned chair, closing his heavy-lidded eyes, relaxing for the first time in months. Before going to bed, he probably went to the writing table in his bedroom and scribbled a draft of the message he would send Wilson the next morning. It was a short, joyful dispatch bearing no mark of the doubt and vexation felt so long. Page praised Wilson's "prompt action after . . . patient efforts to avoid a rupture," and told of many wonderful things that would happen to the United States and the world. He turned and read it to Mrs. Page, who still was awake. More scribbling: "Mrs. Page thinks this telegram too impersonal. So it may be, but I am afraid to let myself go."[50] He sent it that way.

For a few days everything in London seemed to go right. Page now took pleasure in reading newspapers which a few days earlier had been so critical of the United States. "An event of measureless

---

[48] For the attitude of Wilson and other officials see Lansing, *Memoirs,* 212–13, David F. Houston, *Eight Years with Wilson's Cabinet, 1913 to 1920,* 2 vols. (Garden City, N.Y., 1926), 1: 229.

[49] Hendrick, *Page,* 2: 215.

[50] Feb. 4, 1917, ibid., 3: 318–19.

importance . . . in the history of mankind. The nation has 'found itself,' " said the *Times*.[51] One of the most exciting experiences was Page's conference with the prime minister. When Page entered that historic residence at 10 Downing Street he found a stocky man of medium height, gray hair, and a stringy mustache. The ambassador had some idea of what to expect, for Lloyd George had a reputation for frequent profanity, vigor, and enthusiasm—American characteristics, some people said. Page once had called him "one of the most energetic projectiles" he ever had seen, and the story went about how Conservative gentlemen (Lloyd George was a Liberal) used to grumble that he would be a poor companion on a tiger hunt (he would have been on the side of the tiger).[52] The prime minister was full of energy that day, excitedly shaking Page's hand, anxious for the United States to get into the fight. Nothing Page did could bring him out of the clouds, not even the statement that America thought about peace, not war. "It is well to look a little ahead," replied Lloyd George with great rapidity. "Are your shipyards on the Great Lakes doing their utmost? . . . Is there any way we can serve you? . . . come see me at any time." Calming somewhat, the prime minister said that his major reason for wishing American participation was to obtain Wilson's cool and humane counsel at the peace conference. Page, of course, was delighted to hear such talk, and if he could not discuss war plans with Lloyd George, he could not conceal the fact (if he tried) that he too was happy.[53] About this time the president had Lansing answer Page's query about replacement, expressing hope that the ambassador would not leave "at the present time." Page answered that he was happy to serve "at any sacrifice," and was making arrangements to stay until the end of the war.[54] It was a longer commitment than

[51] Feb. 5, 1917.

[52] Page to Wilson, Dec. 30, 1916, Hendrick, *Page*, 3: 309–10. For a description of Lloyd George see George Dangerfield, *The Strange Death of Liberal England 1910–1914*, Capricorn Books edition (New York, 1961), 18–19.

[53] Page to the secretary of state, Feb. 6, 1917, *For. Rels., 1917, Supp. 1*, 119–20.

[54] The secretary of state to Page, Feb. 5, 1917; Page to the secretary of state, Feb. 6, 1917, *The Lansing Papers*, 1: 716.

Wilson had asked or wanted, but at that joyous time one can excuse Page for not analyzing Lansing's message.[55]

There was, however, one feature of the president's position, if interpreted properly, which could nullify all the good things happening in Britain. Wilson had gone before the Senate on February 3 to explain that a break in relations was not an automatic declaration of hostilities, that he intended to wait for "overt acts" which would prove the hostile intent of the Imperial Government.[56] The question was: What was an overt act? For several days Page and American consular officials in Britain kept the wires hot with reports of torpedoed ships—the *Evestone,* the *California,* the *Turino,* and many others. Mostly the vessels were British or ships of neutral nations other than the United States; some were armed merchantmen, some unarmed; Americans died on some vessels, escaped from others.[57] Certainly the attacks violated the *Sussex* pledge. They were overt enough for Page, who began to grumble. "I am now willing to record my conviction that we shall not get into war at all," he noted on February 19. "The P. is constitutionally unable to come to such a point of action."[58]

Moreover, the break in relations seemed to be backfiring. Germany's threat to sink all shipping in the war zone was anything but an incentive to unprotected American shippers, and vessels kept to the ports. Not only did this activity lessen danger of a decisive incident, supplies did not reach England. The British were beginning to feel a pinch for food. The United States thereby was helping enforce the German proclamation. "We are practically blockaded—held up, held in, driven off the seas by the German threat!" Page exclaimed, irritated at the government's unwillingness to arm merchant ships.[59] The incidents continued.

[55] A few days later Wilson told House he had written Page he would not make any change for the moment, but Wilson feared Page had misconstrued it to mean he would not make a change until the war was over. House Diary, March 5, 1918.

[56] Ray Stannard Baker and William E. Dodd, eds., *The Public Papers of Woodrow Wilson,* 6 vols. (New York, 1925–1927), 4: 422–26.

[57] The vessels were too numerous to itemize. For reports see *For. Rels., 1917, Supp. 1,* 112–49.

[58] Page Diary.

[59] Diary, Feb. 25, 1917, Hendrick, *Page,* 3: 323.

On February 25 a submarine sank the Cunard liner *Laconia*. Among the victims were a Miss and Mrs. Hoy of Chicago, who perished in a lifeboat. Another *Lusitania*, if on a smaller scale; "surely an overt act," Horace Plunkett wrote;[60] did the president think so? Mr. Hoy (brother and son of the deceased) came by the embassy, wanting a gun. He wished to join the American army if the United States went to war, the British army if war did not come. He was going to wire the president. Page could have explained that he had been doing that for almost two years without any effect, but he probably only sympathized with the bereaved man.[61] Grey wrote from his house in the country to express disbelief and remark that a failure to act would grievously depress the future of America.[62] What was one to do?

It is an ironic fact that, much as Page disliked them, no individual or group of individuals did as much as the Germans for fulfillment of the ambassador's grandest schemes. Germany's latest gift was the Zimmermann Note, which Balfour presented Page in late February 1917. It was, the aging Britisher later remarked, "as dramatic a moment as I remember in all my life."[63] The Zimmermann dispatch was an incriminating piece of evidence, and it must have quickened the pulse of the ambassador. The note from the German foreign secretary to his minister in Mexico stated that in case of war with the United States, Germany would favor alliance with Mexico. Mexican reward was to be recapture of territory lost in the war with the United States in 1846–1848, which the dispatch explained to mean Texas, New Mexico, and Arizona. (Strangely, the Germans did not offer California and other states from the Mexican cession.)

Almost as alarming as the content was Zimmermann's method of transmission. The British had obtained the note through secret sources and were anxious for the United States to have it, but the State Department could obtain another copy by checking its files. During the *Lusitania* negotiation Bernstorff had obtained occa-

[60] Plunkett Diary, Feb. 27, 1917.
[61] Page Diary, Feb. 27, 1917, Hendrick, *Page,* 3: 324.
[62] Feb. 26, 1917, Page Papers.
[63] Blanche E. Dugdale, *Arthur James Balfour,* 2 vols. (New York, 1937), 2: 137–38.

sional use of American cables, since German channels were un-
trustworthy and slow. The administration had continued this
courtesy, and Zimmermann had sent his dispatch, among other
methods, through Bernstorff and the department. When Wilson
heard these details, he could only exclaim "Good Lord!"[64]

For all its drama and intrigue, the affair failed to have the
effect Page desired. The ambassador sent the telegram to Washington on February 24. He made the accompanying message simple and factual, cautious not to spoil a stroke of good luck with an
overabundance of advice.[65] The facts seemed clear enough, that is,
for anyone but Wilson. "This would precipitate a war between
any two nations," he noted. "Heaven knows what effect it will
have in Washington."[66] Wilson on February 26 asked Congress for
authority to arm merchant ships, which without protection still
refused to venture out. The note probably hastened this move,
but the president had been considering such action and soon
would have done so. The government released the message to the
press on March 1 and a great uproar resounded through the
nation. That was fine to Page, convinced that the people wanted
war. "I have never abandoned the belief that if the President
were really to lead, all the people will follow," he noted March 2.
"Whether he will even now remains to be seen."[67] Days then
passed with no new action. Wilson's second inauguration came on
March 4. Page saw accounts of the president's speech. One newspaper commented that "Dr. Wilson's second inauguration will
pass into American history as an event as dramatic as that of the
first inauguration of President Lincoln." "No—no!" scribbled
Page beside the sentence.[68] The ambassador surely hoped that the
Zimmermann Note was indisputable proof of the German intent,
the end of Wilsonian pacifism, but except for exciting American
opinion, and perhaps hastening the arming of merchant ships
(the bill ran aground in the Senate but Wilson armed them anyway) , it caused no change in American foreign policy.

[64] Lansing Diary, March 4, 1917; *Memoirs,* 227–28.
[65] *For. Rels., 1917, Supp. 1,* 147–48.
[66] Feb. 24, 1917.
[67] Hendrick, *Page,* 3: 325.
[68] The newspaper is in Page's Papers.

The persistent ambassador had one more large gun to fire. The day following the inauguration he sent an urgent telegram to explain the economic reasons for America's going to war. The problem stated simply—and few individuals could state a problem as simply, its solution as clear—was that the world faced financial disaster due to a gigantic imbalance of gold reserves. One hemisphere (the western) had much of the gold and supplies, and the other needed them. The Allied powers could not continue to purchase supplies in the United States because gold was short and what they had, they did not wish to send for fear submarines might send it to the bottom of the ocean. The solution, probably possible only through declaration of war, was credit in such large quantity that only the American government could supply it. The alternative was collapse of American trade, economic panic in the United States and the world.[69]

While the United States never fully tested the truth of Page's statement, it is beyond doubt that he had pointed to an important problem of the Allies and to a lesser degree, the Americans. The Allies were in poor economic condition in 1917, and if neither Page nor the American government knew the full story, the closer the United States came to war, the more the Allies were willing to let the Americans know about it. If there was a solution short of intervention, the United States never had to discover it. Had the president's policy of armed neutrality continued a few weeks longer, he could have tested Page's thesis, and if found accurate, Wilson would have had to decide if prosperity was justification for war. As it was, the message of March 5 had no visible effect on American policy—at least it did not hasten the president's decision for war—and two weeks after he wrote it the ambassador still was trying to obtain an answer.[70] The decisive fact is that there were other reasons for war which Wilson could not ignore, if he wanted to.

While the story of American intervention is a many-sided,

---

[69] Page to the secretary of state, March 5, 1917, *Papers Relating to the Foreign Relations of the United States, 1917, Supplement 2,* 2 vols. (Washington, D.C., 1932), 1: 516–18.

[70] Page to the secretary of state, March 24, 1917, ibid., 519.

complicated account, the most important immediate influence on Wilson was what happened on and beneath the waves of the Atlantic Ocean. There time ran out on the president. If he never had explained what he considered an overt act, his performance since February 3 indicated that he would act on nothing less than a deliberate attack upon an American vessel. News came in on March 18 that torpedoes had struck not one, but three American ships.[71] Two days later the president polled the cabinet. Some members responded with vigor, some with sorrow and hesitation, but all declared that war already was upon the United States. The president did not say anything and his grave manner seemed to indicate that he had not yet decided; when cabinet officials filed out of the room they had no indication of what Wilson was going to do.[72] They learned the next day that he had called Congress into special session for April 2.

If the final two months of neutrality was for Page a period of fluctuating emotion, a time when success seemed so near and yet beyond grasp, from the standpoint of his diplomatic duties it was one of the easiest times since the war began. He automatically had shed the evil-sounding title of German ambassador and with the title went some time-consuming duties. After February 3 the problems with Britain almost came to a standstill. The British seized few American ships during that period because few vessels left port, and if some old cases remained on the docket the United States did not worry about them. Though Page made frequent trips to the Foreign Office, especially after Wilson had called Congress into special session, it was to lay the groundwork for Anglo-American cooperation, not to pester Balfour about ships, mail, or other problems. With detachment the ambassador could have sat back and enjoyed the relief which the German government granted him. No one who knew Page would expect him to do that, not when his nation and president were under such close public scrutiny; when the British and Page himself could see clearer than ever Wilson's view of the Germans and the war;

[71] New York *Times,* March 19, 1917.
[72] A memorandum of the cabinet meeting, dated March 20, 1917, is in Lansing's Papers.

when the ambassador saw Germany challenge the president to stand up and fight, and Wilson sought every possible way to avoid the challenge. Viewing the issue thus, Page could not stand off unconcerned, and he did not, although there was little he could do to influence the course of events. Except for a few ineffectual dispatches, the ambassador had to content himself with private memorandums, and while these jottings and little essays never reached the president, they do show Page's mind at the time the United States entered the conflict; they show that for the ambassador, perhaps the greatest casualty of neutrality was the respect and admiration he long had held for Wilson. "He has not breathed a spirit into the people: he has encouraged them to supineness," Page wrote the day before Congress met to receive Wilson's war message. "He is *not* a leader, but rather a stubborn phrasemaker. His chief counsel is with—House, as timid a dependent-in-thought as one man ever found in another."[73]

[73] Diary, April 1, 1917.

Chapter Nine

Victory and Death

I'LL TELL YOU," Rudyard Kipling remarked to Page a few months after America's fateful decision, "your coming into the war made a new earth for me."[1] Page failed to record his answer to the famous English poet, but he could have replied "for me also," because there was no happier man on April 3. No longer could his government procrastinate; no longer need he explain Wilson's policy. Along the way to the Foreign Office he could see the American flag displayed on public buildings, and entering Balfour's office he watched the foreign secretary rush forward to shake hands and remark: "It's a great day for the world."[2] Britons used almost every imaginable means of expressing delight that America was in the war, and Page celebrated along with them. The ambassador sat solemnly erect at a ceremony at St. Paul's Cathedral, and at a private party which followed the ceremony he yelled at the top of his voice for five minutes. It might have been unusual behavior for an ambassador, but it was an unusual time.[3]

American intervention almost ended Page's job and initiated a new, brief, and final phase of his embassy. The great transformation of diplomatic function had begun when the United States severed relations with Germany, but not until the act of April 1917 could Page know that the problems of neutrality were gone for good. Indeed, the old troublesome policies of blockade and blacklist now became parts of American procedure. Confronted with no neutral nation powerful as itself, the American government in some cases imposed even more rigid rules than had the British. "Mr. Balfour," Frank Polk remarked when the foreign secretary visited Washington in April, "it took Great Britain three years to reach a point where it was prepared to violate all the laws of blockade. You will find that it will take us only two months to become as great criminals as you are."[4] Page felt no embarrassment at his government's reversal, for he long had contended that necessity and not law should guide a nation's foreign policy, at least that of Anglo-Saxon nations. Besides, it allowed him to shed the mask of neutrality he had worn with such discomfort. Of course, his sympathies had not been exactly unknown. As the king assured: "Ah—ah—we knew where you stood all the time."[5]

This is not to say that the United States and Britain adopted at a single stroke the fraternal relationship of Page's dream, or that the ambassador had nothing to do after April. The United States scarcely had entered the war when Page had to admit that the Allies were in such desperate financial need, the submarine campaign so effective, that Germany might yet win. When it appeared during the spring and summer of 1917 that the submarines might starve out the British, the ambassador rushed several messages to Washington asking for antisubmarine craft of all sorts. "It is the most serious situation that has confronted the Allies since the Battle of the Marne," he cabled in June with a tone of urgency now familiar to the State Department. Similar messages came from Admiral William S. Sims, the ranking American naval officer in Britain and a man in close contact with the Admiralty. The American government was hesitant. At first it sent six destroyers. Page wanted all the destroyers and "hundreds of armed seagoing

[1] Page Diary, Jan. 22, 1918.
[2] Ibid., "The Day" (April 3, 1917).
[3] These experiences were related by an unnamed friend of Page, *Times* (London), Aug. 28, 1918.
[4] Hendrick, *Page,* 2: 265.
[5] Page Diary, May 1917.

tugs, yachts . . . , any kind of swift small ships."[6] Discussing the matter with Sims, he supposed the administration considered him hopelessly pro-British and discounted much of what he said.[7] Balfour tried next, saying virtually what Page and Sims had advised.[8] The president was suspicious. "I have been greatly surprised," he cabled, "by failure of the British Admiralty to use Great Britain's great naval superiority in an effective way."[9] Nonetheless, by August the United States had thirty-seven destroyers and several converted vessels in European waters, and in December Britons were delighted to hear that a squadron of battleships—superdreadnoughts, some enthusiasts liked to call them—was coming. The submarine menace never vanished, but the Allies reduced it, and with a great boost in the American merchant marine they solved the problem of supply.

A problem of equal concern, although more readily susceptible to solution, was Britain's finances. Shouldering much of the burden for the other Allies as well as itself, the British government found in 1917 that it had overdrawn the account with the J. P. Morgan firm by $400,000,000. Page again swung into action. "Unless we come to their rescue we are all in danger of disaster," he cabled, intimating that the future of the world depended on the administration.[10] The same day Balfour sent a similarly urgent cable to House: "If we cannot keep up the exchange neither we nor the Allies can pay our dollar debts, we should be driven off the gold basis, and all purchases from the United States would immediately cease and Allied credit would be shattered."[11] The case of the Morgan overdraft exposed American reluctance to grant its new associates a blank check, and reemphasized that the

[6] Page to the secretary of state, June 20, 1915, *For. Rels., 1917, Supp.* 2, 1: 106–107; Page to secretary of state, April 27, 28 (two messages), June 27, 1917, ibid., 46–47, 111–12.

[7] Hendrick, *Page,* 2: 284.

[8] The British embassy to the Department of State, July 1, 1917, *For. Rels., 1917, Supp.* 2, 1: 115.

[9] The secretary of state to Page ["For Admiral Sims from the President"], July 4, 1917, ibid., 117–18.

[10] Page to the secretary of state, June 28, 1917, ibid., 532–33.

[11] Balfour to the consul general in New York (Bayley), June 28, 1917, the Papers of Arthur Balfour, Public Record Office, London.

United States entered the war to fight Germany, not as Page had hoped, to preserve British friendship. It showed also that the mere presence of Page's name on a dispatch, especially a message requesting assistance for Britain, almost automatically weakened its argument. The administration grumbled about the financial problem through the summer of 1917, then bowed to the inevitable and picked up the check.

With an easing of the submarine onslaught, and with financial arrangement between the United States and its allies, Page's war diplomacy virtually was over. In the numerous problems of winning the war and arranging for peace, Wilson bypassed Page—indeed, in some cases even the State Department—and worked through House and the British government. House took up quarters on the ninth floor of the same New York hotel in which lived Lord Reading and Sir William Wiseman, chief of British military intelligence in the United States. The colonel obtained information through a direct telephone line to the White House and State Department, passed it on to Reading who relayed it to Wiseman; the intelligence officer then sent the messages to the Foreign Office. Wiseman cautioned colleagues in London to make these unusual channels known to the fewest people possible. "We should remember particularly Page's position," he wrote.[12] During the greatest of all crises, the race to get troops to France in 1918, the ambassador was more a spectator than a participant, nervously watching to see if American intervention had been too late.

Whatever the course of the battles, Page now was very much *persona grata* in London, in demand for speaking engagements and public appearances. In some respects it resembled the first year of his embassy; in some respects it was better, for he could glow with pride as the British witnessed conclusive evidence that America had taken its place in the world. Sims was the first military official to arrive in London and almost immediately became a favorite with the Admiralty. General John J. Pershing and staff passed through in June, amid parades, receptions, and other celebration, through which Page proudly led the American

[12] Sir William Wiseman to Sir E. Drummond, Oct. 4, 14, 1917, ibid.

general. Arrival of each uniformed group of Americans, even a group of nurses, sustained the warm feeling that for the first time the new world had stepped forth to the rescue of the old.[13] To be sure Page retained some resentment at Wilson's peacetime behavior. "History will not give him the place of a real leader," he noted in February 1918. "He was pushed in and once in, his incomparable gift of expression enabled him to state the case in a masterful way."[14] But except for an occasional disclosure to his son, he kept these feelings to himself. Letters to Wilson were full of flattery, proclaiming the president's soaring prestige in Britain and how, once the Allies had won, Wilson would stand first among the leaders of the world.[15]

Now that Anglo-American cooperation was established, Page renewed efforts to assure that this relation was not merely a marriage of necessity, but the foundation of perpetual understanding and world leadership. He was much encouraged when Balfour journeyed to the United States in April 1917. Essentially a good will visit, Balfour explained to a colleague how he planned to proceed: "The mission starts out with the immense advantage that it is unique and will appeal enormously to American vanity. A little civility to the press on the way to Washington—a little flattery and a few assurances that we contemplate no 'entanglement' of the U. S.—will give us the start we need." But in addition to these gestures, the foreign secretary felt there needed to be something specific, some idea of what the Allies expected of the United States.[16]

While Balfour was in America the war cabinet decided that

[13] "This our-new-ally business is bringing to me a lot of amusing problems," Page wrote. "Theatres offer me boxes, universities offer me degrees, hospitals solicit visits from me, clubs offer me dinners—I'll have to get a new private secretary or two well-trained to say 'no' politely, else I shall not have my work done." To Wilson, May 4, 1917, Hendrick, *Page,* 2: 62; see also Page to Wilson, June 8, 1917, ibid., 3: 376–77.

[14] Diary, Feb. 3, 1918. See also Page to Arthur Page, March 8, 1918, Hendrick, *Page,* 2: 336–37.

[15] For example, Page to Wilson, May 4, 1917, Hendrick, *Page,* 2: 262–63; June 8, Sept. 25, 1917, Jan. 16, 1918, ibid., 3: 379, 408, 416–17.

[16] "Some Platitudes for Sir E. Drummond," undated [probably April 1917], Balfour Papers.

there needed to be a permanent agent, "an influential and energetic man," in the United States to supervise and coordinate work of various British departments. Some persons mentioned Grey, and Balfour wrote from the United States that the former foreign secretary would be a popular and effective special envoy. But other officials, including the prime minister, objected: they thought Grey too much a pacifist, and Lloyd George wanted to send a businessman.[17] In process of selecting a person (the choice was Lord Northcliffe) there arose a small disturbance with Page. Lord Curzon, speaking in the House of Lords, had mentioned in passing that the government had received Page's approval of Northcliffe's appointment. The ambassador protested to Balfour that he had given an opinion personally and unofficially, and Curzon's remarks placed him in a bad position with his government.[18] The fears turned out to be ill founded: Curzon said the ambassador had misunderstood him; the State Department made no mention of the episode.[19] Once in the United States, Northcliffe confirmed what the British government knew to be true, that Britain's image was not what it should be. He complained that the French army received most of the publicity, and people in the United States rarely heard of the British fleet. Northcliffe passed along House's suggestion that Britain should have prominent naval officers visit America.[20]

Long convinced that personal confrontation of Americans and Britons would do much to destroy suspicion, Page was prime mover in a campaign to bring to England distinguished Americans who would lecture about the United States. As the group, headed by former President William Howard Taft, was about to embark, Taft stopped by the White House to explain the purposes to Wilson. The president was not at all agreeable. He was not certain he wished closer relations with Britain. Told about Page's part in the plan, Wilson reportedly complained: "Page is really an Englishman and I have to discount whatever he says

[17] Lord Cecil to Balfour, May 17, 1917, Balfour to Lord Cecil, May [?] 1917, ibid.
[18] Balfour to Lord Curzon, July 7, 1917, ibid.
[19] Lord Curzon to Balfour, July 7, 1917, ibid.
[20] Lord Northcliffe to the premier and cabinet, Aug. 15, 1917, ibid.

about the situation in Great Britain."²¹ The program came to a halt. Not only was Page suspect in the United States, but he lost strength as adviser to the British government. Spring-Rice frequently reminded the Foreign Office of Page's pro-British reputation in Washington and warned against taking the ambassador's opinion as the wishes of the American government.²²

Perhaps the months of American participation showed that, unlike Page, Wilson did not believe that Anglo-American friendship held the world together. Perhaps this period showed also that Page's advice was ignored in Washington, sometimes when it should not have been, but to the ambassador these were tolerable matters. The United States was "in"; that was the important thing.

Increasingly Page's problem became less the war than his health. Perhaps a man less sensitive, less dedicated to principle, could have handled the London embassy with little physical difficulty, but Page could not. He did not possess the luxury of detachment, and the gaunt body, now sixty-two years old, began to show effects of almost five years at his post. "No human creature was ever as tired as I am," he wrote in October 1917, only a few months after the United States had entered the war.²³ Despite a steadily worsening condition, he stayed on the job, complaining only about fatigue and (jokingly) a daily diet of cabbage: "Cabbage and Germans belong together: God made 'em both the same stinking day."²⁴ He endured the winter of 1917–1918, but in March had to take off a few days and go to St. Ives on the coast of Cornwall. There, looking across the Atlantic in the direction of the United States, he rested and caught up on correspondence. The letters pondered the old themes, and creeping into the pages with noticeable frequency were thoughts of the United States and North Carolina.

Before March was out, Page was back in London, handling his chores and keeping anxious watch on events. The final German

²¹ Hendrick, *Page,* 2: 348.
²² Spring-Rice to Balfour, July 27, Sept. 20, 21, Oct. 12, 1917, Spring-Rice Papers.
²³ To Frank N. Doubleday, Hendrick, *Page,* 2: 324.
²⁴ To Ralph W. Page, March 4, 1918, ibid., 334.

offensive was underway in France and Americans were pouring into the western front by the hundreds of thousands, among them Frank Page, Charles G. Loring, and several other relatives. Letters from Page were full of cheer and optimism, but they dropped hints, such as a complaint about a diet of cream, that the illness was not going well.[25] His doctors were worried. Resign and go home, they said. Not yet, he always replied, not until the war was over and his job done, but he did consent to take off several weeks for another rest.[26]

This time he stayed in the home of the Waldorf Astors at Sandwich, Kent, on the English Channel, a poor choice if Page had any thought of forgetting the war. Distant but distinct rumbles of guns drifted across the channel from battles in France. Trenches and barbed wire ran along the beach, and not more than fifty yards from the house was a large artillery piece which occasionally let out thundering belches as it fired at enemy planes on the way to London.[27] Such atmosphere did little for a man attempting to coax back his health, but to the struggle in France —the Germans again were approaching Paris—Page hardly could remain oblivious. There were more letters to Wilson, House, Arthur, and Ralph about the war and home. Overwhelmingly the major topic was the future and Anglo-American friendship. He rarely talked about his condition, but he occasionally did confess: "I do get tired—my Lord! how tired."[28]

He returned to London in the middle of June to have one last go with the embassy; it was a short experience, for his failing health was evident to almost everyone. In July Frank (now Major Frank Page) came over from France. Almost immediately he summoned Arthur from the United States. Together with the doctors, the two sons were able to prevail over vigorous protests and persuade the ambassador to resign. On August 1, 1918, Page performed the agonizing task of informing the president that while he expected eventual full recovery, his health demanded a

---

[25] To Arthur Page, April 7, 1918, ibid., 369; to Ralph Page, April 7, 13, 1918, ibid., 371–72.

[26] Ibid., 376.

[27] As Page described the place to Ralph Page, May 19, 1918, ibid., 382–83.

[28] To Arthur Page, May 27, 1918, ibid., 388.

surrender of the post. Some weeks later Wilson accepted the resignation and assured the ambassador he had performed his duties "with distinguished success."[29]

When the news became public the British went to great length to send off the ambassador with full knowledge of their appreciation. He had been "a great ambassador" was the consensus of editorials. Most notable of these messages was an article in the *Times* by a "personal acquaintance," so written as to suggest the author was a high official in the government, perhaps even Balfour. Calling Page "a lovable human being" it announced how the ambassador had been "heart and soul" in the war long before the United States was a belligerent, and how he "contrived to bevel the edge of many a sharp note."[30] There were personal messages from Lloyd George, Grey, the king, almost every high official. The English so opened their hearts to their stricken friend that had Page's health been better, those last weeks would have been an experience of the fullest pleasure.

Deterioration continued so rapidly that for a while it appeared that Page would spend his last days in London. Too ill to help with packing, he left that chore to Mrs. Page and went with Arthur to Scotland to rest. The wait for transportation was unexpectedly long, and by the time he could obtain a suitable ship he had grown so weak that doctors thought the voyage a risk. Deciding that the ambassador's willpower would compensate for a weakened body, they consented to the journey.[31] It seemed a safe time to leave. Almost two million American soldiers now manned the western front, and together with the newly inspired British and French troops they were driving the Germans to the fatherland. The success of Allied arms made Page's departure from Waterloo Station the more touching. Several members of the government were present, as was the embassy staff, to bid farewell to a friend and associate, now so weak he needed assistance onto the train. No one in the crowd which watched silently was more

[29] Page to Wilson, Aug. 1, 1918; Wilson to Page, Aug. 24, 1918, ibid., 393–96; Ray Stannard Baker, *Woodrow Wilson: Life and Letters*, 8 vols. (Garden City, N.Y., 1927–1939) , 8: 356–57.
[30] *Times* (London) , Aug. 28, 1918.
[31] As explained by Frank Page, New York *Times*, Oct. 13, 1918.

affected than Balfour, who confessed that he almost wept when Page moved away.[32]

As the ship headed into the ocean that October day there was no certainty Page would live to reach the United States. The obliging captain did his best to hasten the voyage, but the tossing Atlantic was far from beneficial to a man near death; and the voyage was long. The doctor intermittently had to apply oxygen to keep the patient breathing, and for perhaps a third of the voyage Page was delirious. The ship steamed into New York a full day ahead of schedule, its principal passenger still alive.

October 12, 1918, was a day of irony for Walter Page. Victory and peace seemed only days away. It was Saturday, and New York was in a gay mood to greet the president who was in the city for a Liberty Day parade. An American flag draped over his right shoulder, Wilson marched along brightly decorated streets to an ovation such as no president had received in the city. "The Wilson smile," said the *Times*, "was in evidence from start to finish." In another section of town an ambulance rushed through the streets carrying a critically ill Page to St. Luke's Hospital.[33] While the man lay dying who, perhaps more than any other individual, had labored to bring the United States into the war, unaware of the excitement of the city, the person who had exerted such great effort to avoid participation was having a jubilant day.

For a few days Page lingered between life and death. He did not realize that the flowers in his room were from President and Mrs. Wilson. When he could make sense he was obsessed with seeing the president and making a final report, a task which Wilson asked relatives to tell him was not necessary.[34]

In November he again was able to hold a pen. His first letter went to Wilson. The armistice had been signed, and as the ambassador wrote, the president prepared for a momentous journey to Europe to help arrange the postwar settlement of the world. "What I w^d not give to be in England when you are there," Page wrote. Now his grandest dreams were coming true. America had

[32] Hendrick, *Page,* 2: 403.
[33] New York *Times,* Oct. 13, 1918.
[34] Baker, *Wilson,* 8: 484.

broken its isolation. Best of all, England was going to get a look at the president of the United States. Perhaps Page could not see the president and the king of England side-by-side, but he could enjoy the thought that he had had a part in fulfillment of his world plan: "My regret is the measure also of my profound appreciation for your giving me the most interesting and (I hope also by far) the most useful experience of my life, an experience that I hope to turn to good use and to your credit as long as I live. You will find the heart of England most grateful to us; and the admiration of your extraordinary management of the world's most extraordinary events—beyond bounds. It would be the greatest joy of my life to see them receive you. You have set the moral standard for the world to become a new world."[35] Forgotten was the agony of the days of neutrality; only the future was important; Anglo-American cooperation had begun and Page, unaware of his condition, was anxious to keep it moving.

But Page's part in the world plan had ended. The recovery for which he showed optimism did not occur. The doctors gave up hope and granted his request to return to North Carolina. There, with almost all the family present, he died peacefully on December 21, 1918, five days before King George welcomed Wilson to Buckingham Palace. Page left the world during the brief interval when American prestige and influence was at its highest peak, before the nation retreated to old ways.

[35] Nov. 23, 1918, Page Papers. A complete photostated copy of the letter is in Baker, *Wilson*, 8: 566–69.

Chapter Ten

The Ambassadorship of Walter Page

THE STORY OF Walter Page did not end with the ambassador's death; indeed he became a more popular, albeit controversial figure in the years which followed the World War. The military battles in France prefaced equally important, and in some cases more frustrating diplomatic battles at Paris. The quarreling victors agreed upon a settlement which presaged another conflict between scholars and statesmen who set out to refute or support the famous war guilt clause of the Versailles Treaty, which stated that Germany had caused the war. Governments published documents to prove their countries' innocence and historians, delighted at so much primary evidence so soon, began to rehash the First World War. Among the most important and surely one of the most interesting of these works was the published letters of Walter Page, the first two volumes of which appeared in 1922. Before the eyes of the world the ambassador pleaded his case of German barbarity, British sanctity, the need for a world-saving Anglo-American alliance. His sympathetic editor concluded that Page had done as much, perhaps more than any individual to make the world a safe place.

An enormous financial success, *The Life and Letters of Walter Hines Page* inspired a large group of Page admirers in the United

States and abroad. Delighted at reading such good things about themselves, the English responded with a plaque in Westminster Abbey.[1] The volumes also inspired detractors who, alarmed at the ambassador's independent behavior in London, felt him anything but a credit to his nation and the diplomatic service.[2] Surrounded with vastly differing interpretations, the ambassador's name then slipped into limbo; the volumes of exciting letters gathered dust in college libraries and used-book stores.

One must hope, however, that Page will not be forgotten. He was a talented, colorful individual who sought the best for his region and nation. His efforts to reform the South and revitalize periodical literature did credit to himself and his movements. He was aware better than most individuals that a prosperous, industrialized America could not remain tied to old ideas of international relations. His was the clearest expression of a view of the war which, while not dominant in the United States, found strong support among many of his compatriots. He understood that the war was destroying the old order, that if the United States was to be satisfied with the new order, it ought to have a hand in shaping it. He was a master with the pen; and the student who studies the World War, however far in the future, will find in Page's letters from war-torn London accounts of the conflict seldom equaled. Finally, Page's ambassadorship, while not the key to America's destiny at the time, sheds light on the diplomacy of the war, the attitude of President Wilson, and the diplomatic profession.

It must be evident by now that Page will not be remembered as the person who drove Wilson to belligerency. The simplest explanation is that the German policy of Page and Wilson were not

[1] "If there had been in Page even a touch of cynicism, of selfishness, of vanity, or of irritability," wrote one British friend, "the whole history of mankind might have been changed. Happily there was no such flaw in his nature. It was refined gold throughout." J. St. Loe Strachey, *The Spectator* (July 7, 1923): 4. See also Viscount Esher, "A Great Ambassador," *The Quarterly Review* (April 1923): 307–17.

[2] C. Hartley Grattan, "The Walter Hines Page Legend," *American Mercury* 6 (Sept. 1925): 39–51; "Walter Hines Page—Patriot or Traitor?" *Nation* 121 (Nov. 4, 1925): 512; *Why We Fought* (New York, 1929); Walter Millis, *Road to War: America 1914–1917* (Boston, 1935); Charles C. Tansill, *America Goes to War* (Boston, 1938).

the same, that when Page urged one course, the president almost invariably did something else. The ambassador hinted at a break in relations as early as May 1915; he openly urged it in January 1916; the break did not come until the following year. The German policy of Page and Wilson parted at the time of the *Lusitania*'s sinking. They would not meet again until April 1917, and then it was so late and under such compelling circumstances that Page hardly would regard Wilson's policy as his own.

Even so, in his war message of April 2, 1917, Wilson did explain American participation in terms strikingly similar to the way Page had been justifying intervention. The war, Wilson said, was a battle for civilization, a crusade of good against evil, a war to make "the world . . . safe for democracy."[3] Doubtless the President did feel, as he told Page in the dark days of 1916, that the political system of Germany was not in accord with American ideals, and that a group of aggressive militarists directed the Second Reich. The mistake is to say that Page placed these thoughts in Wilson's mind and that they were the dominant reasons for going to war. Some of the ideas Wilson had as early as the ambassador; he frequently heard them from the people in Washington, but of all the anti-German expressions which the president heard from time to time, frequently from such individuals as House and Lansing, only Page's became irritating. And one must doubt if German philosophy and the German political system were major forces behind the decision for war. Wilson did not find these factors compelling in 1914–1916 and almost not so in 1917. There now is some doubt that Wilson's famous conversation with Frank Cobb of the New York *World,* in which the president is supposed to have uttered "if there is any alternative [to war], for God's sake, let's take it," ever took place.[4] Even if the

[3] *For. Rels., 1917, Supp. 1,* 201.

[4] For many years students accepted the idea that this meeting took place the evening of April 1, 1917. Arthur Link (*Wilson: Campaigns for Progressivism and Peace, 1916–1917* [Princeton, N.J., 1965], 399) contended that the conversation occurred March 19, when Wilson was pondering the decision for war. Jerold S. Auerbach doubts that the discussion ever took place. See Auerbach, "Woodrow Wilson's 'Prediction' to Frank Cobb: Words Historians Should Doubt Ever Got Spoken," *Journal of American History* 54 (Dec. 1967): 608–17.

meeting is fiction, the words seem a fair statement of Wilson's feelings at the time. Britain fighting for civilization; Germany an enemy of humanity? Perhaps, but there was good possibility that Britain would continue to fight civilization's battle and Germany the battle of inhumanity, without American intervention, that is, if the Germans had refrained from sinking American ships and killing American citizens.

America's German policy was one side of the diplomatic story of 1914–1917, hence only a part—the lesser part—of the ambassadorship of Walter Page. What Wilson did with Germany was little more important than what he did not do with Britain. Germany's policy toward the United States failed; Britain's succeeded. The question is: what was Page's part in Anglo-American relations? Did he, by keeping the president alert to the issues and especially by clever arrangement of American affairs in London, stave off serious difficulty, perhaps even war between his two favorite nations?

It is fair to say that his impact was not nearly as great as his admirers have contended. If he had any influence in Washington, it came during the first months of war, before Page had branded himself a hopeless anglophile. He probably had influence on such issues as the Declaration of London, although there is no assurance that without Page in London the settlement would have been different. After the first weeks of 1915 Page was so obviously pro-British, so much more interested in British diplomatic success than American, that the administration usually treated his messages with disinterest or disgust. The behavior of Wilson and Lansing gave Page so much torment that it was, one must suspect, partly responsible for his illness.

British sources verify what Grey years ago said was the object of British policy: to exert strongest pressure possible without inciting American reprisal. The Foreign Office, however, had great difficulty determining how much the Americans would tolerate. Grey believed Wilson was not anxious to promote sharp turns in relations with Britain, but aware of the huge pressure on the administration, he never could be certain what the United States was going to do. Officials in the Foreign Office expressed frequent bewilderment at the many directions American policy seemed to take. Page often pointed to one reason for such confusing diplomacy: too many individuals undertook responsibility for interpreting, if not attempting to guide, American policy. Of course the ambassador contributed to this state of affairs; so occasionally did House and Lansing. The situation in the first weeks of 1916 is the obvious example. House came to London bearing his complicated peace proposal; Lansing offered the plan for disarming merchant ships; Page pleaded with his government to accept the blockade; all the while Spring-Rice kept alive the danger of embargo. For good reason a British official could ask House what the United States wished Britain to do; and House's response, however jolly it sounded, was no answer at all. If the situation were not confusing enough Lord Bryce at the same time contributed letters from "responsible" Americans, also offering advice as to what the Foreign Office should do. Small wonder that Sir Eyre Crowe would exclaim, "How extraordinary these American busybodies are! They all take their mouths full of professions of the absolute sympathy for the Allies animating the whole of America. They all suggest that there [sic] information and understanding is imperfect. They all say that unless England does something in accordance with this imperfect understanding the U.S. will practically treat us as an enemy. The shoddiness of thought and superficiality of knowledge are really hopeless."[5]

There was another reason for the unclear nature of America's British relations. Given the sympathy of members of the Wilson administration and the growing dependency on the munitions traffic, American policy had a built-in contradiction. Wilson wished respect for American commercial rights, but weapons which would compel this respect the president could not, or did not wish to, use. While the State Department never ceased to protest interference with trade destined for European neutral nations, the administration was not prepared to insist that all such interference stop, knowing it probably would weaken the Allied war effort. Above all it was not willing to impose an embargo. Thus while the administration let it be known that it

[5] Foreign Office Minutes, Feb. 22, 1916, Grey Papers.

was dissatisfied, it never was able to explain in a convincing manner precisely what measures would be satisfactory.

Bewildering as this situation was for Page and officials in the Foreign Office, it was a major source of strength for American policy. There were two ways the United States could have made its policy consistent and clear. One method was to force Britain to meet American demands, and be prepared to accept consequences of economic readjustment and in the weakened Allied military posture. The other alternative was agreement about acceptable methods of restriction, perhaps the sort of policy Grey considered in 1915 an alternative to the blockade, or perhaps Page's recommendation that the United States establish a legal basis for claims, then stand off and watch. Either agreement would have given official sanction to broad measures of trade restriction. By keeping the Foreign Office guessing—without any general plan to do so—the United States maintained a token restraint on the British, kept public opinion appeased enough that it did not compel strong measures, and strengthened the hand of Bethmann and moderates in the German government.

About Page's much-publicized collaboration with British officials, it is possible to make the following observations. He could not have made important changes, and certainly no change in substance, in the major notes sent to Britain. Newspapers carried verbatim accounts of these notes a few days after dispatch, and substantive change would have been immediately obvious to the State Department. While he did alter sentences to conform with high British standards of diplomatic ritual, the purpose was to "civilize" the note and not change its meaning.[6] Of course, smoothing language might have had a softening effect. When the State Department sent short messages, instructing the ambassador to read them to the foreign secretary, available evidence suggests that Page did as directed. For the most part, the ambassador's

[6] Examples of this type of alteration are Page's letter to Asquith, April 2, 1915, to correct "errors and omissions" in the American note, and Page's letter to Grey, Nov. 6, 1915, in which he changed the phrase "in the words of the American note of November 7" to read "in the words of the note which my Government had the honour to address to His Britannic Majesty's Ambassador in Washington on November 7th 1914." F. O. 382/186, 12.

collaboration with the foreign secretary lay not in his changing messages, but in interpreting them and seeking ways to circumvent the purpose. His manner often was to suggest that a dispatch was not as demanding as it sounded, that Wilson had to make periodic gestures for sake of public opinion. Occasionally Page went further and attempted to help Britain gain diplomatic advantage over the American government. How frequently he was guilty of such behavior, it is impossible to say, for while Grey's Papers and Records of the Foreign Office—indeed, what seems to be all the British and American sources—are open to public scrutiny, it is not possible to obtain full account of Page's conversation at Whitehall. The foreign secretary left no record of this discussion, and while he occasionally sent Spring-Rice the drift of conversation, he did not tell his ambassador all that had transpired between him and Page. The best-known examples of collaboration—the case of the *Dacia* and the time Page offered his assistance in answering an American dispatch—come not from the public record but from Grey's memory as set down in the published memoir. From such circumstances it is reasonable to assume there were similar occasions the world never will know about.

The question is: Did Page's advice make a difference in British policy? Was the ambassador helpful in Grey's attempts to steer American relations on a safe course while tightening restrictions on neutral commerce? To begin with, it is impossible to find in British or American sources a dramatic upheaval, or threat of upheaval, which Page kept from becoming dangerous. Burton Hendrick believed that the *Dacia* and controversy over the Declaration of London were such episodes, but it now is possible to say that in neither case was Page the vital factor. He had not the slightest effect on the outcome of the *Dacia* affair. There remains the general scope of British-American relations 1914–1917, the fact that Britain, without effective American resistance, did steadily tighten its hold on German trade. If Grey listened primarily to Page, the ambassador should receive substantial credit for this successful policy. Of course the foreign secretary did not do so; he received information from House, Spring-Rice, Crowe, and other

officials, a wide variety of sources. One is struck with the way Page
fades to the background when House appeared on the London
scene. The Foreign Office responded quickest to leaks from Lansing in Washington. The most important general influence on
British policy was belief that Wilson and his advisers in the
United States, while not always predictable, were basically pro-
British.

Inasmuch as Page was an amateur, not a career official, his
ambassadorship points to some merits and pitfalls of filling high
diplomatic posts with political patronage. He brought to his position freshness and a willingness to explore new ideas—characteristics frequently absent in professional diplomats. He made the
London embassy an exciting and a typically American place. But
from his virtues stemmed some vices. Lacking experience, he did
not understand that frustration often is part of the diplomat's lot.
He failed to appreciate the fact that while his position close to a
problem shed some bright light, it also shed a narrow light, that
he did not have the information or perspective to devise or modify
policy. He did not realize that while his country sent him abroad
to manipulate a foreign government, that government also sought
to manipulate him. The only aspect of his job which interested
him was fostering friendship; other duties were important only to
the degree that they sustained the original task. Page knew that
he sometimes acted with dubious propriety, but thought that the
issues were great enough to justify everything he did. He never
ceased to contend, and there is no reason to doubt his sincerity,
that his actions were the purest expression of Americanism. If he
was excessively generous with British leaders, it was because of a
conviction that the fate of the United States, indeed the fate of
the world, was in jeopardy if Britain did anything but win,
Germany anything but lose. Policy that would inhibit these ideals, though it appeared to serve immediate American interests,
was by his interpretation un-American in the long view of events.
Obsession with this goal of Anglo-American leadership led him
first to lose sight of, and later interest in, the precariousness of
America's neutral position.

The ambassador placed too much faith in his judgment, too

little in the judgment of his government. Americanism is a matter for personal interpretation; intensity of feeling does not, as Page seemed to think, guarantee truth. American policy had to depend on someone's interpretation of Americanism, and for good reason that person was not the ambassador in Britain. Page had an obligation to pursue the objectives of his government, although he had the right to question those objectives and by proper means, attempt to change them. Unable to do so, the obvious recourse was resignation. But the failure to leave his post was not fully Page's choice. While he could have stated his position stronger, or simply sent an unequivocal resignation, he did stay in London believing he had the acquiescence, if not the approval, of the president.

Viewed alone, Wilson's failure to relieve Page is baffling; within the context of his British policy, there is consistency. The president never was able to bring British relations to a showdown. He talked about the "totally indefensible course" of British policy, had the State Department press for release of detained ships, sent notes of protest, spoke of stronger ones, threatened to restrict trade with the Allies, but did little or nothing to halt the steadily restrictive course of British measures. Fortunately for Wilson's troubled mind, German submarine policy relieved him of the need to decide. So it was also with Walter Page. The president sometimes grumbled that Page was more British than the British. Up to the time the United States entered the war, he considered recalling Page; he asked House to suggest a replacement and evidently sounded Cleveland Dodge on the post.[7] But he did no more. He never replaced him because he never made the decision to chart Anglo-American relations along a new course. If Page was no help in London, he was at least predictable (or so Wilson thought), assurance that relations with Britain would not worsen beyond the president's design.

Those individuals who prefer to classify diplomatists in schools

[7] So Dodge told House, Feb. 22, 1917, House Diary. On March 28, Wilson remarked to House that in a "misguided moment" he had told Page he could remain, and supposed "we would be compelled to have a British-American representing the United States at the Court of St. James'." Wilson also remarked that he could not find a suitable man to replace Page; ibid.

of thought will find placement of Page a difficult task. It might be tempting, judging from Page's admiration for the British fleet and his obsession with Britain's remaining a powerful nation, to call him a realist, interested solely in protecting American security. To be sure the ambassador did understand the value of power as a weapon of diplomacy; he did think Britain was important to American strategic interests. But he also admired that nation for moral and cultural reasons, and it is doubtful he would have thought any different had the United Kingdom, instead of standing between America and the Continent, rested in Scandinavia or South Africa. He had little faith in that major instrument of realist diplomacy, the balance of power, and wished to see Germany eliminated as a European military force. His statements on relations with Mexico and other Latin-American states are the strongest professions of missionary idealism. He saw a good many things wrong in the world and would not be fully content until the United States, hopefully in collaboration with Britain, set them right. He was indeed concerned with the national interest; so was Wilson and presumably all other Americans; the problem, as always, involves not ends but application, and Page wished to pursue the national interest with more ambition than one usually associates with diplomatic realism.

The war was for Page, no less than for the world, an unfortunate event. It shortened his life, led him to alienate, temporarily or for life, some old friends. An honorable man, his zeal for the British led him to positions that were not honorable. Neutrality produced its moments of pleasure but largely it was a time of frustration during what might have been the most enjoyable years of the ambassador's life. Had the world, instead of exploding into chaos, continued the way it began in 1914, allowing Page to continue as he had the first year in London, he would have had a delightful and surely a productive embassy.

Bibliographical Note

PRIVATE PAPERS AND GOVERNMENT COLLECTIONS

PAGE'S PAPERS ARE scattered throughout the United States. The major collection is in the Houghton Library, Harvard University. Here are housed most of the letters Page received, copies of many he wrote, a number of interesting if sporadic diaries, and part of the London embassy files. Duke University Library has a small collection of Page Papers and other letters in such collections as the Papers of Benjamin N. Duke, the Papers of Robert Newton Page, and the Papers of Thomas Nelson Page. The Edwin A. Alderman Collection, in the University of Virginia Library, has several long letters from Page; and the Mary Johnston Collection, also in the Virginia Library, carries the story of Page's flirtation with the occupation of playwright. Many of his best letters have been published.

Second in importance only to Page's Papers are the Diary and Papers of Edward M. House, Yale University Library. House was a go-between for Wilson and Page, and each said things about the other to House which they would not say personally. House's Papers are the best source for Wilson's reaction to the ambassador, sometimes in letters, but usually in conversation which the colonel had his secretary record in diaries.

Wilson's Papers in the Library of Congress are massive, and contain letters from Page, House, and many other individuals. Although this collection is a good, perhaps the best, source for a study of the era of the World War, it does not equal House's Papers for the story of Walter Page.

Collections of other public officials, while important for the period, fail to rival these gigantic sources for a study of Page. Perhaps the most useful were the Papers of Frank L. Polk, Yale University Library. Polk became counselor for the State Department in summer of 1915, and was one of those people most interested in getting Page back to the United States for a rest. When Page did return to the United States in 1916, he met frequently with Polk, and while he disagreed with Polk's view of American policy, the ambassador seems to have gained respect for the counselor. After returning to England, Page corresponded regularly with Polk, something he did not care to do with the secretary of state. The Papers of William Jennings Bryan and Robert Lansing, both in the Library of Congress, are disappointing. Lansing kept diaries which show the secretary's view of the war and Wilson, but say little about Page. Lansing left many of his papers with the State Department files in the National Archives, the most important of which have been published. Bryan evidently failed to preserve many of his papers. The Bryan-Wilson Correspondence in the National Archives consists of four large letter books, which include some well-known documents but on the whole say little about Page and the World War.

On the British side, historians can rejoice that the Foreign Office Papers at last are open to inspection in the Public Record Office. This collection is so huge that one must doubt if a single person ever will be able to master it. There are virtually countless diplomatic dispatches, but even more interesting, and sometimes more revealing, are scribbled notes and minutes passed from one Foreign Office official to the others. Even though much information in these records already has been made public, much remains that is unknown, and it seems likely that students for years to come will be extracting tidbits of new material.

Also in the Public Record Office are papers of individuals involved in foreign policy during the war. The largest and most important collection is that of Sir Edward Grey, which overlaps and in some cases supplements the Foreign Office Papers. Perhaps the most striking feature of the Grey Papers is what is absent, for the foreign secretary saw fit to keep from the public depository such private correspondence as the letters from Colonel House. Even so, these papers combined with the Papers of Sir Cecil Spring-Rice are important guides to foreign policy and here the student will find discussion of British-American relations, including occasional reference to the behavior of Page. The Papers of Arthur Balfour and the Papers of Viscount Robert Cecil are smaller and less useful collections. These papers occasionally yield a unique document or letter, but cannot be regarded as rich sources for Anglo-American diplomacy.

An English source now easily accessible to American researchers is the Diary of Horace Plunkett, microfilm copy of which is, among other places, in the Princeton University Library. Plunkett noted occasional visits with Page in London, but more important, he had frequent conversation with House in which the colonel often spoke frankly. Unfortunately, Plunkett's handwriting was so poor that it is in some places almost impossible to read.

OFFICIAL GOVERNMENT PUBLICATIONS

Indispensable for a study of this period is the excellently edited series *Papers Relating to the Foreign Relations of the United States* (Washington, D.C., 1920–). The regular series covers Page's first year in London. *Supplements, 1914–1917,* 6 vols. (Washington, D.C., 1928–1933) provide masses of official correspondence of the war. *The Lansing Papers, 1914–1920,* 2 vols. (1939–1940) include much intergovernment communication, as well as some of Page's best messages. All told, these volumes offer amazingly complete information about the period, and omit few important papers in the files of the department.

CORRESPONDENCE AND COLLECTED WORKS

It would have been difficult to proceed with the present study without the groundwork of Burton J. Hendrick. His volumes, *The Life and Letters of Walter Hines Page,* 3 vols. (Garden City, N.Y., 1924–1926), and *The Training of an American: The Earlier Life and Letters of Walter Hines Page* (Cambridge, Mass., 1928), reproduce many of Page's best letters, excerpts from diaries, and other writings. Though written in fine literary style, the work has some faults. Of necessity selective, Hendrick leaves out large sections of many letters, omits some of Page's verbal mistakes, and sometimes makes other errors of reproduction. The author's interpretation is sheer hero-worship. But again, my study owes much to the work of Hendrick.

Charles Seymour, ed., *The Intimate Papers of Colonel House*, 4 vols. (Boston, 1926–1928) is another valuable published collection. Seymour did a careful job of including many important excerpts from House's papers and diary, as well as adding interesting narrative. The work generally accepts the interpretation of the war of Hendrick and Page, and while it is objective about Page and Wilson it finds little fault with House.

Ray Stannard Baker rounded out the triumvirate of published works. In collaboration with William E. Dodd he edited *The Public Papers of Woodrow Wilson*, 6 vols. (New York, 1925–1927), largely a competent job, and later published *Woodrow Wilson, Life and Letters*, 8 vols. (Garden City, N.Y., 1927–1939). Partly biographical, Baker's last work contained several of Wilson's letters. Character of the volumes changed with passage of time. Frequently critical of Page, Baker saw little wrong with Wilson in his first four volumes. This interpretation changed somewhat in the next two, and in the final volumes Baker dropped the biographical narrative and published daily excerpts from Wilson's papers and published sources. A final collection of published letters is Stephen Gwynn, ed., *The Letters and Friendships of Sir Cecil Spring Rice*, 2 vols. (London, 1929). The ambassador's letters from Washington often give a cynical view of American policy, but they frequently advise Britain's granting concession.

MEMOIRS, AUTOBIOGRAPHIES, CONTEMPORARY WORKS

On Wilson's election to the presidency, three works are worth notice, partly because of their differing views, partly because they referred to Page's work. William McCombs's *Making Woodrow Wilson President* (New York, 1921) is by Wilson's campaign manager who, feeling that he did much to secure Wilson's election, later became bitter toward the president. Frank Parker Stockbridge, "How Woodrow Wilson Won His Nomination,"

Current History 7 (July 1924) : 561–72, is by the man Page chose to be Wilson's publicity agent. David Lawrence's *The True Story of Woodrow Wilson* (New York, 1924) is an account by a newspaperman who knew Wilson and Page and reported numerous interviews with the president.

Almost all Wilson's cabinet members and advisers left personal accounts. Bryan's *The Memoirs of William Jennings Bryan* (Philadelphia, 1925), edited with the aid of his wife, gives the view one would expect of the former secretary of state—defending neutrality, and critical of Wilson's English bias. Bryan's successor also left writings. Lansing's *War Memoirs of Robert Lansing* (Indianapolis, Ind., 1935), supplemented with "The Difficulties of Neutrality," *The Saturday Evening Post* 203 (April 18, 1931) : 6–7, 102–105, present the most critical view of Page by any member of the Wilson administration. Lansing's memoirs incorporated many essays from his diaries and also gave retrospect comment about Page and American neutrality. "The Difficulties of Neutrality," one must suspect, was written not long after Lansing read Page's unflattering published letters, and is partly the reason the secretary was so critical of the ambassador.

David F. Houston's *Eight Years with Wilson's Cabinet, 1913 to 1920,* 2 vols. (Garden City, N.Y., 1926) is by a man in whom the president had much confidence. Houston's work is useful as a guide to Wilson's thinking on important issues, such as a successor for Bryan, and the cabinet meetings. Two other works by members of the administration, Josephus Daniels, *The Wilson Era: Years of Peace, 1910–1917* (Chapel Hill, N.C., 1944), and Joseph P. Tumulty, *Woodrow Wilson as I Know Him* (Garden City, N.Y., 1921), refer occasionally to Page, but generally one must use them with caution.

Some original information came from the other side of the Atlantic. This largely means Sir Edward Grey's memoirs, *Twenty-five Years, 1892–1916,* 2 vols. (New York, 1925), which tells how Grey as foreign secretary received Page's aid and advice. Another member of the British government, David Lloyd George, in *The War Memoirs of David Lloyd George,* 6 vols. (London, 1933–1936), supplements Grey's explanation of British foreign policy. Lloyd George gives none of the intimate information about Page that Grey did, and his description of the ambassador came largely from published letters.

WRITINGS BY PAGE

I will not attempt to list all Page's early writings; Hendrick's volumes contain some of the best. While editor of *The Forum* Page occasionally contributed an article, examples of which are "Mr. Cleveland's—Failure?" *The Forum* 19 (April 1894): 129–38, and "Political Career and Character of David B. Hill," *The Forum* 26 (Nov. 1894): 257–69. In *Atlantic Monthly* two of his articles defended the war with Spain, "The War with Spain and After," 81 (June 1898): 721–27, and "The End of the War and After," 82 (Sept. 1898): 430–32. He wrote most of the editorials for *World's Work* during the years 1900–1913, and followed the career of Wilson in that journal. After attaining success in the literary world he published three books. *The Southerner,* which appeared in 1909, was partly a novel, partly autobiography, and it carried the message that despite great problems, there was hope for the South. More ideas about the South came out in the collection of speeches *The Rebuilding of Old Commonwealths, Being Essays towards the Training of the Forgotten Man in the Southern States* (New York, 1902). In 1905 he explained some of the pitfalls of publishing, as well as ways to improve writing, in *A Publisher's Confession* (republished Garden City, N.Y., 1923). Aside from letters Page's literary output ended in 1913.

NEWSPAPERS AND PERIODICALS

The best American newspaper, perhaps the world's best newspaper for twentieth-century world events, is the New York *Times*. In 1913–1918 this paper presented broad coverage of news, as well as comment from other leading American and foreign newspapers. Also I used the *Times* (London) for 1913–1918 and more sparingly, *Punch*. For British opinion after Page's letters became public, *The Spectator* and *The Quarterly Review* are useful.

World's Work and the other journals Page edited are important for a study of his early life.

It would be meaningless to list all the books about American neutrality and the men involved. The following list does not include all the books I consulted, but those found most useful and, I hope, representative, because of quality, points of view, or emphasis.

The best description of Page's life in the United States comes from Hendrick's volumes. Edwin Mims, "Walter Hines Page: Friend of the South," *South Atlantic Quarterly* (April 1919), 97–115, gives another laudatory view of the author's old friend. Useful for its brief view of Trinity College at the time of Page's attendance is Earl W. Porter, *Trinity and Duke 1892–1924: Foundations of Duke University* (Durham, N.C., 1964). An excellent description of England before the war comes from George Dangerfield, *The Strange Death of Liberal England, 1910–1914,* Capricorn Books edition (New York, 1961), a witty and perceptive study of English domestic politics.

For the period of neutrality a good starting point would be Richard W. Leopold, "The Problem of American Intervention, 1917: An Historical Retrospect," *World Politics* 2 (1950): 405–25, which analyzes the popular writings and views of American intervention. Ernest R. May also concentrates on the literature concerning the United States's entry into the First World War in his nineteen-page pamphlet *American Intervention: 1917–1941* (Washington, D.C., 1960). May is able to include some works which Leopold's earlier publication did not permit. Among these is May's account of American neutrality, *The World War and American Isolation, 1914–1917* (Cambridge, Mass., 1959). Basing his research on foreign as well as American sources, May agrees with Wilson's policy and stresses the submarine as the major determinant of American intervention. His is the best single volume on the period.

Arthur Link is the foremost authority on Woodrow Wilson.

His *Wilson the Diplomatist: A Look at His Major Foreign Policies* (Baltimore, Md., 1957), and *Woodrow Wilson and the Progressive Era* (New York, 1954) are brief but excellent accounts. Link's multivolume study of Wilson now has reached the period of American intervention. Earlier volumes, *The Road to the White House* (Princeton, N.J., 1947), and *The New Freedom* (Princeton, N.J., 1956), take the president to the time of the World War. The three latest works, *The Struggle for Neutrality, 1914–1915* (Princeton, N.J., 1960), *Confusions and Crises, 1915–1916* (Princeton, N.J., 1964), and *Campaigns for Progressivism and Peace, 1916–1917* (Princeton, N.J., 1965), place heavy emphasis on the president's foreign policy. Perhaps the work's major discrepancy is the title, for it is more than a biography; it is an account of worldwide events which affected the United States. Based on broad domestic and foreign materials, the work carries the message that Wilson's policy, while not flawless, was as neutral as it realistically could be.

Older but sound in interpretation are Charles Seymour's *American Diplomacy during the World War* (Baltimore, Md., 1934), and *American Neutrality: 1914–1917* (New Haven, Conn., 1935). Seymour was one of the first writers to stress the submarine in American intervention. Another fairly recent account, which emphasizes Wilson's friendship with the Allies and the importance of American intervention in international politics, is Edward H. Buehrig, *Woodrow Wilson and the Balance of Power* (Bloomington, Ind., 1955), and by the same author, "Wilson's Neutrality Re-examined," *World Politics* 3 (Oct. 1950): 1–19.

Debunking writers have had much to say. C. Hartley Grattan began major revisionist literature with his *Why We Fought* (New York, 1929). Disillusioned with the war, Grattan contended that Wilson's policy was unfair, unneutral, unwise, that a truly neutral policy would have kept the United States out of war. Grattan is the leading debunker of Page. In *Why We Fought* and earlier articles—"The Walter Hines Page Legend," *American Mercury* 6 (Sept. 1925): 39–51, and "Walter Hines Page—Patriot or Traitor," *Nation* 121 (Nov. 4, 1925): 512—he implies not so much that Page was ineffective but that he was influential in the wrong way, and for benefit of the wrong country. Walter Millis in *Road to War, America 1914–1917* (Boston, 1935) followed Grattan's revisionism. In interesting, satirical style Millis lampooned intervention and the interventionists, including Page. Revisionism received added respectability in the long and deeply researched volume of Charles C. Tansill, *America Goes to War* (Boston, 1938). Although one must admire Tansill's efforts, he does seem to have set out with the purpose of devastating the Wilson administration, including Page, has disregarded some important documents, and, as Link has shown, based his conclusion on weak evidence. Finally there is Alice M. Morrissey's *The American Defense of Neutral Rights, 1914–1917* (Cambridge, Mass., 1939), a scholarly, legalistic account which states with some accuracy that Wilson did not defend American rights against Britain as well as he did against Germany.

Among special studies and biographies one should mention Daniel M. Smith's *Robert Lansing and American Neutrality, 1914–1917* (Berkeley, Calif., 1958), and "Robert Lansing and the Formulation of American Neutrality Policies, 1914–1915," *Mississippi Valley Historical Review* 43 (June 1956): 59–81. Smith seeks to raise Lansing to a place of much importance in the making of American policy. Two biographies about the foreign secretaries Page dealt with are George M. Trevelyan, *Grey of Fallodon* (Boston, 1937) and Blanche E. C. Dugdale, *Arthur James Balfour*, 2 vols. (New York, 1937). A special study on British opinion is Armin Rappaport, *The British Press and Wilsonian Neutrality* (Stanford, Calif., 1951). On the whole a commendable work, Rappaport makes frequent but little original reference to Page. Richard W. Van Alstyne in "The Policy of the United States regarding the Declaration of London at the Outbreak of the Great War," *Journal of Modern History* 7 (Dec. 1933): 434–47, feels that the United States gave up a good legal case too easily, and has little respect for the American ambassador. Special studies written with lively novelistic style are Barbara W. Tuchman, *The Zimmermann Telegram*, Dell Paperback edition (New York, 1965), and A. A. and Mary Hoehling, *The Last Voyage of the Lusitania* (New York, 1956). Three articles of interest are Jerold S. Auerbach, "Woodrow Wilson's 'Prediction' to Frank Cobb: Words Historians Should Doubt Ever Got Spoken," *Journal of American History* 54 (Dec. 1967) : 608–17; Ross Gregory, "The Superfluous Ambassador: Walter Hines Page's Return to Washington 1916," *The Historian* 27 (May 1966) : 389–404; and Ross Gregory, "A New Look at the Case of the *Dacia*," *Journal of American History* 55 (Sept. 1968) : 292–96.

Index

Adams, John, 64
Aix-la-Chapelle, Germany, 59
Alaska-Canada boundary dispute, 32
Allies: and House peace plan, 1916, 141, 145; financial state of, 181, 194, 198, 199–200; and war aims, 185–86; American sympathy for, 212
American embassy. *See* London embassy (American)
Ancona, 137
Anderson, Chandler P., 59, 70, 158
Arabic: sinking of, 109, 110, 112; mentioned, 125, 189
Arabic pledge: offered, 110, 112; and British-American relations, 132; mentioned, 154
armed merchant ships: controversy over Lansing's proposal, 149–52, 177. *See also* Foreign Office (British) ; Lansing, Robert; Page, Walter H.
army, American, 192
Asquith, Herbert, 130, 144, 183
Atlanta Exposition, 1882, 7
Atlantic Monthly, 9, 11, 14–15
atrocity stories: circulated, 59; and Wilson, 59–60; and Page, 60
Austria-Hungary: assassination of heir-apparent, 49; Page takes embassy of, 52; declares war, 57; and Declaration of London, 64; and *Ancona* incident, 137–38

Baker, Newton D., 23
balance of power: and Page's diplomacy, 46, 153
Balfour, Arthur: sees Page's dispatch, 153; becomes foreign secretary, 180; relations with Page, 180; and Zimmermann note, 192; and American declaration of war, 197; visit to Washington, 1917, 198, 201–202; and submarine warfare, 1917, 199; and financial crisis,

1917, 199; and Page's departure, 1918, 205–206; mentioned, 181, 195
Balkan peninsula, 132
Belgium, 57, 59, 60, 171
Bernstorff, Johann von, 110, 112, 144, 188, 192–93
Bethmann Hollweg, Theobald von, 154, 178, 188
Bismarck, Otto von, 58
blacklist controversy: 162–63; and Page, 163, 171–72, 175–76; and Wilson, 166; mentioned, 177
blockade: proclamation of, 1915, 114–15; Page's message on, 116; American irritation at, 119, 120, 121; Grey considers abandoning, 1915, 124–25; and submarine warfare, 131; protest of October 1915, 133–36; proposed changes in, 146–48, 146–47n, 148–49n; and France, 148, 148n
Bonaparte, Napoleon, 56, 64
Bordeaux, France, 61
Boston *Monitor,* 136
Brandeis, Louis, 24
Breitung, Edward N., 85
Bremen, Germany, 85
Bremerhaven, Germany, 118
British ambassador to United States, 63. *See* Spring-Rice, Cecil
British embassy: and transfer of ships' registry, 84
Bryan, William J.: presidential candidate, 16, 16–17n; and election of 1912, 20, 21; placement in cabinet, 22; and Mexico, 37; and Panama tolls, 40; and outbreak of war, 52; and Page's messages, 78; and note of December 1914, 81–82; and *Dacia* case, 84, 88; proposes *modus vivendi,* 1915, 92; and *Lusitania,* 99; resigns, 100; attacks on, 101–103; spokesman for pacifists, 103; mentioned, 58, 64, 66
Bryce, James, 32, 40, 212

Bryn Mawr, 10, 17, 25
Buckingham Palace, 207
Bull Run, battle of, 133
Bunkering policy, 177

Calhoun, John C., 3
California, 192
California, 191
Canada, 147
Carden, Lionel, 37, 38
Casement, Roger, 159, 163, 164
Cecil, Robert: counseled by American
embassy, 136; and Spring-Rice's re-
ports, 148n; and German peace pro-
posal, 1916, 181–82; and war aims
proposal, 182, 183, 184–85
Central Powers, 68, 153
Chamberlain, George E., 41, 42
China, 146
China, case of, 161, 161n
Choate, Joseph, 127
Civil War (American): Page's remem-
brances of, 1; impact on South, 2–3;
impact on Page, 2, 3; and neutral
rights, 115
Clay, Henry, 3
Clayton-Bulwer Treaty, 43
Cleveland, Grover, 16, 154n
Cobb, Frank, 210
Commoner, 103
Congress: and neutrality, 131; passes
retaliatory legislation, 1916, 166–67;
mentioned, 137, 195
Congressional Government, 17
Conservative party (British), 180, 190
Constantinople, Turkey, 185
continuous voyage, doctrine of, 147n,
148n
contraband: in Declaration of London,
64; list expanded, 65, 79; aboard
Lusitania, 96, 100; seizure of, 118;
cotton defined as, 125. *See also* block-
ade
cotton: interception of, 124, 125
Crewe, Lord, 124, 137
Crowe, Eyre, 118, 147, 184–85, 212, 214
Cunard line, 90, 95, 113, 192
Curzon, Lord, 202
Cushing, 95

Dacia: case of, 83–89; transferred to
American registry, 85; creates controversy with Britain, 85–86; attitude of

Page, 86–87; British discussion of, 87–
88; captured by French, 88; and
British-American relations, 88–89;
mentioned, 214
Daniels, Josephus, 19n, 24
Declaration of London. *See* London,
Declaration of, 1909
Democratic party, 16, 18, 19, 21, 30, 40,
43, 97
Diaz, Porfirio, 33
Dixon, Frederick, 136
Dodge, Cleveland, 31, 43, 162, 216
Dooley, Mr. *See* Dunne, Finley Peter
Doubleday, Frank N., 9, 25
Doubleday, Page and Company, 9
Dublin, Ireland, 159
Duke University. *See* Trinity College
Dumba, Constantin, 110–11
Dunne, Finley Peter: article on Page's
ambassadorial indiscretion, 42–43

Easter Rebellion. *See* Irish question
East Prussia, 65
election, presidential: of 1912, 19–21;
of 1916, 178
Eliot, Charles W., 24, 127
Euston Station, 90, 97
Evestone, 191

Falaba, 95, 97
Falmouth, England, 141, 145
Foreign Office (British): strengthens
policy, 1914, 78–79; records of, 87,
214; rejects *modus vivendi*, 1915, 93,
94; and American message of April
1915, 117–18; and note of October
1915, 136; and economic reprisals,
137, 147; and House peace mission,
144–45; and armed merchantman proposal, 151–52; and dependency on the
United States, 174–75; policy of November 1916, 177; and war aims proposal, 184–85; bewilderment at American policy, 211–12, 213. *See also*
Cecil, Robert; Crowe, Eyre; Grey,
Edward
Foreign Office (German), 100
Forum, 9, 11
Fowler, Harold, 76–77
France: and seizure of *Dacia*, 87, 88; and
reprisals against United States, 1915,
137; and House peace mission, 1916,
142, 145, 145n

Gallipoli, campaign at, 130, 133, 149
Galveston, Texas, 85
General Education Board, 13
George V, 28, 183, 198, 205, 207
Gerard, James W., 52n, 92, 105, 120
Germany: Page visit to, 1877, 6; Page takes embassy of, 1914, 51; approves Declaration of London, 64; politics within, 57–58, 131, 154–55, 156, 188; and *modus vivendi*, 1915, 92, 120; and House peace proposal, 141, 142; and *Sussex* pledge, 156; proposes peace conference, 1916, 178, 181–82; and war aims proposal, 185–86; and Zimmermann note, 192–93; declaration of war on, 197. *See also* submarine warfare
Gettysburg, battle of, 133
Gildersleeve, Basil L., 5, 6
Gilman, Daniel C., 5
Great Britain: economic dependency upon United States, 1916, 174–75; change of government, 1916, 180; praise for Page within, 209, 209n. *See also* Allies, the; blockade; Foreign Office (British); Grey, Edward
Greek, studies in, 4, 5, 6, 11
Grey, Edward: relations with Page, 29, 33, 56–58, 126–27, 161; and Mexico, 34, 35, 37, 38; and Panama tolls, 39, 39n, 41; and outbreak of war, 52; comments on importance of United States, 56–57; and Declaration of London, 66–72; and restriction of trade, 79–80, 82; and *Dacia*, 84, 85–89; and *modus vivendi*, 1915, 93, 119–20; and sinking of *Lusitania*, 98; and difficulties of blockade, 115, 116, 117, 118, 122–24; considers abandoning blockade, 124–25; Page's collaboration with, 126–27, 127n, 213–15, 213n; impact on Colonel House, 129–30; and objects of British diplomacy, 131, 211–12; and note of October 1915, 134, 135, 136; and House peace plan, 141, 143n, 144, 145; and armed merchantman proposal, 149–52; protests retaliatory legislation, 167; negotiation on blacklist, 176; and economic problems, 176, 181; leaves office, 1916, 180; advises reconsideration of peace plan, 181; disturbed at American inaction, 1917, 192; considered as special envoy

to United States, 202; mentioned, 132–33, 153, 157, 205, 213
Gulflight, 95, 97

Haldane, Lord, 86
Hale, William B., 20, 52n
Hamburg, Germany, 118
Hamburg-Amerika line, 85
Harper, House of, 9
Hart, Albert B., 14
Hay-Pauncefote Treaty, 32, 38, 39
Hearst, William R., 41
Hendrick, Burton J., 74–75n, 87, 214
Hesperian, 110–11, 189
Hindenburg, Paul von, 188
Hohenzollern dynasty, 188
Holland, 65, 85
Houghton Mifflin Co., 9, 12, 17–18
House, Edward M.: tells anecdote about Page, 10; and cabinet appointments, 22, 23, 24; and appointment of Page, 25; sends funds to Page, 31; and Panama tolls, 40, 43; "mission" to Europe, 1914, 45–47; comments on Page's indiscretion, 48; speaks of Page's naivete, 58, 120; and protest of September 1914, 67, 67n; and Page's anger at American policy, 71, 72, 75; warns Page about unneutrality, 78; and *modus vivendi*, 1915, 93, 119–20; and *Lusitania* controversy, 96–97, 98, 139; recommends Page for secretary of state, 104; tries to maneuver vacation for Page, 107–108; and problems of blockade, 115–16, 119, 121; collaboration with Britain, 127, 127n; influenced by Grey, 128–29; criticism of Page and Grey, 130; problems with Page, 133, 134, 135–36; and "mission" to Europe, 1916, 140–45, 149, 152, 157; and *Sussex* crisis, 155; thinks Page should resign, 158, 162; and Page visit the United States, 158, 163, 164–65, 170–71; and mediation, November 1916, 178–79; discusses Page's resignation with Wilson, 179, 180, 180n; urges break in relations with Germany, 188; and diplomacy, 1917–18, 199, 200, 202; influence in Britain, 214, 215; mentioned, 60, 132, 138, 172, 201, 212
House-Grey memorandum, 144
Houston, David F., 23, 127, 162

Huerta, Victoriano, 33–34, 35, 36, 50
Huxley, Thomas H., 5

international law: and American neutrality, 72, 82; and armed merchant ships, 150
Irish question: in British politics, 29, 159, 163–64; Page's opinion of, 164
Italy, 137, 150

Japan, 45, 146
Jefferson, Thomas, 64, 179
Johns Hopkins University, 5, 6, 7, 17
Johnson, Cone, 81
Johnston, Joseph, 1
Johnston, Mary, 11–12

kaiser. See William II
Keynes, John Maynard, 175
Kipling, Rudyard, 11, 197

Laconia, 192
Ladies' Home Journal, 14
Lane, Mrs. Franklin K., 119
Lansing, Robert: writes note, September 1914, 66–67; and Declaration of London, 67, 68, 72; attacked by Page, 68, 71, 142, 143, 166; reaction to Page, 75, 78, 103, 107, 108, 134, 149, 162; note of December 1914, 81–82; and Lusitania case, 99; becomes secretary of state, 103–105; and Arabic crisis, 110, 112; and blockade, 121, 123, 134, 146; and House "mission," 1916, 140; and armed merchant ship proposal, 149–52; and submarine crisis, 1916, 154–55; and Page visit home, 165, 166, 167, 168; moves to soften retaliatory legislation, 167–68; and war aims proposal, 182; and peace without victory, 186; and break in relations, 1917, 188, 189; asks Page not to resign, 190–91; leaks information, 215; mentioned, 158, 171, 174, 179, 210
Laszlo, P. A., 10
Latin-American states, 217
Laughlin, Irwin, 70, 168
League to Enforce Peace, 159
Lee, Robert E., 133
Liberal party (British), 29, 30, 190
Life and Letters of Walter Hines Page, 208, 209
Lincoln, Abraham, 193
Liverpool, England, 88

Lloyd George, David: Chancellor of Exchequer, 29; conference with House, 144; becomes prime minister, 180; and peace negotiation, 186; conference with Page, 1917, 190; letter to Page, 205; and special envoy to United States, 208
London, Declaration of, 1909: proposed by United States, 64, 67–68, 69; approved by Central Powers, 64; British modification of, 65, 66, 72; Page's opposition to, 67, 68–69, 70–71; controversy ends, 72–73; analysis of controversy, 73–74; impact on relations between Page and Washington, 74–75; mentioned, 89, 92, 107, 151, 160, 211, 214
London, England: description, 1913–1914, 27, 29; and outbreak of war, 50–51; atmosphere in, 130
London Daily News, 82
London embassy (American): unsatisfactory state of, 1913, 30; and outbreak of war, 51–52; moved, September 1914, 62; leaks to foreign office, 78–79; "a nest of disloyalty," 158; Page returns to, 1916, 173; supports Page, 179; Page impact on, 215; mentioned, 203
Loring, Charles G., 107–108, 204
Loring, Mrs. Charles G. See Page, Katherine Alice
Louisville, Kentucky, 7
Louisville Age, 7
Ludendorff, Erich, 188
Lusitania: torpedoed, 90, 91, 95–96; American response to, 99–100, 105, 108, 109, 139, 140; Page response to, 90–91, 96–97, 98, 105–106, 112–13; and Bryan's resignation, 101; and British-American relations, 119; mentioned, 119, 120, 121, 137, 151, 153, 156, 169, 173, 189, 192, 210

McAdoo, William Gibbs, 104
McClure's, 14
Madero, Francisco, 33
Madison, James, 64
Marne, battle of, 61, 198
mediation (American), 52, 103, 157, 182–85
Mediterranean Sea, 139
Mexico: and British-American relations,

27, 33–38; and Zimmermann note, 192; mentioned, 217
modus vivendi: on submarines and blockade, 1915, 92–94, 119–20; on armed merchant ships, 150
Morgan, J. P., 199
muckrakers, 14

navy, American, 198–99
navy, British, 65, 78, 85, 91, 118, 132
Negro problem: Page's views on, 8, 13, 128
neutral rights. *See* blockade; contraband; London, Declaration of, 1909
New Freedom, 40
New Hampshire, 164
New Jersey, 18, 19
New Mexico, 192
New York: Page's arrival in, 1916, 164; Page's arrival in, 1918, 206
New York *American,* 41
New York *Times,* 82, 85, 163
New York *World,* 7, 8, 210
Nicolson, Arthur, 78–79, 88
Norfolk, Virginia, 85
North Carolina. *See* Page, Walter H.
North Carolina, University of, 7
Northcliffe, Lord, 202
North Sea: Britain's mining of, 91

O'Gorman, James A., 42
Old Head Kinsdale (Ireland), 90, 113
Olney, Richard, 24
Order-in-Council, of March 1915. *See* blockade

Page, Allison F., 1, 3
Page, Mrs. Allison F., 3–4
Page, Arthur W., 10, 31, 127, 204, 205
Page, Frank C., 204
Page, Mrs. Frank C., 164
Page, Katherine Alice, 25, 107–108, 122
Page, Robert N., 49–50
Page, Walter H.: childhood in North Carolina, 1–2; early education: local, 3, at Trinity College, 4, at Randolph-Macon College, 4, at Johns Hopkins University, 5–6; early employment: at University of North Carolina, 7, in Louisville, 7, in St. Joseph, Missouri, 7, with New York *World,* 7–8, with Raleigh *State Chronicle,* 8, with *Forum,* 8, with Houghton Mifflin, 8,

with Harper, 8, with *World's Work,* 8; personal and professional characteristics, 10–12; views on Negro problem, 8, 13, 128; and American politics, 15–16; boosts Wilson for presidency, 18–21; and cabinet appointments, 22, 23, 24; appointed ambassador, 24; qualifications for post, 24, 25; leaves for London, 25–26; introduction into British society, 27–28; financial difficulty, 30–31; policy in Mexico, 34–38, 49; and Panama tolls issue, 39–41, 43, 44, 49; arouses controversy, 41, 43; lampooned by Mr. Dooley, 42–43; Wilson's approval of, 43, 47; and House "mission," 1914, 47; and outbreak of war, 50–51, 52; and mediation, 52–53; and meaning of war, 54–56, 59–60; Grey's influence on, 57; and German atrocities, 60; predicts British victory, 61–62; and Declaration of London, 66–72; criticism of Lansing, 69, 71; reprimanded by Wilson, 69; troubles with State Department, 75–76, 78, 80–81; and restriction of trade, 79–80; and note of December 1914, 83; collaboration with Grey, 83; and *Dacia* case, 83, 84, 85, 86, 87, 88, 89; suggests that French take the *Dacia,* 87; and *Lusitania* controversy, 90–91, 95, 96–97, 98, 100, 101, 106, 106–107n, 108; and *modus vivendi,* 1915, 92–94, 103; attacks Bryan, 101, 102–103, 103n; considered for secretary of state, 103–104; approves selection of Lansing, 105; favors war, 1915, 106; relations with Washington, 1915, 107, 108; and *Arabic* crisis, 109–10, 111, 112–13; and Dumba incident, 110–11; Wilson's response to, 1915, 110, 111–12; and case of *Hesperian,* 1915, 114, 115–16, 117, 122–24; collaboration with Grey, 126–27; thoughts on Anglo-American unity, 127–28; complaints about American policy, 1915, 128, 132–33, 134–36, 134n, 137–38; rumor of resignation, 134–35; and submarine crisis, 1916, 139–40; advises break with Germany, 139, 152–54, 154n; opposes House "mission," 1916, 140, 141, 142–43, 144, 145, 161; supports blockade, 1916, 146–49, 146n; opposes armed ship proposal, 149–52;

and *Sussex* crisis, 155–56; on relations with Grey, 161, 162; visit home, 1916, 163–72; attacks Lansing, 166; attacks Wilson, 166; conference with Wilson, 1916, 168–70; conference with House, 169–70; attacks blacklist, 171–72, 175–76; plans to resign, 1916, 172; on return to London, 1916, 173–74, 176; offers resignation, 1916, 178, 179–80; and German peace proposal, 181–82; and American peace note, 182, 183–85; and "peace without victory," 186, 187; and break with Germany, 189–90; agrees to stay at post, 190–91; assessment of Wilson, 191, 196, 201; and Zimmermann note, 192–93; and financial crisis, 1917, 194, 199, 200; last weeks of neutrality, 195; criticism of House, 196; and declaration of war, 197–98; and submarine warfare, 1917, 198–99; attitude in Washington toward, 199, 200, 202–203; diplomatic duties, 1917–1918, 200, 202; failing health, 203–205; resigns, 204–205; popularity in Britain, 205; returns home, 205–206; last letter to Wilson, 206–207; dies, 207; letters published, 208–209; analysis of impact: on German policy, 209–11, on British policy, 211–15; collaboration with British, 213–14; significance for: foreign service, 215–16, Wilson's diplomacy, 216; diplomatic philosophy of, 216–17

Page, Mrs. Walter H., 10, 205

Palmerston, Lord, 32

Panama tolls: act, 39, 40, 41, 43; controversy, 27, 38–43

Parliament Act of 1911, 29

Percy, Eustace, 148, 174–75, 177

Pershing, John J., 200–201

Persia, 139, 150

Philadelphia, Pennsylvania: speech at, 98

Phillips, William, 164

Pless, Germany: conference at, 188

Plunkett, Horace, 153, 192

Poland, Russian, 185

Polk, Frank L.: wants to call Page home, 158, 162; and blacklist, 163; and Page visit home, 1916, 164, 165–66, 167; letter from Page, 1917, 176; writes Page, 177–78; on American wartime policy, 198; mentioned, 171

Port Arthur, Louisiana, 85

Price, Thomas R., 4, 5

Princeton University, 18, 19

progressivism: definition of, 16

public opinion (American), 99, 131, 136

public opinion (British), 98, 105–106, 107, 112–13, 122, 132, 139, 149

Punch: quoted, 98

Raleigh *State Chronicle*, 8, 13, 17

Randolph-Macon College, 4–5

Reading, Lord, 144, 200

Realism, philosophy of: and Page, 217

Republican party, 16, 21, 159

Retaliatory legislation, 1916: passed, 166–67; and Lansing, 167–68; impact in Britain, 167, 174; and Wilson, 169

Rockefeller, John D., 13

Roosevelt, Theodore, 14, 16, 32, 127

Rotterdam, Holland, 84, 85, 118

Royal Navy. *See* navy (British)

Russia, 56, 62, 121, 137, 185

St. Joseph, Missouri, 7

St. Luke's Hospital: Page's arrival at, 1918, 206

St. Paul's Cathedral, 197

Scandinavia, 65, 217

Serbia, 57

Shadow Lawn (New Jersey), 168, 169, 170

Sharp, William G., 165

Sherman, William T., 1

Sims, William S., 198, 199, 200

Skinner, Robert, 126, 134, 162

Social Darwinism, 127–28

South Africa, 217

South America, 86

Southerner: published, 12; quoted, 13

Spanish-American War, 14–15

Spring-Rice, Cecil: and moralism in American diplomacy, 35; letter from Wilson, 62; and American profiteering, 63; and Declaration of London, 67n, 70n, 71; and note of December 1914, 82; comments on Bryan, 101; approves Lansing as secretary of state, 105n; warns of possible embargo, 117, 137, 146; and restriction on trade, 127, 127n, 160; and note of October 1915, 136; perturbs foreign office, 147–48; and armed ship proposal, 150, 151; and mediation, 159; and Page visit the United States, 166; and German peace proposal, 181; and war aims proposal, 183; warns against accepting Page's advice, 203; mentioned, 32, 40, 58, 167, 174, 212, 214

State, Department of: Page's criticism of, 47, 74, 75, 76, 86, 128, 142–43, 176; approves war trade, 63; proposes Declaration of London, 64; and Robert Skinner, 126; and note of October 1915, 133; and German peace proposal, 181; and "peace without victory," 186; and Zimmermann note, 192–93; and instructions to Page, 213; mentioned, 66, 101, 107, 108, 119, 122, 130. *See also* Bryan, William J.; Lansing, Robert; Polk, Frank L.

Steffens, Lincoln, 14

Stockbridge, Frank P., 19, 21

submarine warfare: and Page's ambassadorship, 90–91; proclamation of, 1915, 91; difficulty of, 94–95; and *Arabic* pledge, 110, 112; and British blockade, 115, 131; and armed merchantmen, 150; resumed, 1916, 154–55; and *Sussex* crisis, 155–56; decision to resume, 1917, 188; and American intervention, 195; campaign, 1917, 198–99

Sussex: torpedoed, 155; controversy over, 155–56; mentioned, 157, 173, 189, 191

Taft, William H., 16, 39, 40, 127, 202

Tammany Hall, 21, 154n

Tarbell, Ida M., 14

Tennessee, 51–52

Texas, 192

Times (London), 190, 205

To Have and to Hold, 11–12

Trinity College, 4

Triple Entente, 56, 63

Turino, 191

Tyrrell, William, 37, 38

U-53: case of, 177

Venezuela boundary dispute, 32

Verdun, battle of, 149

Versailles, Treaty of, 208

Victoria Street: site of American chancery, 1913, 30

Wallace, Hugh C., 157–58, 180

Washington, George, 45

Waterloo Station, London, 205

Western front: mentioned, 76, 204, 205

Westminster Abbey, 132, 209

Whitlock, Brand, 162

William II, 188

Wilson, Willia Alice: married Page, 10

Wilson, Woodrow: meets Page, 7; publishes in *World's Work*, 14; early association with Page, 17–18; early academic and political career, 17–19; campaign for presidency, 1912, 19–21; and cabinet appointments, 22–24; and appointment of Page, 24–25, 26; offers financial aid to Page, 31; "missionary" diplomacy in Mexico, 34, 36, 37; and Panama tolls issue, 40, 43; praises Page, 43, 47–48; declines to visit Britain, 45, 46, 46n; and outbreak of war, 52, 53; neutrality policies, 1914, 53, 60–61, 66–67, 69, 72, 75, 81, 81n, 82; sympathy for Allies, 61, 61n, 62; relations with Page, 1914, 68–69, 75, 78; and "strict accountability," 91, 95; and *Lusitania* crisis, 98, 99–100, 101, 108; thoughts on replacement for Bryan, 103, 104, 105; relations with Page, 1915, 107, 108, 110, 111–12, 128, 133, 134–35, 137–38; and *Arabic* crisis, 109, 110; and note of October 1915, 133; and House "mission," 1916, 141, 144; Page criticism of, 142–43, 172; and armed ship proposal, 150, 151; and *Sussex* crisis, 155–56; and mediation, summer 1916, 157, 159; considers replacing Page, 162; attacks blacklist, 163; calls Page home, 163; and Page visit home, 165, 166, 168–70; and mediation, fall 1916, 173, 178, 179; and Page resignation, 179–80, 180n, 190–91, 191n; and war aims proposal, 182–85; "peace without victory" speech, 186–87; breaks with Germany, 189; and "overt" acts, 191; and Zimmermann note, 193; Page criticism of, 196, 201; and financial crisis, 194; asks for declaration of war, 195; diplomatic channels, 1917–1918, 200; calls Page an "Englishman," 202–203; accepts Page's resignation, 205; and Page's return home, 206–207; analy-

sis of war policies, 209–11; analysis of relations with Page, 216, 216n; mentioned, 9, 16, 129, 132, 137, 204, 217
Wilson, Mrs. Woodrow, 179, 180n
Wiseman, William, 200
World's Work: founded, 9; described, 11; purposes of, 14; and election of 1912, 20, 21; mentioned, 12, 13
Worth, Nicholas, 12, 13

Zimmermann, Arthur, 192
Zimmermann note, 192–93